THE
STRUGGLING STATE

*Nationalism, Mass Militarization,
and the Education of Eritrea*

JENNIFER RIGGAN

TEMPLE UNIVERSITY PRESS
Philadelphia • Rome • Tokyo

TEMPLE UNIVERSITY PRESS
Philadelphia, Pennsylvania 19122
www.temple.edu/tempress

Copyright © 2016 by Temple University—Of The Commonwealth System
 of Higher Education
All rights reserved
Published 2016

Library of Congress Cataloging-in-Publication Data
Riggan, Jennifer, 1971– author.
 The struggling state : nationalism, mass militarization, and the education
of Eritrea / Jennifer Riggan.
   pages cm
 Includes bibliographical references and index.
 ISBN 978-1-4399-1270-6 (cloth : alk. paper) — ISBN 978-1-4399-1272-0
(e-book) 1. Civil-military relations—Eritrea. 2. Militarization—Eritrea.
3. Militarism—Eritrea. 4. Teachers—Eritrea. 5. Education and state—
Eritrea. 6. Nationalism—Eritrea. 7. Eritrea—Politics and government
—1993– I. Title.
 JQ3583.A38R54 2016
 320.9635—dc23
                                                                2015013666

♾ The paper used in this publication meets the requirements of the American
National Standard for Information Sciences—Permanence of Paper for Printed
Library Materials, ANSI Z39.48-1992

Printed in the United States of America

9 8 7 6 5 4 3 2 1

The Struggling State

For Ermias

Contents

Acknowledgments		*ix*
	Introduction: Everyday Authoritarianism, Teachers, and the Decoupling of Nation and State	*1*
1	Struggling for the Nation: Contradictions of Revolutionary Nationalism	*33*
2	"It Seemed like a Punishment": Coercive State Effects and the Maddening State	*57*
3	Students or Soldiers? Troubled State Technologies and the Imagined Future of Educated Eritrea	*89*
4	Educating Eritrea: Disorder, Disruption, and Remaking the Nation	*122*
5	The Teacher State: Morality and Everyday Sovereignty over Schools	*155*
	Conclusion: Escape, Encampment, and the Alchemy of Nationalism	*193*
	Notes	*211*
	References	*221*
	Index	*231*

Acknowledgments

I have tried to write this book with honesty, integrity, and compassion. It has been a long process, and I am deeply indebted to many people who have provided support, insight, and advice along the way. Many Eritreans at all levels—Ministry of Education personnel, school directors, teachers, students, and others—were gracious enough to share their observations, their analyses, their experience, and sometimes even their lives and friendship with me. All were working hard to make Eritrea the best country possible for its young people. I admire and deeply respect each individual I spoke with in the process of researching this book for all the struggles they took on. I am very grateful to all those who enlightened me with their visions, hopes, and criticisms. I especially thank the teachers and others who shared so much with me over the course of several years.

I was fortunate to receive a postdoctoral fellowship from the National Academy of Education and Spencer Foundation, which was invaluable in the completion of this book. I also received funding from a Social Science Research Council International Dissertation Field Research Fellowship and a Fulbright/IIE student fellowship to complete this research. The National Academy of Education and Spencer Foundation provided an opportunity for wonderful mentoring. I am particularly grateful to Aurolyn Luykx and Leslie Bartlett for their encouragement.

The title of and several long segments from Chapter 2 are from Jennifer Riggan, "It Seemed like a Punishment": Teacher Transfers, Hollow

Nationalism, and the Intimate State in Eritrea," *American Ethnologist* 40, no. 4 (November 2013): 749–763. I thank Angelique Haugerud and the anonymous reviewers for their feedback on the ideas that shaped that article, which are also integral to this volume as a whole. An earlier version of Chapter 3 was published as Jennifer Riggan, "Avoiding Wastage by Making Soldiers: Technologies of the State and the Imagination of the Educated Nation," in *Biopolitics, Militarism, and Development: Eritrea in the Twenty-First Century*, edited by David O'Kane and Tricia Redeker Hepner, pp. 72–91 (New York: Berghahn Books, 2009). I am grateful to the volume editors for their feedback on that work. Earlier versions of various chapters in this book were also presented at numerous conferences. I am indebted to panel organizers, discussants, fellow panelists, and audience members who provided feedback on this work. I also thank Sara Cohen at Temple University Press for her enthusiasm for this project and the anonymous reviewers who provided insight on the draft manuscript.

This book was shaped by comments, feedback, and conversations with an eclectic group of scholars and thinkers. I am grateful to my dissertation committee, a group of powerful intellectuals and fine human beings who supported me as a scholar and a person and have very much shaped who I am in both regards. Kathleen Hall is not only an intellectual role model but also a nurturing friend and mentor who inspires me through her ongoing search for meaningful, critical academic engagement with issues that we care about in the world. Over the years, Sandra Barnes has shaped my thinking through coursework and conversations, provided ongoing inspiration and encouragement, and continued to provide extremely supportive and helpful mentoring over the past decade. Guidance by Ritty Lukose helped shape much of my early thinking on this project; most notably, I am grateful to her for pushing me to focus explicitly on the relationship between the nation and state. I am very fortunate to have benefited from the support, encouragement, and guidance of three such accomplished anthropologists, each of whom brought a distinct perspective to my work.

I am also blessed to have the support of many friends who are distinguished intellectuals and excellent editors. My thinking on teachers and, indeed, my decision to focus on teachers, would never have taken its current form without my long conversations with Aiden Downey about his brilliant work on teachers in the urban United States. He and I exchanged lengthy e-mails across the world as I typed up field notes with a view of the Red Sea and he wrote about schools on the East Coast of the United States while looking out over snowy Montana. Maia Cucchiara and Dana Holland both generously edited, in its entirety, much earlier versions of what became this book. Both have always been wonderful friends, and Maia is a great writing companion. The book could not have come to fruition without consistent support from Thea Abu El-Haj, with whom I met regularly during the writing phase. She read the entire manuscript as it evolved, sometimes in multiple forms, and had a marvelous way of telling me when to scale back and when to stop. Hilary Parsons Dick, Cati Coe, and Christy Schuetze read several chapters in their near final form and helped me hone them into finished work. Over the years, a multidisciplinary, eclectic group of colleagues read chapters and helped me work through ideas. I am particularly grateful to colleagues at Arcadia: Samer Abboud, Angela Kachuyevski, Sonia Rosen, Peter Siskind, and Amy Widestrom, who read portions of the manuscript. My entire department has been exceptionally supportive in helping me complete this work. I have also been fortunate to have many wonderful talented research assistants at Arcadia. I especially thank Hope Kwiatkowski, Josephine Lippincott, and Kate Slenzak for their attention to detail and copyediting.

Scholars who work on Eritrea are a small, intimate, and supportive group. Victoria Bernal, Tricia Redeker Hepner, and Tekle Woldemikael in particular provided professional and personal advice, regularly exchanged information and ideas, and helped me work through the idiosyncrasies of doing research on Eritrea. I also benefited from conversations small and large with fine scholars who study Eritrea—too numerous to mention here—and I am thankful for all the insights that resulted. Amanda Poole in particular has supported and inspired me in a multitude of ways over the past fifteen years. She is a true "multipurpose" friend and colleague for whom I am very grateful.

Finally, I appreciate the support and sacrifices of my husband, Ermias; our children, Yonathan and Samuel; my parents, Ann and John Riggan; my brothers, Matt Riggan and Francis Vargas; and my sisters-in-law, Erin Own and Kim Vargas, all of whom may have grown tired of my working on this book but without whom I could not have completed it. During the years of completing this project, my two sons were born. In so many ways (perhaps not all of them welcome), this book has been a part of their lives from the start. Raising two small children while writing this book would not have been possible without my loving and involved family. I thank you all.

The Struggling State

Introduction

Everyday Authoritarianism, Teachers, and the Decoupling of Nation and State

Assab, May 2000

Teacher Ezekiel woke up and found that his head was resting on a pile of Kalashnikovs. He could feel the rocking motion of the boat and the sun beating down on him, his body soaked in sweat. Squinting, he opened his eyes and scanned his belongings; everything he owned of any worth was in a pile around him. Next to his head, two feet, wearing *shida,* the black plastic sandals emblematic of Eritrean fighters, were anchored on top of his radio. Opening his eyes a little wider in the bright sunlight, he looked up at the fighter who was scanning the crowded boat, calling for someone. The fighter waved, having found his friend, and then stepped down from the radio and moved on, never even noticing Ezekiel waking up from much-needed sleep. Ezekiel put his head back down on his Kalashnikov pillow and closed his eyes.

Three days earlier, it had been a typical blazing hot day in late May in Eritrea's port town of Assab. Having finished marking exams, Ezekiel and his friend had been on their way to the cinema to have a drink and watch a movie to celebrate the end of the school year. "Where are you going?" People they passed asked them.

"To the cinema," Ezekiel and his friend answered.

"You can go, but there won't be any movies. Everyone is leaving."

The presence of the war had loomed over the residents of Assab since the border war with Ethiopia broke out two years earlier in 1998, but this was the first time civilians were evacuated. The front was some sixty kilometers away. The port, which had served as Ethiopia's main access to the sea, closed when the war began, and many of the town's residents returned to the Ethiopian or Eritrean highlands, leaving shops, restaurants, and homes shuttered and empty. The town filled with soldiers. Several times, Ethiopia had unsuccessfully attempted to bomb Assab's airport and the village of Harsile, the area's water source. The school had become a hospital during the first offensive in 1998.

After being told about the evacuation, Ezekiel rushed home to pack. On the way, he ran into his school director, who was heading to the port. In a panic, she ordered him to remain behind to hand back report cards to any students who showed up. He refused, telling her he was going to the same place she was, the same place everyone was going.

Ezekiel and the town's residents had no reason to think the government would not safely and successfully evacuate them. Amid chaos and fear of imminent violence, the residents of Assab hoped and, indeed, assumed that the government would protect them, evacuate them, and provide for them when they were displaced. While these events were occurring in Assab, towns in the western lowlands of the country were also being evacuated, with residents relocated to camps for Internally Displaced People as the fighting forces engaged in a strategic withdrawal in the face of oncoming Ethiopian forces. However, once in the port, where Ezekiel and most of the town remained for several days while the boats were prepared for the evacuation, it was unclear whether anyone was in charge. There was little food. Shops were closed down, and everyone was left to fend for him- or herself. Rumors circulated that the town's top officials had begun to evacuate their own family members and property days before they announced the evacuation to the population at large. At one point, one of the Ministry of Education supervisors showed up with crates of beer that would have been sold at the teachers' club, handing them out to teachers for free while saying, "This is our beer." The implication was that they'd better drink it now, because it would be looted when they left. At one point, while sleeping on the hard concrete surface of the port, Ezekiel and the other teachers woke up to see a military truck suspended overhead from a large crane. The electricity in the port went off while the boats were being loaded by crane, halting the evacuation process. The technicians who worked for the electric company were in a bus, fleeing the town by road, leaving no one to keep the power running.

After the evacuation, when teachers and others arrived in Massawa,

Eritrea's northern port, hungry and exhausted, they were told almost immediately to report for National Service. The government was calling up everyone from around the country for military training and possible combat. Conditions in military training were harsh; trainees were required to engage in extreme physical labor in 120°F desert conditions and to work and sleep outside. They were given limited water and little to eat. Most significantly, they were under the absolute control of commanding officers, all of whom utilized various forms of corporal punishment to discipline trainees, and some of whom believed it was within their rights to beat trainees or tie them in stress positions in the desert sun for hours to punish them for deviation from the strict rules. In the years following these events, conscription into the military would extend well beyond the eighteen months of service outlined in Eritrean law and well beyond the period of actual fighting in the border war. Indeed, the time limits on *service,* a term that includes both national and military service, have become indefinite for many Eritreans who have been "in service" for well over a decade.

Wartime highlights what Begoña Aretxaga (2003) calls the "maddening" nature of the state as people hope that those in charge will take care of them, fear that those in power will hurt them, and experience government institutions unraveling, ultimately muddling the way people imagine the state. During the evacuation of Assab, the state receded. Its institutions and representatives lost the capacity to act "as the state" in the face of chaos and disorder and instead just took care of themselves. Teachers fled before marking their exams. The school director had to abandon her duties. Subsequently, the state, which people thought of as protective during the evacuation, enabled its agents to use force against its people to recruit and train them to be soldiers. A de facto state of emergency was enacted, giving state actors powers of control, coercion, and capacity for violence. Violence and force were used to turn civilians, who thought of themselves as needing protection, into soldiers who would protect the nation. In the process, these civilians were also turned into what I call *coerced subjects*—citizens forced to defend, use, and experience violence for the state.

This book is about how citizens imagine their state *and* nation when they experience the state as turning against them. It is now common among scholars to view nations as imagined communities, but national imaginaries do not simply arise spontaneously, nor are they solely the machinations of governing elites' national projects. The way citizens imagine the nation and their identity as nationals is always a combination of non-national (ethnic, regional, religious) solidarities, lived experiences, and nation-making projects that attempt to bundle these into a neat, unified package. States, meanwhile, are *thought of* as a totality that has sovereignty over national territories and people, including the power to nationalize them, but states are seldom as coherent or cohesive as they seem to be in our imaginations. In reality, states are a configuration of actors, agents, policies, and processes and are only a totality in the imaginations of their citizens, employees, and others who tend to characterize them as such. State actors struggle with each other and with citizens to influence the ways both the nation and state are imagined. When we examine the ways imaginaries of state and nation mutually shape each other, we see that the production of the nation and state is the result of a complex and unwieldy process, particularly when states use force against citizens.

Using the case of Eritrea, I show how citizens' often-coercive encounters with state actors shape their imaginaries of the state, the nation, and the linkage between them. The ideological and imaginative glue that binds nation to state—the hyphen in nation-state—can't be taken for granted, particularly amid conditions of authoritarian rule.[1] National imaginaries are radically altered by state coercion; however, the complex processes through which coercion decouples the nation from the state are understudied. Even when people experience the state as incompetent or dangerous, they hold out hope that the state still cares and has the capacity to care (Aretxaga 2003). These contradictory experiences of the state become even clearer when we understand that even when the state is coercing its subjects, "it" is not a monolith but rather a plurality of actions, actors, and imaginaries, constantly being made and remade in interactions between those who represent the state and those to whom they represent the state.[2]

Most importantly, government employees, who give the state its institutional coherence and materiality, also feel coerced by the state and are responsive to the shifting imaginaries shaped by these experiences. My focus here is on teachers, who are the government employees (state actors) most directly responsible for shaping the nation's young. Teachers and schools provide a unique vantage point through which to understand the dialectic of how national imaginaries get produced in response to feelings that the state is turning against its people, in large part because teachers are situated to do the work of hyphenating, or gluing, nation to state. Those same teachers who experienced the botched evacuation and were subsequently conscripted into a grueling summer of military training in 2000 were released from the military and back in the classroom the following fall, charged, as all teachers are, with inculcating national values and identities into their students, many of whom were also evacuated and had relatives serving in the armed forces. Even as teachers confronted their own maddeningly conflicted imaginaries of the state, they produced the nation for and with their students in schools and classrooms. In doing this, teachers navigated the tension between their charge to educate the nation and their discontent with the party-government program of mass militarization. This book examines this tension at a moment when imaginaries of the coercive state were eroding, unraveling, and changing sentiments about what it meant to be national in Eritrea as a whole.

Education, Nationalism, and the Struggling State in Eritrea

Understanding the relationship between nation and state is essential to understanding Eritrean political and social life and is central to scholarship on Eritrea (Connell 2011; Dorman 2006; Hepner 2009b; Hirt and Mohammad 2013; Müller 2008, 2012b; Riggan 2013b). Indeed, much of the scholarship on Eritrea notes that it is difficult to distinguish between nation and state in large part because the ruling party has worked very hard to synthesize the two (Dorman 2006; Müller 2008, 2012b). Meanwhile, ethnographic work tends to emphasize often quiet, but widespread, grassroots discontent with these efforts at synthesizing the nation with the state (Hepner 2009b; Hirt and Mohammed 2013; Mahrt 2009; O'Kane 2012; Poole 2009; Riggan 2013b; Treiber 2009; Tronvoll 1996, 1998). The predominant version of Eritrean nationalism was carefully crafted and constructed by the ruling (and liberating) party, the Eritrean People's Liberation Front (EPLF), during the country's thirty-year war for independence from Ethiopia, which is referred to as "The Struggle." The EPLF intentionally oriented the Eritrean nation around the revolutionary values of The Struggle: self-sufficiency, an orientation toward "progress" and development, an absolute willingness to sacrifice, and a warrior ethos. The EPLF, which was renamed the People's Front for Democracy and Justice (PFDJ) when independence was won in 1991, embodied both the state and the nation. It enjoyed widespread support during the post-independence years, a moment in history that is described as effervescent for people's widespread emotional coalescence around the party and independence itself (Hepner 2009b).[3] But since the border war with Ethiopia broke out in 1998, the euphoric tone that marked the years between independence and the onset of the border war has been replaced with a sense among many that the government can only bring about a hopeless future. An iconic popular expression, coined by Eritrea's president, Isaias Afewerki, during Eritrea's thirty-year struggle for liberation, describes the country's "warrior ethos": Eritrea is a nation of soldiers. However, for teachers, students, and others, mass conscription has given new meaning to that common expression.

Eritrea's national/military service program, which became controversial at the end of the border war, is central to sentiments that "the government" (*mengisti*), a catch-all phrase that references a wide range of political, bureaucratic, and military policies, practices, and personnel, is turning against, and indeed punishing, its people. National/military service is effectively indefinite for the majority of conscripts. By law, National Service in Eritrea requires citizens, male and female, to undergo six months of military training and twelve months of unpaid, voluntary service, typically in the military, but for educated people, often in a civil capacity. During the border war with Ethiopia (1998–2000), the government mobilized as many citizens as possible; however, despite the fact that there has been no fighting since 2000, those serving in the military have not been demobilized and, at the time of my fieldwork (2003–2005), even those assigned to serve in a civil capacity typically served much longer than the requisite eighteen months. In 2002, the government introduced the Warsai Yikaalo Development Campaign, which allocated the labor of those serving in the military to development projects and extended the term of National Service indefinitely for most conscripts. Following the war, the government began to rely on increasingly coercive measures, such as *gifa,* or mass round-ups, to ensure that Eritreans did not escape from service. Detentions without cause or due process became more frequent, and it was effectively impossible for almost all Eritreans to leave the country. In light of these circumstances, during the course of my fieldwork, Eritreans often referred to their country as a "prison" and depicted the state as punishing. For example, when teachers recounted stories of military training to me, they described it as a punitive experience, telling stories about enduring harsh conditions, sleeping outside, eating watered-down lentils and stale flatbread. They described their fear of commanders who controlled their every moment and movement and could punish them for any failure to follow strict orders at all times of the day, even if they did not know they had done something wrong. Few mentioned the need to defend the nation, despite the fact that a war was going on at the time. This suggests that when the state is imagined as coercive, imaginaries of the nation and national duty also change. The experience of being a soldier became an experience of state violence. Imagining military service as punitive rather than as one's duty to the nation reflected a shifting affective stance toward the nation or, more specifically, toward the government-constructed image of the nation as oriented toward defense, sacrifice, and militarization. Official versions of nationalism were hollowed of effervescence by the government's own policies and practices, which were intended to perpetuate the very sentiments of patriotism that they eroded.

Education in Eritrea is central to the PFDJ's militarized nation-building agenda and to the erosion of populist support for that agenda (Müller 2012b; Riggan 2011). At the time of my longest period of fieldwork in Eritrea (2003–2005), educational institutions were directly implicated in the making of soldiers through the auspices of a dramatic educational reform. In 2003, as part of a comprehensive educational reform package, the Ministry of Education announced that the education system would be expanded from grade 11 to grade 12, but *all* grade 12 students from the whole country would have to attend school in one boarding facility located in Sawa—the nation's military training center. Military training would begin in the summer before grade 12. Additionally, as part of the same package of reforms, the government announced a shift from a system of highly selective promotion in Senior Secondary Schools (grades 9–12) to a system of mass promotion. Thus, the same year in which it was announced that everyone would attend grade 12 in Sawa, it was also announced that everyone would pass. Although there was a complex rationale for this change in promotion policies, which I discuss in Chapter 3, what this policy signaled to teachers and students was that the government no longer "cared about" education, as many of my interlocutors frequently commented. Rather than being rewarded for educational accomplishments, students believed that they were being promoted *en masse* and, furthermore, punished by being sent to military training. Educational policies thus provide a particularly salient example of government programs, which were intended to socialize Eritreans into the party's vision of national duty, being reinterpreted as the government turning against the people.

A state like Eritrea that prohibits citizens from leaving, engages in mass round-ups, detains arbitrarily, permanently conscripts a large swathe of its population into the military, and utilizes schools as a conduit for military conscription might seem like a "strong" state in the sense that it has the capacity to implement policies and enact sovereignty over its people. Such a state might not seem to be "struggling," yet I argue that states in Eritrea and elsewhere struggle in a variety of ways.[4] States struggle to legitimately enact their own nation-building projects. Authoritarianism and state coercion, in particular, reveal weaknesses in the hyphen between nation and state, weaknesses that are present in all states, even those that we might not label as authoritarian or coercive. The case of Eritrea highlights these state struggles in several ways.

Specific to Eritrea, the term "The Struggle" refers to Eritrea's thirty-year war for liberation from Ethiopia, which resulted in Eritrea's independence in 1991. The PFDJ affixes itself to the legacy of The Struggle, a legacy that has fused the creation of a sovereign state, the defense of those sovereign borders, the development of that sovereign nation, and a notion of Eritrean citizenship oriented toward willingness to sacrifice for the nation (Bernal 2014). I explore this legacy in more detail in Chapter 1. The PFDJ envisioned a form of nationalism in which individual citizens in the post-independence nation would *willingly* struggle for the development and defense of the independent nation, but the party eventually had to *force* its citizens to participate in the nation-building project oriented toward these goals. However, as the party turned toward force, it struggled in a different way—to maintain the legitimacy of revolutionary nationalism. As Eritreans came to view the state as punishing, sentiments of national duty and loyalty to the revolutionary legacy were eroded. In this process, as I detail in Chapter 2, the party's rather monolithic definition of what it meant to be Eritrean was challenged. Thus, the second form of struggle illuminated here is the struggle of the party to maintain the legitimacy of its nation-making project.

These challenges to the legitimacy of the party's nation-making project occurred subtly and ambiguously but persistently in the realm of the quotidian, particularly in schools. This brings us to the third manifestation of state struggle. Individuals, including state employees, struggled with their feelings about the state, the nation, and their responsibilities to it. The struggles of state employees, particularly teachers, were especially paradoxical because their struggles occurred in their encounters with students and, thus, constituted and altered the state itself. These everyday struggles in schools are important to explore not only because schools were where divergent meanings of what it meant to be Eritrean clashed but also because teachers' struggles reflected and resulted in a diminished capacity to discipline educated citizens. Schools were alternately spaces of institutional disintegration, the subject of Chapter 4, and spaces of coercion, discipline, and violence, which is examined in Chapter 5. When teachers struggled, the nature and coherence of a key state institution—schools—were at stake.

In short, the Eritrean state struggled to be legitimate, to produce loyal national subjects, to reproduce and reify itself, and to achieve institutional coherence. These struggles are certainly not unique to Eritrea; indeed, all states struggle to produce these effects. But the conditions in Eritrea produced by mass militarization, the party's orthodox adherence to its revolutionary nationalist agenda, and the government's increased reliance on coercion amplify these struggles and expose the paradoxes of state legitimacy and control.

Emergent Authoritarianism and the Imagination of Nation and State

When I first visited Eritrea as a Peace Corps volunteer in 1995, the official National Service program had just begun. Each evening, adults and children from the neighborhood where my host family lived crowded into their small living room to watch footage of National Service recruits completing their military training in Sawa. Extra chairs were brought in for adults, while teenagers stood at the back of the room and young children filled in the floor space between chairs and table. The same scene was repeated in the living rooms of anyone who had a television as well as in many restaurants, hotels, and shops throughout the town. The recruits performed elaborate military drills while the national anthem and patriotic songs played cheerfully. Interspersed with scenes of military unity, interviews with soldiers of both genders and from all nine Eritrean ethnic groups espoused the success of National Service in meeting both of its goals—to develop the nation and to create a sense of national oneness. Meanwhile, that summer, mandatory summer service programs for high school and university students (*ma'atot*) were in full swing. Tent camps had popped up along the sides of roads, and groups of young people were planting trees or building terraces. While there was some debate about these programs, in general Eritreans enthusiastically supported the idea of service (Hepner 2009b; Müller 2008; Reid 2009). It seemed to me that every family had at least one (or more) member involved in National Service or summer service.

In the years prior to and immediately following independence, the Eritrean government engaged its population in a highly effective nation-building program. During the war for independence, the party created a national ideology and a state apparatus to disseminate it, which together effectively galvanized and unified the population (Hepner 2009b; Pool 2001; see also Connell [1993] 1997 and Iyob 1995). Eritrea is a country where the party leadership has been engaged in a long effort, one that predates independence by well over a decade, to produce institutions to govern, educate, and generally manage and look after the welfare of Eritreans. These institutions of governance were also intent on instilling a particular sense of *Eritrean-ness* in the population. Given the effectiveness of a nation-building project that fused nation to state, Eritrea might appear to be a strange place to interrogate the weakening relationship between the two.

Eritrea was quite different from most other African states at independence (and, indeed, states in Africa and elsewhere today), where societal forces and relationships are often densely intertwined with state institutions, leading to what Goran Hyden (2006) has called "politics in people" and what others often gloss as "clientilism" or "patrimonialism." In contrast, in Eritrea "the state" is quite strong and well emancipated from society (Chabal and Daloz 1999). Eritrea is also interesting because, unlike many countries in Africa where attempts at fusing nation and state fell apart because of either the institutional weakness of the state apparatus or because of the lack of coherent, populist nationalism, in Eritrea the PFDJ/EPLF adeptly hyphenated them. Eritrea's leadership quite intentionally created institutions of governance to produce and promote a version of nationalism that enabled Eritreans to imagine their national community and situate the party-run state apparatus at its center. This project of making the nation-state enabled the state and the nation to reify each other, leading to what appeared to be a strong state that at least initially produced strong attachments between its people and the nation.

However, the state is not the only entity with the capacity to produce imaginaries of the nation; the ways in which citizens think and feel about the state directly affect the ways in which they imagine the nation, and vice versa (Appadurai 1996; Gupta 2012; Herzfeld 1997; Wedeen 2008). Imagination is a social process that gives us a profound and powerful collective capacity to think through our interconnections with other people, times, and spaces that are unknown to us and spread across a national territory and, at times, the globe (Appadurai 1996). One example of this is Benedict Anderson's (1991) famous assertion that nations are imagined communities, but imagining the national community is difficult without placing an imaginary of the state at the center of what the nation is. The understanding of a territorial entity called the nation, a community of people attached to that territory, and the sovereignty of a state over that community and territory (even if it is not the state all the people want) is central to defining the nation (Wedeen 2008). The state, thus, plays a critical role in nationalizing the nation, but when the state is not imagined as benevolent, it loses its hold over *how* people imagine the nation, leaving nationalism fragmented, conflicted, and susceptible to skirmishes over the meanings of the nation and national belonging.

In the years following Eritrea's 1991 independence, Eritreans tended to imagine the state as benevolent despite initial evidence of authoritarianism. The ruling party argued that it was inventing its own form of governance, which would be uniquely suited to Eritrea's own historical circumstances. Indeed, Eritrea's leaders rather self-assuredly asserted that they were not going to repeat the mistakes of other newly independent African nations (an assertion the government used and continues to use to give license to many of its coercive and authoritarian tendencies). In the years between independence and the border war, the government announced a date for elections; engaged Eritreans in a grassroots, collaborative process of constitution making; and implemented a number of highly progressive policies to promote gender and ethnic equality (Müller 2005). During these years, education and health care were expanded into rural areas, and the National Service program was implemented. Party leaders, along with many foreign diplomats and Eritreans themselves, saw tendencies toward authoritarian consolidation of power at that time as actions of a regime that was "in transition."

Up to and through the border war, this bond between nation and state in Eritrea remained strong; it only began to disintegrate in the year after the border war ended (roughly 2000–2001). In fall 2001, prominent party insiders wrote an open letter critiquing the government's management of the war and the country. They were subsequently arrested. Shortly thereafter, the private presses were closed, and several journalists were arrested as well. This trend began to delegitimize the party's governing strategies and nation-making project. The 2002 implementation of the Warsai Yikaalo Development Campaign, which effectively extended national-military service indefinitely, and the mass round-ups (*gifa*) that followed further challenged people's loyalties toward and trust in the state.

By the time I began fieldwork in 2003, it had become quite clear that many Eritreans inside Eritrea did not believe that the government would transition to democracy. Indeed, people commented that the government no longer cared for the people, only for itself. Elections were postponed again and again. *Gifa*, which made it clear that the government had the capacity to detain without cause, was enacted with a new ferocity (as I discuss in Chapter 2). A form of extensive but low-tech surveillance became common (Bozzini 2011), and there was increased paranoia about internal opposition, especially within the ruling party (Hepner 2009b). People felt constrained and forced by the state. Coercion, or the sense of being *forced*, is one of the key modalities through which the state is encountered in authoritarian regimes.

The idea that states have a legitimate capacity to use force (against their own citizens, if need be) is central to conventional understandings of what the state is, yet anthropological work on the state pays surprisingly little attention to the nuances, complexities, and paradoxes of coercion. The way coercion reworks citizens' national identities and imaginaries of the state is seldom examined. (Additionally, we know little about how and why state actors choose to utilize force and violence. I address this below.) With some very notable exceptions, the trend toward examining the state through the lens of poststructuralist or Foucauldian approaches has tended to illuminate forms of discipline that do not use physical force, on the one hand, but emphasize the disciplinary capacity of physical force to create docile subjects on the other.[5] Coercion does not simply produce docile, disciplined subjects, however, but subjects who are simultaneously docile, discontented, unruly, and disorderly. Coercion is a form of productive power—in other words, a state effect, but one that produces effects that are hard to control.

Many authoritarian regimes have power over the bodies of their subjects, including the power to relocate, detain, harm, and kill; however, this power creates conditions in which state subjects imagine themselves individually and collectively as coerced subjects, or subjects who can be forced.[6] Conversely, they imagine the state as not only able but willing to use force. The state imagined in this manner becomes illegitimate precisely because it is experienced as turning against its people. At the same time, coerced subjects develop a set of strategies to avoid coercion, and solidarities form around evading the state. An affective climate in which fear intermingles with humor and ridicule of authorities emerges. Furthermore, the humor, ridicule, fear, and evasion that emerge to cope with state coercion undermine and unravel the national projects that states often enlist to legitimize their use of force. The coercive state, thus, cannibalizes the legitimacy of its own national project.

Over time, fewer and fewer Eritreans regarded the state as legitimate, and yet lingering and maddening desires for a benevolent state have arguably prevented people from engaging in broader resistance to such repressive conditions. This condition is reminiscent of what Achille Mbembe (2001) calls "impotence." According to Mbembe, when subjects perceive the state as having the capacity to absolutely command them—to tell them when, how, and where to walk, stand, dance, talk, work, fight, and so on—they will comply, but only to the extent that they are forced. Mbembe notes that as these state commands are enacted, symbolic and disciplinary realms join to produce docility and obedience, but they never quite produce complete compliance among citizens, and thus the seeds of transgression may emerge in subtle ways as symbols are transformed, rituals subverted, and narratives quietly rewritten. Citizens evade state commands and ridicule those in power with all sorts of humorous and vulgar forms that delegitimize their power. According to Mbembe, ridicule, ribaldry, and other subtle but powerful ways of symbolically diminishing the grandeur of the state render both the state and its subjects impotent. Rather than undoing official power, this situation results in what he calls "mutual zombification" (2001: 111). Ruler and ruled are caught in a sort of bizarre, grotesque dance that leaves them both sapped.

Coercion produces what I think of as a vicious cycle of impotence. When a regime must rely on force to govern, it strips itself of legitimacy, thereby further necessitating its reliance on force and further undermining its legitimacy. As Eritrea's leaders became more and more reliant on force, particularly to conscript Eritreans into National Service, but more generally to command Eritreans to do their "duty" as national subjects through ongoing National Service, they made the very concept of the state impotent. As the Eritrean leadership became more reliant on *forcing* its citizens to defend and sacrifice for the nation, Eritreans quietly ridiculed the state and developed evasive tactics to avoid and escape from its demands.

Attempting to consolidate power over state institutions while building coherent national identities is a delicate balancing act under the best of circumstances, but authoritarian regimes face particular challenges in doing so precisely because their subjects believe they are forced to perform "as if" they are compliantly patriotic (Wedeen 1999: 15–16). For this reason, authoritarian regimes often produce hollow nationalisms that are performed but not felt and thus never achieve emotional resonance or legitimacy. Fearing disloyalty or disunity, authoritarian governments may actually turn on their nations, violently cleansing and attacking parts of their populations and, in doing so, cannibalizing the nations by symbolically stripping away the capacity for their populations to imagine themselves as part of the national communities (Appadurai 1996; Aretxaga 2003). Additionally, coercive practices designed to force citizen bodies to comply with performances of obedience can backfire, producing an empty performance, an illusion of compliance, and an imaginary of an illegitimate state (Mbembe 2001; Wedeen 1999). It is precisely because of their power to coerce citizen bodies that authoritarian regimes undermine national loyalties.

Authoritarian regimes, like any regime, want to appear legitimate and thus must "manage the symbolic world"—in other words, they must control not only the symbols of the nation but also what these symbols signify to citizens and how nationals feel about these symbols. These regimes do so by exerting disciplinary, coercive, *and* symbolic power (Wedeen 1999: 32), but what the Eritrean case shows us is that often the efforts to exert disciplinary power are overly reliant on coercion and result in delegitimating the symbolic world of the nation. Authoritarian regimes are adept at commanding citizens to perform in and observe national rituals but often fail to be perceived as legitimate representatives of the nation (Mbembe 2001; Wedeen 1999). They produce a display of power, docility, and obedience, but the fact that coercion is necessary in the first place reveals the limitations of coercion—it produces empty displays of loyalty (Mbembe 2001:

110). Coercion of the body and the production of national ideology thus coexist in a mutually constitutive but troubled relationship.

To understand the complex and nuanced process of how once-effervescent Eritrean nationalism began to cool in the face of coercion, one must step away from the official project of nation-state formation and examine the informal spaces in which people transgress these disciplinary-symbolic systems of (state) power to produce alternative imaginaries of state and nation (Wedeen 1999: 151). Powerful, but not entirely coherent, national imaginaries circulate outside the official national project. Alternatives to the official national project always exist, but they take on a new salience when citizens come to imagine the state as increasingly incompetent or dangerous, as the state in Eritrea came to be imagined. But even more interestingly, in Eritrea, I found that these alternatives to the state project could be and were produced within state institutions themselves, most remarkably in schools.

Teachers in the Middle

In late summer 2000, teachers were released from military training. One evening around that time, I was in a small nondescript bar on one of the back streets of Asmara where teachers from the South Red Sea region tended to congregate at all times of day for cappuccino, tea, soft drinks, or beer. I was with several teachers and other civil servants from the region and noticed a teacher who often sat with us but on this night was sitting across the room with a man I did not know. He was talking intently with this man, huddled over their beer bottles. Half an hour or so later, the teacher joined us and said, "That was our commander when we were in military training. I saw him here and I wanted to buy him a beer. To just talk to him as a person."

He paused, and I let the significance of what he had just said sink in. Military training varied in its level of harshness, with some trainers using relatively little force and violence while others used a great deal. Military training, which involved intimidation and hierarchical authority, was an intense encounter with the coercive state, particularly for teachers, who were more accustomed to being the authority figure than to having authority wielded against them.

"I am very happy tonight," the teacher noted. "Now I know this man as a person. Military was very hard. They don't treat you like a person. I was happy to talk to him and know who he is."

This brief anecdote, a unique occurrence, gives us a rare insight into the state that is coercive, authoritarian, and often violent but also intimate and personal. Exploring the motivations of this civil servant and former military trainee buying a beer for his former military commander, who had wielded authority over him and had used force and possibly violence against him, allows us to disentangle the state as people from The State writ large. The teacher's desire to know the person who had caused him pain on behalf of the state illuminates the fact that the state, ultimately, comprises people, albeit people who are imagined as part of a much larger totality.

The language commonly used to talk about the state in Eritrea illustrates a similar interplay between the state and the people who constitute it. The word *mengisti*, which translates as "government," is typically used to describe the state and more often than not refers to a realm of officialdom—the president, the leaders of the party, and mandates, practices, or policies that were passed down from the top. For example, various forms of service, *gifa*, and educational reforms were all attributed to "the government," and, indeed, these policies and practices did emanate from on high. *Mengisti* typically was not a word used to describe intimate encounters with the state but rather a term to depict a form of higher power—The State. This is an important distinction because it suggests that Eritreans made scalar distinctions regarding how they thought about where and what The State was; however, these scalar distinctions broke down and became blurry in practice. I recall a conversation I had with several teachers and lower-level Ministry of Education bureaucrats about what and, more precisely, who constituted *mengisti*. Everyone agreed that the head of the South Red Sea branch of the Ministry of Education was the government, but aside from agreement that the head was "government," there was great disagreement about where the government ended and the people began. A lively debate ensued as some contended that the lower-level bureaucrats around the table were also *mengisti*, while these bureaucrats themselves strongly disagreed. (Indeed, my argument throughout this book is that teachers *are* the state because of their particular positioning and the role they play, but most teachers would disagree with this viewpoint.) Although Eritreans drew a clear distinction between *mengisti*, which was clearly thought of as existing at a higher level, and their own encounters with those endowed with state power, these distinctions were in reality very blurry, in large part because very little in Eritrea was the result of clear "policy." Blurriness around what was and what was not *mengisti* came, in part, from the lack of rule of law in Eritrea, which manifested itself at all levels and made it impossible to know who or which entity was responsible for how people were treated. This ambiguity contributed to the sense of arbitrariness surrounding being coerced and punished. Eritreans talked about *mengisti* as "out there" or "up there," but *mengisti* also had very direct effects on people's lives because it forced them to do things. At the same time, there was uncertainty and debate as to where/who/what *mengisti* was. It was simultaneously intimate and transcendent.

When the state is coercive or violent, we seldom examine its ambiguity or explore the complex agency of actors carrying out violence. Instead we reify an imaginary of a powerful state that *is* violent. In material terms, The State does not act on bodies; rather, individual state agents do.[7] But through state agents' interactions with the bodies of state subjects, everyone involved—agents and subjects alike—come to imagine the state and their relationship to it.[8] For this reason, it is crucial to understand the state as the people who act on its behalf and to explore the belief systems and contradictory experiences that shape these people's actions.

I refer to these actors, who are in the employ of but not necessarily empowered by the state, as *middle actors*. Middle actors may be military commanders or police, but they may also include bureaucrats, civil servants, or teachers. They are *in the middle* by virtue of being both powerful and disempowered. They are influenced by the same quotidian social, political, and economic processes as the broader citizenry, but they also have power to shape this citizenry's actions, beliefs, and imaginaries of the state. They often hail from dominant groups in terms of ethnicity, race, religion, class, region, or gender, but their position as frontline state agents means that they are typically not among the elite of these groups.

I look at teachers as a particularly important type of middle actor, for they are situated in the middle in some particularly paradoxical ways. Teachers produce and reproduce both state and nation. Teachers are often students' first encounters with the state (Luykx 1999; F. Wilson 2001). They inculcate national identities and a sense of citizenship duties in students but are often critical of the very state that they help constitute. In Eritrea, teachers were caught in the middle as they tried to navigate between their desires to help the nation develop while contending with the state's project of mass militarization and its assumption, which they were highly critical of, that both students and teachers were soldiers. Teachers had their own educational nation-building project but were pressed to comply with government policies. They tried to negotiate the de facto merger of educational and militarized identities but were affected by state coercion and, in turn, coerced students on behalf of the state.

A variety of types of state actors could be analyzed to understand this dialectic of being coerced/coercing. Other ethnographies of the everyday state focus on other types of middle actors, such as members of the military

(Bickford 2011; Glaeser 2011; Kanaaneh 2009; Macleish 2013), customs agents (Chalfin 2010), bureaucrats and civil servants (Gupta 2012; Herzfeld 1992), and artists (Adams 2010; Frederik 2012). Additionally, a series of studies of vigilantes shows how those outside the state do the work of the state but also respond to state incompetence and impotence in an attempt to make society more moral (Goldstein 2003; Hellweg 2011; Smith 2004). These studies and others all recognize the importance of understanding how states are imagined and experienced by examining the actors situated ambiguously in the middle—citizens experience these actors as representing a state, but the actors themselves may be disillusioned with the state or have motivations that differ significantly from government policy. All of these middle actors constitute an arm of the state, but their social positions are also often ambiguous. For quite some time, anthropologists have been studying up, focusing on the beliefs, cultures, and practices through which the upper echelons of power become manifest (Nader 1972); however, the mandate to study up in many ways sets up a false dichotomy between those who are empowered and those who are disempowered, between the elite and the subaltern. More often, state actors who engage with the population are simultaneously powerful and lacking in power. For this reason, I suggest that a framework that emphasizes the ambiguity of power among those situated liminally between the state and the people is important, yet few theoretical frameworks are explicitly designed to allow us to do so. A study of teachers, like other middle actors, is neither a study up of those with power nor a study down of those who are disempowered, but a study of the intersections of both.

Eritrean teachers have an elite status because they predominantly come from the dominant gender (male) and ethno-religious group (Tigrinya); however, teachers do not consider themselves to be elite members of society for a variety of reasons, and many Eritrean teachers argued compellingly that they were disrespected by society in large part because of the way they were treated by the government. Eritrean teachers are predominantly male and from the dominant Tigrinya ethnic group. Tigrinya people comprise 50 percent of the Eritrean population, reside primarily in the central highlands of the country, and are mostly Christian. The other eight ethnic groups are predominantly Muslim and are scattered around the coastal and western lowlands as well as the more remote northern highlands. Teachers are also elite by virtue of being educated in a country where higher education has been a rarity. Thus, they have a good deal of power and stature in Eritrean society. Teachers are role models for many Eritreans because they have succeeded educationally. However, teachers also believe that their social status is much lower compared to that of other educated people and argue that they are paid less and treated worse than other comparable civil servants. They are thought to be noble by virtue of their education but also in a lower-status profession, constantly under the thumb of the state. Teachers often feel maligned by the government, often comparing themselves to police and soldiers—other groups of state employees thought to be even more poorly treated and regarded.

For Eritrean teachers, the experience of mass militarism, the recent war, and the coerciveness of the government in general played significant roles in shaping how they acted as the state, but in different ways for different teachers. There were two categories of Eritrean teachers in Assab during the two years I conducted fieldwork—"service teachers" and professional teachers.[9] The distinction between service and professional teachers was blurry. The Ministry of Education had hired the older generation of professional teachers in the early 1990s. This generation was conscripted into National Service at the end of the border war in 2000, and their demobilization was finalized in spring 2004. They were, first and foremost, teachers and considered themselves professionals. In contrast, a younger generation of teachers, referred to as "service teachers," had been recruited as part of their National Service obligation following completion of university or teacher training. Members of this group were not demobilized during my time in Eritrea, although they had been released from active military duty to teach. While all teachers were unhappy about their extended National Service, service teachers, who did not know whether they would ever be demobilized, were particularly discouraged. In reality, the distinction between a professional teacher doing National Service and a National Service conscript serving as a teacher (service teacher) was a blurry one, and quite a few teachers fell between the two categories. Nonetheless, the categories determined how quickly one was demobilized and, as I discuss in more detail below, teachers' attitudes toward the government.

In Assab, most teachers came from elsewhere. As I discuss in more detail below, Assab was a somewhat transient place. So, too, was teaching a transient profession. Eritrea's National Service program and civil service jobs displaced and relocated many people. Transfers of civil servants were not limited to a few isolated cases but were widespread, particularly within the Ministry of Education. As of 2003, when I began fieldwork, all teachers in the South Red Sea region had already experienced a transfer at some point or expected to be transferred in the future. To be a teacher meant not counting on being able to settle, put down roots, or imagine a future independent of a state that could relocate you. Although in many respects moving people around the country, particularly under the auspices of service projects, was a strategy of nation building, because teachers felt coerced into moving, it actually undermined their ability to imagine the state as benevolent.

Thus, teachers were in an ambivalent position—relatively elite and privileged compared to Eritrea's population as a whole, but thwarted in their aspirations compared to other educated people in Eritrea. As symbols, teachers simultaneously represent the lived embodiment of people's hopes for a good future and their disappointments in the actual future. For this reason, studying teachers allows us to understand the contradictions of state power as it is imagined as oppressive to teachers while being enacted by them. This complex social status shapes teachers' beliefs, which in turn influence how they act "as" the state. Michael Lipsky's ([1980] 2010) sociological study of "street-level bureaucrats" documents the beliefs and prejudices that certain state employees bring to their work on the street. On top of all this, they bring their own prejudices and belief systems to bear on their work as the state in a process that Michael Herzfeld (1992, 1997) has called "cultural intimacy." As both Akhil Gupta (2012) and Herzfeld (1992) note, bureaucrats often use the power they are allocated not to help but to produce indifference. Extending these arguments, I suggest that the "social production of indifference" (Herzfeld 1992) emerges not because state actors are bad people who want to hurt others but because they are responding to a combination of their own beliefs about what is right and moral, their disillusionment with the state that they are unwittingly and inadvertently a part of, and the structural/institutional constraints of their job. But, ironically, middle actors themselves are often not happy about the roles they play for one reason or another. They are keenly aware of the limits of their power and, at times, of the injustices around them. They often feel alienated, disenfranchised, and victimized by the state that they represent.

Middle actors are also often empowered to utilize force in the name of the state, but their decisions about whether to do so are framed by their ambiguous status. Under conditions that are violent and coercive, it is important to ask how and why state actors behave coercively and violently. Drawing on Giorgio Agamben's (2005) work on the state of exception, which itself is derived from Carl Schmitt's ([1922] 2005: 1) assertion that "sovereign is he who decides on the exception," scholars have focused on the devolution of sovereignty and, specifically, the devolution of decision making about the use of force and violence to state actors (Das and Poole 2004; Hansen and Stepputat 2005). Middle actors are often in a position to decide on the exception and, thus, be sovereign, particularly under conditions in which the state is impotent and incompetent. The violence that results is often seen as a necessary means to produce moral communities, often bringing together public actors and institutions with private relationships (Buur 2003; Lyons 2008; Peteet 1994). In this vein, forms of violence can be seen as attempts to retain order, justice, and morality in times of anxiety. Teachers at times seek to reinscribe morality by using violence, through corporal punishment in particular.

Teachers are also complex and interesting because even when they disagree with government-mandated educational policies, they must comply with them, because resistance to these policies might undermine the quality of education. Teachers may abhor government policies that are largely imposed on them, but they believe in education and schools as a moral good, even if a tainted one, and, ultimately, have to make a choice between resisting distasteful policies and doing their best to maintain the school as a good, moral space. Teachers in Eritrea and elsewhere thus simultaneously resist *and* do work in a way that they think is morally correct and in the best interests of the students (Downey 2007) or in the best interest of the nation (Silver 2007; Wilson 2001). In Eritrea, they had what they regarded as a moral mandate to produce educated citizens for the nation despite conditions that were out of control, even though these same teachers, in some cases, contributed to the chaotic and out-of-control atmosphere.

Studying middle actors requires examining how structures constrain and produce certain actions but also exploring alternative structures and variegated ways in which middle actors respond to structures. The move to merge military training with secondary education was one such structural constraint that teachers had to contend with. The government command that education should shuttle students into military service, which was enacted through both National Service and educational policy, certainly placed structural constraints on how teachers could educate. But at the same time, teachers' beliefs about what their work was for—to produce national subjects—also profoundly shaped what they were willing and not willing to do in classrooms. Teachers responded to these various structures in what were often contradictory ways. At one extreme, some teachers resisted everything associated with being a teacher, showing up for the school year late, arriving late and leaving early almost every day, not disciplining students, and not planning lessons. At another extreme, some teachers appropriated and tried to understand the new policies and help students understand why being sent to the military did not preclude their working hard to have a bright future. Most teachers' responses were far more complex and contradictory. On many days, the same teacher would drag his feet and show up late for class but then afterward express anxiety about how disorderly the school had become and think of ways to create order and improve the quality of education. Times of moral crisis, flux, or change highlight the paradoxes of middle actors by showing how they wield power, how they are disempowered, and how the tensions between their empowerment and disempowerment mutually constitute each other. The government's merging of secondary education with processes of military training produced such a crisis, ultimately revealing that teachers and the government had radically different notions of what an educated national subject should be.

The Paradoxes of the Making of Educated Military Subjects

In light of the 2003 educational policies that embedded educational institutions into broader processes of militarization, we might assume that schools would become somehow like the military in the sense that they would discipline and produce soldier-students. Indeed, had this merger of education and the military been more seamless, this result might have been the case. However, what was striking in Eritrea was that the opposite happened, in large part because teachers refused to take on the role of making students into military subjects. Instead, these policies produced a moral crisis, because there were substantial differences in how Eritreans imagined the future and national duties of educated people and the way they imagined the future and duties of soldiers. While educational institutions are teleologically and developmentally oriented, military institutions are oriented toward sacrifice and the absence of a future. Education cultivates and nurtures subjects to work hard for both self-improvement and, by virtue of self-improvement, national development. In contrast, military institutions produce and rely on disciplined subjects oriented toward sacrificing the self for the defense of the nation. While educated citizens are encouraged to imagine pathways to a hopeful and bright future and to situate themselves on these pathways, those in the military, ever ready to sacrifice themselves for the nation, cannot really imagine a future at all.

Despite these key differences, schools and the military forge attachments to the nation in a variety of similar ways in Eritrea and elsewhere.[10] School curricula legitimate Eritrea's military history and normalize the creation of a militarized citizen. The goal of national curricula everywhere is to directly and indirectly produce a common historical memory, to categorize particular types of (ethnic, gendered, religious) national subjects, and to delineate the rights and duties of citizens (Kaplan 2006). Eritrea's curricula recount military exploits, craft narratives that glorify past violence, and legitimate the need for future military exploits as well as teach students what their roles in the militarized nation might be. In schools, students learn a version of national history that legitimates the military and develops a particular subject position for the fighting citizen. Additionally, both schools and the military train subjects to behave in particular ways, thereby learning to adopt the behavior of a particular type of person—be it a student or a soldier. As Michel Foucault (1995) has noted, subjects in both the school and the military are subject to a microphysics of temporal and spatial discipline as they are trained to move their bodies in particular ways, think in particular ways, adapt to a very specific timetable, and organize their learning in particular ways that are specific to being educated. Finally, education and the military also produce an experience of simultaneity that is profoundly nationalizing. Anderson (1991) notes that nationalist sentiments arise from a sense of simultaneity and commonality as citizens move to different parts of the country, encountering other types of nationals with whom they discover they have had a common experience. Students move "up" to higher levels of education and different parts of the country, and as they do so, they become aware that others from other parts of the country have had remarkably similar experiences of schooling and share very similar life trajectories and aspirations. Soldiers are trained and mixed up with others from around the country and become aware of their common experience of being a national soldier.[11] In Eritrea, creating a sense of simultaneity through collectively developing the nation is quite intentionally part of the nation-building strategy. Its National Service project, summer work projects for students, and the move to set up the final year of high school in the military training center are all means to draw together Eritreans from diverse religions, ethnic groups, and regions and provide them with a common nationalizing experience.

The ruling party in Eritrea has long seen education and militarism as paired. Militarism[12] and developmentalism (an orientation toward developing the country, of which education is a key component) compose the twin core of Eritrean nationalism (O'Kane and Hepner 2009). Eritrea has been oriented toward military goals (first liberating the country and later defending its borders) since The Struggle for independence began, but defense and development have long been fused. The PFDJ liberated territory and then set up schools, clinics, and other developmentally oriented programs in the liberated areas. The government continues to pair defense and development through the goals and work of National Service conscripts. Through the auspices of the National Service program, military experiences are infused into the lives of all Eritreans.

In Eritrea, education has always been central to the PFDJ/EPLF's developmentalist project, but tension has also always existed between "fighters" (*tegadelti*) and educated people. The EPLF prioritized literacy campaigns and education for civilians and fighters alike, and immediately following independence, the PFDJ continued these programs and rapidly expanded formal education into the remote corners of the country (Gottesman 1998; Müller 2005). Following independence, the PFDJ created massive weekend and summer work projects that all students were required to participate in, thus utilizing educated people as part of its mass of labor for development projects, such as terracing hillsides and planting trees. This requirement signaled to students that physical labor to develop the country was also part of their duty as educated people. In doing this, the party was trying to disseminate the idea that educated and uneducated people were equal and that everyone had a part to play in developing the nation. Another way the party operationalized this ideal of egalitarianism was by promoting fighters, who had been educated in the field during the war, to supervisory positions following independence. Many educated people chafed at this assertion of egalitarianism between the educated and the uneducated. Some teachers complained about "uneducated" fighters being placed in positions of authority over them and also believed that these fighters might mistreat them out of jealousy or bad feelings for those who were not fighters. Teachers' and students' anxieties and complaints about the government incorporating high school into National Service drew on their beliefs that that educated and uneducated people were distinctly different.

Through National Service, militarism and developmentalism are not only tightly intertwined but also promulgated biopolitically (O'Kane and Hepner 2009). Biopolitics refers to strategies of governance oriented around mass management of the population as a whole (Foucault 1997). As David O'Kane and Tricia Redeker Hepner (2009) note, the Eritrean government organizes and manages the "broad masses" to defend and develop the nation. This version of state-sponsored defense/developmentalism is top-down, requiring a mass of obedient conscripts whose labor is rigorously managed. With the policies introduced in 2003, the government thought that schools could be incorporated into this project of biopolitically managing, militarizing, and educating the population, but schools proved to have a very different orientation from that of biopolitical developmentalism/defense, in large part because of Eritrean teachers' beliefs about what it meant to be an educated person. This discrepancy largely explains why schools failed to work effectively in service of this biopolitical project.

Teachers navigated these contradictions between producing educated, aspirational subjects and sending students off to the military to become sacrificial subjects in paradoxical ways. Teachers evaded and demonized a state that was thought of as punitive toward its citizens and then utilized remarkably similar forms of punishment on students. They also tacitly and subtly joined with students in mocking the government's national military project and then helped students debate alternative ways of being national. Each of these strategies resisted the government's version of what it meant to be Eritrean but simultaneously reproduced forms of state power and, specifically, encounters with a state imagined to be punitive and unfair to their students.

As I make clear throughout this book, teachers themselves understood the ambivalent position they were in. They were clearly positioned to carry out the government's program of mass militarization by preparing students to be sent to Sawa, but teachers also had a deeply held sense of how they were supposed to produce educated national subjects. For Eritrean teachers, these two roles were diametrically opposed. Although many teachers did resist new educational policies, resistance had its limits because teacher resistance erodes teaching, learning, and other components of the educational process that teachers believe in deeply. Thus, teachers could not completely resist policies of mass militarization without schools entirely falling apart, so resistance was always partial, stunted and held in check by teachers' own sense of their moral mandate to educate the nation.

Studying the Nation-State from Its Margins

The vast majority of literature on Eritrea has focused on fighters, The Struggle for liberation, and its legacy.[13] When I set out to conduct research in Eritrea, the literature was almost entirely dominated by a preoccupation with the war for liberation; the unique qualities of the liberating, and later ruling, party; and Eritrea's near miraculous capacity for self-liberation and self-sufficient and tremendously organized rule. Scholars expressed fascination with sentiments of nationalism that emerged from The Struggle, which were notable for their powerful capacity to draw people together and often described as "effervescent," and the capacity of the leadership to cultivate and nurture that sense of nationalism (Hepner 2009b).[14] Now many scholars are raising questions in an emerging body of work about why what initially seemed to be such an effective project of nation-state formation is unraveling so dramatically (for examples of this work, see Hepner 2009b; O'Kane and Hepner 2009; Woldemikael 2013). Studies that look at nation-state making within Eritrea itself (rather than from the vantage point of the diaspora) but outside the party's project of nation-state making are largely missing from the literature. Examining nation-state making from this vantage point helps us understand how an increased reliance on coercion unraveled the party's nation-state making strategy in Eritrea.

My entry point into the study of Eritrea was quite different from that of most scholars. I entered Eritrea from its margins, the town of Assab. I also first came to Eritrea not as a researcher but as a teacher myself (and a Peace Corps volunteer) and later as a girlfriend, fiancée, and wife of an Eritrean teacher. When I arrived in Eritrea, it was not fighters who came to be emblematic of the country for me but educational administrators, teachers, students, and their families. I set out to do a study that did not place the fighters or the liberation war at its center but instead showed the ordinary experiences of Eritreans who aspired to educate the country and become educated for the country. This, from its outset, was a study of the nation from the vantage point of a group (teachers) often regarded by scholars of both Eritrea and nationalism as marginal to the process of nation-state making. I suggest that this marginal population, in hindsight, has proven to be remarkably predictive of the changing nature of Eritrean nationalism and needs to be thought of as central to these changes. However, because of the focus in the literature on the processes by which Eritrea became independent, initially I found little literature that could frame my understanding of this new, emergent Eritrean nationalism, a nationalism that engaged the powerful sentiments emergent from The Struggle for liberation and the architecture of nation building put in place by the leadership, but in unpredictable ways.

I was a Peace Corps volunteer from 1995 to 1997, serving as an English teacher in the Senior Secondary School where I later conducted my research. I returned to Eritrea eight times between summer 1997, when my Peace Corps service ended, and summer 2003, when I moved back for an extended period of fieldwork from 2003 to 2005. I married an Eritrean teacher in 2000, the same year I started graduate school. My research thus emerged out of a ten-year relationship with the country and the town of Assab and with the Eritrean educators in it.

Throughout the course of my fieldwork, in answering a question or explaining something to me, research subjects would say, "Well, you are like an Eritrean, you understand." Usually they said this when making a point about the political conditions or about the conditions of the schools. What they meant by this statement was that I had been around long enough to have an intuitive understanding of the macropolitics of the country and the micropolitics of the schools and the Ministry of Education. I also understood the ways in which teachers made sense of the problems facing the schools, and, in a sense, felt teachers' pain, frustration, and disillusion because my own life was being disrupted by the same factors. Throughout the war, I was in and out of Eritrea, often traveling to the country when other nonessential foreign personnel had evacuated. And after the war, as the noose of National Service tightened, I was bound to the country because my husband was stuck in the country, like so many others. Knowing that I had experienced the recent turbulence in Eritrea and that my life was deeply affected by the war built a sense of solidarity with my research participants.

At the same time, I clearly am not Eritrean. Throughout the war and the years following, I could leave and return to the country (although my husband could not). At some level, I chose to be there. Even more significantly, I was not dependent on the Eritrean government for my livelihood, my future, or my education, but instead could secure research funding and work toward a degree elsewhere. Most significantly, I was not required to do National Service, pay taxes to the Eritrean government, or remain bound to the Eritrean state in any way.

My conversations and interviews were conducted in English, the medium of instruction of Eritrean schools. Students and teachers were far more fluent in English than I was in Tigrinya and Amharic, and given the complexity of issues involved, I, and, more importantly, teachers and administrators, preferred to use English. The language issue also marked me as non-Eritrean. I did often listen in on informal conversations in Tigrinya and Amharic.

My research itself consisted of three components. First, in Asmara, I conducted interviews with officials and staff in the curriculum office and the Department of General Education who were involved in the creation of new curricula and the logistics of implementing new policies in schools. I also collected policy documents and attended training sessions for teachers and directors related to the 2003 curricula and policy changes. Second, in Assab, I conducted in-depth life-history interviews with teachers and directors in the Senior Secondary School and Junior Secondary School. During these interviews, I asked about teachers' own education and training, how teachers came to be teachers in Assab, their experiences moving to and settling in Assab, and their current experiences as teachers. Inevitably, what came across in these interviews was, on the one hand, a sense of what education ideally could and should accomplish and, on the other hand, a deep sense of discontent with current conditions that prevented teachers and the education system from accomplishing as much as it could. The new policies, the political climate, and, above all else, the National Service program were deeply implicated in what teachers perceived as the problems with education.

Finally, the most important component of my research consisted of participant observation in and out of schools with teachers throughout the two years of my fieldwork. I observed and participated in the daily life in these two schools by regularly observing and occasionally teaching classes; watching ceremonies, such as the flag ceremony; and participating in and noting informal interactions among teachers and between teachers and students. I also noted the routines and rituals that occurred at particular times in the school year and the ways in which the current educational and political conditions seemed to be altering the annual rhythm of school life. Additionally, I spent a good deal of time socializing with teachers outside the school both in Assab and during summer vacation in Asmara. In addition to casually socializing with teachers, I attended their weddings, mourning gatherings, holiday celebrations, and children's baptisms and birthday parties.

The background to teachers' lives, their hopes, dreams, and disappointments, was the presence of war and dictatorship. Teachers remembered the struggle for liberation and life under Mengistu Haile Mariam's communist dictatorship (known as the Derg regime), from which they had been liberated. This background both did and did not contextualize the way they narrated their lives and the meaning of education. Independence and the onset of the border war were clearly significant events, yet at the same time, the value of education often loomed, disembodied and hopeful, above and apart from the war—which is part of the reason why it was so bitterly disappointing when the government merged military training and education in 2003.

Assab was not only an ideal site in which to examine this profound rethinking of Eritrean nationalism but also the place that very much shaped my thinking on the subject. Indubitably an Eritrean city, yet close to the Ethiopian border and, prior to the border war, full of Ethiopians who had lived in Eritrea all their lives and Eritreans who had lived in Ethiopia most of their lives, Assab was a place where the dominant, state-produced form of nationalism was in question long before it was elsewhere in Eritrea. Yet it was also a profoundly nationalistic place that was important to the nation. It was here that the Italians first arrived in 1869, and it was the place from which they launched their colonial takeover of Eritrea, working their way up the coast and eventually colonizing all of Eritrea by 1890. Many suggested that Assab, separated from the Eritrean capital by six hundred kilometers of coastal desert and, until 1998, barely accessible by road, "felt" more like an Ethiopian town than an Eritrean one prior to the start of the border war. The town of approximately fifty thousand was then linked economically and socially to both Eritrea and Ethiopia. The border war, however, changed this arrangement significantly.

At independence, when relations between the newly independent nation of Eritrea and the new government of Ethiopia were amicable, Eritrea granted Ethiopia free use of the Assab port. This seemed a logical arrangement at the time, considering that the two liberating parties had fought side by side for the dual purpose of gaining Eritrea's independence and overthrowing the Derg regime in Ethiopia. Assab had long served as Ethiopia's main port, having been developed into a modern port largely with Soviet funding as a result of Ethiopia's close relations with the Soviet Union. Additionally, Eritrea's northern port of Massawa had always been sufficient in meeting the needs of Eritrea's small population. Furthermore, the "road" from Assab to Eritrea's northern coast and the highlands was little more than a series of shifting, dry riverbeds until Eritrea began constructing a better road in 1998, after the border war cut off travel from Assab to Ethiopia.

The border war transformed Assab. The wide tree-lined streets in the port section of the town changed from an area full of thriving businesses, bars, and restaurants into a ghost quarter. The squawking of crows replaced the formerly incessant rumble of trucks heading to and from the road to Ethiopia. In 1998, when the border war began, the hinterland between Eritrea and Ethiopia was transformed from a bustling transportation route to a front line. The port was closed. Lacking jobs in the port, the first wave of Assab's Ethiopian residents left in 1998. Thousands of soldiers soon replaced them, leaving the town feeling quieter but not quite empty.

Assab was a town that few residents "came from." As I noted above, teachers in Assab were an ethnically homogenous group who were transferred there from the mostly Christian and Tigrinya highlands. But while the Eritrean teachers in Assab were an ethnically homogeneous group, the student body was increasingly diverse. The demographics of Assab's Senior Secondary School began changing in 2000. Many of the Tigrinya, highland residents in Assab, left the town due to the closure of the port. At the same time, the government expanded access to schooling in the region and strongly encouraged Afar children—who were indigenous to the area but underrepresented in educational institutions—to go to school. Whereas in 1998 approximately 10 percent of students in Assab's schools were Afar, by 2005 Afar students composed more than 50 percent of the school population. Assab's Senior Secondary School was the only Senior Secondary School in the region, and thus any Afar student wishing to attend Senior

Secondary School had to travel to Assab. Some Afar secondary school students lived in a boarding home run by the Ministry of Education, but many lived with relatives.

Although Assab, with its close links to Ethiopia, was culturally peripheral to Eritrea, it was symbolically and politically important. There is no doubt that Eritreans viewed Assab as an integral part of Eritrea, but it was a hybridized place formed at the intersection of nations and cultures by people who came there from different places, different countries, largely for economic reasons. It was a place, as one of my research subjects told me, where people felt "free" of the constraints of "culture" and the expectations of family and more traditional communities. It was a place at the borderlands, in the margins of Eritrea, where a new way of being Eritrean could be imagined, but it was also a place where the reach of the Eritrean state could increasingly be felt.

Before I continue, it is important that I provide a couple of qualifications and disclaimers. First, some readers may be critical that this study has so much to say about mass militarization in Eritrea and yet is not a study of the military *per se*. The lack of explicit focus on those in active military units and on military installations is in part a problem of access (I tried several times to visit Sawa and was not given permission). But even more importantly, my emphasis on mass militarization is a result of the entire country being overtaken by these processes. I did not set off to study militarization, yet it was such an all-pervasive component of everyday life in Eritrea that I would be remiss if I failed to make it a central focus of my ethnographic examination of schooling and nationalism in this context. In a place like Eritrea, one can study a form of militarization *without* studying the military itself or focusing exclusively on soldiers because the militarization of the country is so pervasive. Indeed, it is impossible not to.

My second disclaimer is that it is not possible to take up every issue related to nationalism and the state in a book of any reasonable length, and so there are a few concepts, some of which have been central to other studies of nationalism and the state, that I address but do not give a central role in this book. Gender, ethnicity, and religion, while addressed periodically throughout the book, are not central to my discussion. Several other scholars of Eritrean nationalism have begun to examine questions of gender, ethnicity, and religion in Eritrean nationalism (see, for example, Bernal 2014 and Müller 2005). These perspectives on nationalism are essential to understanding nationalism in Eritrea and elsewhere and are certainly worthy of more in-depth discussion in their own right, but, given my focus on the relationship between nation and state, between teachers and militarization, they are beyond the scope of what I can cover in depth in this particular book.

Finally, it is also important to note that when researching in a place like Eritrea, extra care needs to be taken to protect identities of human subjects, given that one is never entirely sure what the surveillance capacity of the government is. At times, it appears to have extensive reach and capacity to gather information about its subjects, keep records about whom they talk to and why, and enact consequences against them should they speak too freely. At other times, the government appears to be unconcerned with what ordinary citizens say privately; indeed, I found Eritreans spoke quite openly about their feelings about their country. But because of this uncertainty, in addition to the typical measures taken in keeping with human subjects' protocols (using pseudonyms for interlocutors), I have also blurred other characteristics that would personally identify these individuals. For this reason, I do not note dates and places of my interviews or attach quotations to any other information that would be identifiable.

Overview of the Book

Taken together, Chapters 1 and 2 look at how coercive state effects in the post–border war years eroded the government's own national project, resulting in a need for more coercion but also mass evasion. The first chapter provides an overview of the genesis of Eritrea's revolutionary nationalist project, which was the creation of Eritrea's ruling party during The Struggle for independence. During the early years of independence, as I noted above, the party's efforts to forge a unified national ideology were tremendously effective, resulting in a populist nationalism. As I show in Chapter 1, one of the problems with the party's national project was the way in which the ruling party sought to make all Eritreans be like the fighters and punish anyone who resisted. As a result, this populist effervescence began to erode in the face of increased state coercion, violence, and crackdowns on political dissent. All of this led to a reimagining of the state, its revolutionary leadership, and the fighters in power as dangerous and punishing, a topic that I take up in Chapter 2. The second chapter examines everyday coercive encounters with the state and the constellations of rumors and commentary on these encounters through which Eritreans tried to reconcile their earlier popular and powerfully emotional support for those who liberated the country with their experiences with the punishing state.

The second half of the book looks at the interplay of coercion and evasion in schools. Schools, in some respects, were a microcosm of the nation as a whole in the sense that as students were forced to enter the military through schools, a culture of evasiveness ensued. However, because teachers still championed the role of schools in producing educated national subjects, distinct from soldier-subjects, and because students still aspired to become these educated subjects, the interplay of coercion and evasion in schools was complex. Chapter 3 explores the clashing versions of what the nation and its citizens should be—educated or militarized? Here I show how and why teachers found the two choices incompatible and provide an overview of the complexities of the new educational policies introduced in 2003. This chapter also illustrates the disconnect between the disciplinary work of teachers in shaping and cultivating individual students to be highly trained, knowledgeable, and morally superior educated people and the biopolitical efforts of the government to produce a mass of student-soldiers. Teachers chafed not only at the idea that students should be soldiers but also at the new techniques they were directed to use to mass-promote (and, theoretically, to mass-educate) their students. The subsequent chapters look at how this incompatibility between being a soldier and being a student played out in schools, resulting in divergent responses among teachers to new policies. On the one hand, the educational state became coercive but impotent; on the other hand, schools turned into sites where the meaning of being national could be debated.

Chapter 4 shows how a climate of evasion took hold in schools. This climate was marked by not only disorder and mockery of all forms of officialdom but also an increased informality and a blurring of the lines of authority between students and teachers as both teachers and students began to believe that they would never "grow up" and achieve the status and stature appropriate to successful, educated people. Here my focus is on how teachers' authority was subverted in part as a result of perceptions that everyone—teachers and students—was leveled by the National Service mechanism. School-based rituals and routines changed as a result of tacit student and teacher resistance, resulting in changing relationships of authority between teachers and students.

Chapter 5, in contrast, looks at teachers' responses to conditions of disorder. Here I show how teachers behaved coercively and claimed their authority *as* the state to rectify what they saw as the moral crisis of students not acting like students. The chapter raises questions about how and why teachers came to act as everyday sovereigns under Eritrea's state of exception. Here I also explore the dialectical relationship between teachers' beliefs about what was good for students, how teachers imagined the state (and imagined it as inhibiting their ability to do what was good for the students), and, finally, how they were imagined *as* the state. Teachers took control, often in violent ways, over schools that they thought had become out of control. While they thought they were acting in the good, moral interest of their students and the nation, students and parents often imagined this teacher state quite differently.

As a whole, the book explores the tenuous hyphen between nation and state under lived conditions of everyday authoritarianism. Chapters 2 and 5 look at how encounters with often-violent state actors reshaped imaginaries of the state. Chapter 1 provides an overview of official nationalism, while Chapter 4 looks at the bottom-up reworking of that official version of the meaning of the nation. Taken together, the chapters comment on how imaginaries of the state altered imaginaries of the nation and raised questions about the legitimacy of the official version of the nation produced by its leadership. Meanwhile, the book examines how middle actors, such as teachers, remain in an awkward position. They have the power to shape the way in which the Eritrean nation-state, and the nation in particular, is imagined. Their power and their legitimacy come from the fact that they are close to their students and their communities and, in many respects, regarded as being part of those communities. In this regard they are, arguably, more powerful than the country's leaders, who have lost their legitimacy. But teachers' power is always partial and intimate; they do not have the biopolitical machinery that the government possesses to produce a national population en masse.

1

Struggling for the Nation

Contradictions of Revolutionary Nationalism

In the middle of Sema'atat Square in Asmara is an unusual sculpture. The size of a small car, surrounded by flowering hedges, made of metal, is the *shida*—a tribute to the commonly worn plastic sandals. Bicycles, taxis, cars, buses, even the occasional donkey cart pass by this heavily trafficked circle at a major intersection in Asmara. Pedestrians walk past hurrying on their way to somewhere else, many of them wearing *shida*. The *shida*—an object common to every household and everyday life—is at once a symbol of the Eritrean everyman and everywoman and a glorification of Eritrea's *tegadelti*, or fighters, who liberated the country during the thirty-year struggle for independence. During The Struggle, many fighters wore them instead of military boots; they enabled the fighters to move quickly, lithely, and stealthily through the rough mountainous terrain where much of the war was fought. *Shida* are tough, versatile, and inexpensive. Fighters could easily repair torn *shida* by melting down the plastic and reattaching it, meaning they often wore the same pair for long periods of time. In the 1980s, the Eritrean People's Liberation Front (EPLF) began manufacturing *shida* themselves in the liberated areas of the country along with other necessities. The party and many Eritreans are proud of these factories, which indicated the EPLF's capacity to govern, fight, and liberate itself without any significant support from the outside world. The history of plastic sandals, worn by fighters, repaired, recycled, and eventually manufactured behind the front lines during The Struggle for independence, references the national ethos of self-sufficiency and sacrifice, while *shida* themselves are a symbol of fighters' stealth, resilience, and ability to win the war against great obstacles. The *shida* statue, thus, transforms a quotidian object into a symbol of the nation that embodies the core values of The Struggle. It is literally and metaphorically larger than life but also reflected in everyday life. The *shida* is a military symbol but also an ordinary one, and, most importantly, it is ubiquitous throughout the country.

The *shida* statue is but one example of what we might think of as the quotidian nature of Eritrean nationalism. Quotidian nationalism fuses symbols, narratives, and performances that reference the legacy of The Struggle for independence with the lives of ordinary Eritreans. This quotidian nationalism has enabled the ruling People's Front for Democracy and Justice party (PFDJ) to forge a particular sense of personhood, creating Eritrean subjects who are supposed to think of themselves as willing to sacrifice (and kill and die, if need be) to not only defend their nation but also develop it (Bernal 2014; Hepner 2009b). Processes through which Eritrean men and women are socialized into becoming this ideal national subject are also supposed to ensure that the nation is a central part of Eritreans' everyday lives. To do this, the party drew on the lived experiences of Eritreans during The Struggle, validated and valorized experiences of suffering, gave meaning to sacrifice, and nationalized that meaning. To further make the nation part of citizens' everyday lives, the party created service programs that were intended to inculcate the values of The Struggle in Eritrean youth by loosely (and sometimes directly) simulating the experiences of the fighters in the war for liberation. However, the party's revolutionary nation-making program not only drew on past experiences of The Struggle but also set out to craft a sense of the future and an ideology of how society would change in its aftermath. This included promoting egalitarian gender and class norms and also an idea of a multicultural, multireligious, unified national whole. As with many other revolutions, liberation was but the first step of social transformation.

The PFDJ, previously known as the EPLF, emerged as the liberators of the country at the end of the thirty-year struggle for liberation. One of the EPLF's key accomplishments was to construct a cohering sense of Eritrean nationalism and to bind that to state institutions even before the country was liberated (Pool 2001). A good deal of literature has detailed the nature of the Eritrean revolution, and my objective here is not to repeat the contributions that this literature has made, although I draw substantially from it (see, for example, Connell [1993] 1997; Hepner 2009b; Pool 2001; Reid 2005). Rather, I hope to highlight a few key points about the strengths and shortcomings of Eritrean revolutionary nationalism to lay the groundwork for my exploration of the unraveling of effervescent support for the EPLF/PFDJ national project in subsequent chapters.

Eritrea is one of a handful of revolutionary movements that emerged out of a later phase of liberation and anticolonial struggle (Dorman 2006). Sarah Dorman (2006) states that while resistance was common in colonies, prolonged violent conflict was not the norm out of which nations were born in most African anticolonial struggles. The majority of the first-wave anticolonial struggles were relatively nonviolent. In contrast, a second wave of independence movements through the 1980s and 1990s was the result of far more prolonged struggle when colonies or settler states refused to give up power, such as in South Africa, Namibia, and Zimbabwe, or when countries fought to liberate themselves from a second colonizer, such as was the case in Uganda, Eritrea, Ethiopia, and Rwanda. In these later independence movements, the goal was not just wresting the state from oppressive rule but transforming society. During these protracted struggles, Dorman (2006) notes, these regimes acquired ideological legitimacy, a detailed vision of what society would look like, a developmentalist mentality, mass followings, and control of the state. Protracted revolutions thus enabled state building, the development of national identities, and the fusion of the two (Herbst 2000). These revolutionary and postliberation states were quite different from countries that were liberated in the mid-1900s (Dorman 2006). Unlike other African states, these states were relatively emancipated from society and "hard" in the sense that they were able to maintain control over borders and economies (Herbst 2000).

Eritrean official nationalism is revolutionary in the sense that the cooptation of the instruments of governance, the taking over of the state, often through the auspices of the military, was but the first step in the longer process of social transformation (Müller 2005). Both Eritrean revolutionary fronts (the EPLF and its rival and predecessor, the Eritrean Liberation Front, which are discussed below) had the goal of liberating the country, and socialist notions of progress and equality influenced both. But the EPLF was perhaps distinct in its recognition of the importance of crafting a cohering national ideology and creating an organizational infrastructure to promote it. The EPLF did a very effective job of both forging a sense of nationalism and crafting the beginnings of a preliberation state that would later be transformed into a sovereign, internationally recognized state following independence. The EPLF's nation-state formation project was oriented around strong organization; strict discipline within the front; the value of development through self-sufficiency; progressive notions of class, gender, and ethnic equality; and, above all, a willingness not only to sacrifice for the nation but also to do so as the party leadership saw fit.

Ultimately, many of the strategies that were so effective for the revolutionary front that liberated the country were far less effective for a government seeking to work with a diverse and varied civilian population. But the EPLF forged ahead in using these strategies. Utilizing its coherent organizational structure, drawing staunchly on the goals and values forged in The Struggle, and insisting that people continue to promote those goals even in the absence of widespread support for them, the EPLF moved forward with its nation-building agenda. The leadership continued to promote and enforce the party's ideological goals and to try to transform the national subject into a new kind of person, often utilizing the same militarized, disciplinary tactics that it initially used to liberate the national territory. Unfortunately, party leaders found themselves increasingly reliant on force to do this, thus unraveling the gains of their nationalist project. Below, I provide a brief history of the genesis of Eritrean nationalism and the emergence of the EPLF's particular national program from that history. I then give some examples of the quotidian nature of Eritrean nationalism to show the ways in which nationalism tied in with personal and communal effervescence prior to and immediately after independence. I conclude by raising some questions about why revolutionary nationalism is increasingly failing in Eritrea, a theme that I take up in more detail in the following chapter about the state.

The Genesis of the Eritrean Nation and Nationalism

Although much of what we think of as Eritrean nationalism derives from the EPLF/PFDJ's nationalist project, Eritrean nationalism has a robust and multifaceted history that is important to recognize in order to understand the difference between the national narrative produced and promoted by the ruling party and sentiments of nationalism felt by Eritreans. Like many African nations, the formation of the nation-state in Eritrea emerged from late-nineteenth-century colonialism. Italy began its conquest of Eritrea with the purchase of the territory around Assab from the sultan at Aussa in 1869 and then expanded its control, establishing the colony of Eritrea in 1882. Italy planned to take over Ethiopia and therefore unify Eritrea, Somalia, and Ethiopia into greater Italian East Africa, but after Italy lost the battle of Adwa to Menelik II in 1889, the Treaty of Wuchale gave Ethiopia its independence and awarded the territory that later became Eritrea to Italy. Despite Ethiopia's claims that Eritrea has always been an integral part of the Ethiopian empire, this claim is true for only the Eritrean highlands. It was not until Italian colonization that Eritrea as a territorial entity came into existence.

Italy gave Eritrea its territorial shape and a colonial state to govern that territory, but the diverse ethnic, regional, and religious groups in Eritrea had varied histories prior to colonization. Eritrea is approximately 50 percent Muslim and 50 percent Christian. The Christian population is predominantly Abyssinian Orthodox, a form of Christianity encompassing Ethiopia and Eritrea and linked to the Coptic Church in Egypt. Eritrean Christians mainly reside in the central and southern highlands of Eritrea where the capital, Asmara, is located and are traditionally settled agriculturalists. This part of the country has been historically attached to the Abyssinian Orthodox Church as well as successive Ethiopian empires and kingdoms at various times, although these villages have always had strong local forms of governance and, in many respects, have remained quite autonomous from Ethiopian empires. Christian highlanders typically hail from the Tigrinya-speaking ethnic group, also approximately 50 percent of the population and roughly equivalent to the Orthodox Christian population, although some Tigrinya are Muslim, Catholic, and, increasingly, evangelical Christians. The predominantly Muslim Tigre ethnic group resides for the most part in the northern highlands, northeastern lowlands, and western lowlands of Eritrea and comprises approximately 30 percent of the population. The remaining 20 percent of the population is made up of seven other ethnic groups—Afar, Saho, Nara, Kunama, Rashaida, Bilen, and Hedareb. With the exception of the Kunama, who are Christian and Animists, and the Bilen and Saho, some of whom are Christian, these groups are Muslim and reside in the coastal and western lowlands as well as the northern highlands. Geographic, religious, and ethnic differences frame different experiences of nationalism and the state among different populations. When the EPLF gained power in the middle of The Struggle for independence, its supporters took it upon themselves to create a synthetic form of nationalism that would subsume these varied identities to a common Eritrean identity; however, prior to this event, a variety of other ways of imagining the nation were available to Eritreans, and in many ways, the post-Italian politics of Eritrea revolved around the interplay of varied understandings of what Eritrea was.

The period at the end of World War II was a particularly interesting moment during which an array of Eritrean nationalisms circulated. During this interim period, from 1941 to 1952, Great Britain administered Eritrea. The British Military Administration (BMA) was a complex political time; arguably, political divisions that emerged from this period were responsible for the form that the early liberation movements in Eritrea took (Pool 2001). Ethiopia, then under the rule of Emperor Haile Selassie, thought of Eritrea as one of its own provinces, thus equating Eritrean nationalism with Ethiopian nationalism. Ethiopia began negotiating for "reunion" with Eritrea almost immediately, citing deep historical ties with Eritrea's Christian highlands and giving rise to the Unionist Party in Eritrea. Meanwhile, Great Britain favored partitioning Eritrea, giving the Christian highlands to Ethiopia and the lowlands and northern highlands to Sudan, a plan that drew on thinking that Muslim, lowland populations had more in common culturally with ethnic groups in Sudan than they did with Christian highlanders and therefore would be more easily incorporated into the neighboring country. That plan ultimately failed but had the effect of making residents of the lowlands think about which nation they belonged to (Gebremedhin 1989; Markakis 1987; Pool 2001). As a result, an entity called the Muslim League emerged in the western lowlands to challenge the Unionist Party. Meanwhile, a burgeoning independence movement in Eritrea advocated for independent statehood and argued that a distinct Eritrean identity was mapped on to the Eritrean colonial territory (Makki 2011a, 2011b; Pool 2001; Taddia 1994; Trevaskis 1960).[1]

This time period is key because Eritrea's political elites, across ethnic groups and regions, became conscious of the importance of the state and came to understand that even if there was no agreement on what Eritrea was (an independent nation, several nations, or part of Ethiopia), control over the mechanisms of governance was of critical importance (Trevaskis 1960). The question of nationhood and control of the national state brought on religious/regional cleavages that had not previously existed, and competing international interests in control over Eritrea exacerbated these cleavages (Pool 2001). While a cognizance of the nation began to emerge in the BMA period, it did so in different ways among different strata of the population, and few mechanisms existed to spread this sense of nationalism uniformly across the entire geographical territory (Makki 2011b). Eritrean nationalism was emerging through this time period, but doing so unevenly. Still, this time period is key to understanding how disparate movements that began among an urbanized middle stratum in the highlands and among disenfranchised agro-pastoralists in the lowlands eventually came together to frame a movement for independence (Makki 2011b).

These early nationalist sentiments were not simply reflections of religious, ethnic, or regional cleavages, however, but were merged with ongoing class sentiments (Gebremedhin 1989; Markakis 1987). This is important to note because both the EPLF and the Eritrean Liberation Front (ELF;

the liberation front that preceded the EPLF) were deeply concerned with elements of class and inequality in Eritrea and would eventually galvanize class-based grievances into armed insurgencies. The Muslim League actually evolved out of an ongoing serf-emancipation movement in the western lowlands (Gebremedhin 1989). Serfs, who had recently made great strides in achieving greater social equality, believed that union with feudal, imperial Ethiopia would diminish gains that they had made and exacerbate inequalities (Pool 2001). All of this is key because The Struggle for independence initially started in Eritrea's predominantly Muslim western lowlands and, for this reason, is often depicted as stemming from Muslim fear of being federated with Christian Ethiopia. However, as the scholars cited above have compellingly argued, the beginnings of The Struggle not only constituted a religious/regional revolt but also built on ongoing class concerns that related to Eritrea as a whole.

Following the BMA period, despite growing sentiments that Eritrea should be independent, the United Nations agreed to federate Ethiopia and Eritrea, allowing Eritrea to retain its autonomy while incorporated into Ethiopia. It quickly became clear that Ethiopia did not intend to honor the spirit of the loose federation with Eritrea. Ethiopia almost immediately began to undermine the federal agreement and ultimately disbanded the federation and formally annexed Eritrea. While there were initially competing ideas about what *Eritrea* should be in the BMA period, Eritreans' concerns about being dominated by the Ethiopian empire would ultimately galvanize popular support for Eritrean independence; however, what it meant to be *Eritrean* would take much longer to work out.

Sentiments that Eritrea should be independent emerged from different sectors in Eritrea and gained strength as Ethiopia began undermining Eritrea's autonomy. Early opposition efforts began in 1958, when the Eritrean Liberation Movement (ELM), which consisted of mainly urban intellectuals, was formed (Pool 2001). As David Pool (2001) details, by the time the Ethiopian government officially annexed Eritrea in 1962, it had put down the ELM's efforts, but meanwhile another opposition group, the ELF, was forming out of the remnants of the Muslim League in the western lowlands. Thus, liberation movements in Eritrea have roots in both the urban intelligentsia and the disenfranchised in the western lowlands, among the elite and among the periphery.

The ELF began The Struggle in Eritrea's western lowlands, and for many years the western lowlands and northern highlands, which were the regions most disenfranchised by Ethiopian annexation, were the parts of the country that most staunchly supported the ELF. Thus, in the early years of The Struggle, Eritrean nationalism was often seen as a religiously based nationalism. However, as Ethiopian repression in Eritrea increased, larger and larger numbers of urbanized Christians, mainly students, from the central highlands started joining the ELF in the late 1960s and early 1970s. In 1966, new recruits were sent to China, Cuba, and Syria for further training. The group that went to China, which included the current Eritrean president Isaias Afewerki, proved to be particularly influenced by Maoist thought (Pool 2001). Ideas gleaned from the training in China were largely responsible for proposed changes to the ELF that would eventually result in the development of the EPLF and its split from its parent movement. The trip to China was particularly influential in terms of helping the leadership formulate a vision for a more unified national ideology as well as an organizational structure that would allow them to promote this revolutionary form of Eritrean nationalism (Pool 2001). Infighting led to the dissolution of the ELF in the 1980s, leaving the EPLF/PFDJ to eventually win Eritrea's thirty-year struggle for liberation (Hepner 2009b; Pool 2001). Although there were numerous reasons for the EPLF/ELF split, diverging understandings of Eritrean nationalism were significant.

Differences between EPLF and ELF variants of Eritrean nationalism reveal different understandings of the relationship between collective identity, individual subjectivity, the nation, and the state. The ELF is often mistakenly associated with narrow Muslim, lowland concerns, but this association ignores the fact that many Christian, Tigrinya highlanders joined the ELF and that many who joined The Struggle chose which front to join for pragmatic reasons rather than ideological ones (Hepner 2009b; Pool 2001). Both the ELF and the EPLF initially built class-based concerns into their national ethos, the same concerns that had previously sparked the rise of the Muslim League, but the EPLF took up the challenge of forging an explicit national ideology that emphasized unity, equality, and revolutionary thought (Pool 2001). In contrast, the ELF focused more exclusively on liberation and not on the broader task of nation building. Literature on distinctions between the ELF and the EPLF emphasize the exclusionary nature of the ELF, suggesting that this front, with its origins in the western lowlands and support from Arab countries, failed to craft a coherent national identity that would include all of Eritrea's diverse peoples and religions and instead focused narrowly around the goal of independence (Hepner 2009b). However, scholars have noted that another way to understand the ELF's ideological and organizational approach is that it tried to build Eritrean identity around existing social groupings and networks rather than produce statelike structures to promote, disseminate, and subsume state subjects to hegemonic national ideology, as the EPLF did; the organizational structure of the ELF itself reflected the notion of a nationalism oriented around a common goal of liberation rather than a common national identity (Hepner 2009b; Pool 2001). As the ELF developed, it came to be structured along the lines of the Algerian liberation movement, with discrete and homogeneous geographic zones. These zones largely utilized kin, ethnic, regional, and other patronage ties to recruit new fighters, and their organizational structure was rather informal (Hepner 2009b; Markakis 1987; Pool 2001). At times there was even rivalry and conflict between and within the different zones. In contrast, the EPLF prioritized the creation of a nationalist orthodoxy and statelike structures to organize the population and inculcate this ideology in them.

Tricia Redeker Hepner (2009b) makes a compelling argument that the ELF's nationalism was pluralist in the sense that it was able to accommodate a variety of understandings of what it meant to be Eritrean and was, therefore, more flexible and "open-minded" than the form of nationalism ultimately propagated by the EPLF. The ELF's nationalism was less inclined to promote a specific definition of what it meant to be Eritrean, leaving it open for people to be Eritrean in multiple ways. In contrast, what Hepner (2009b: 44) terms the EPLF's "synthetic nationalism" required strict allegiance to a very specific notion of what it meant to be Eritrean that was developed by the party leadership itself. She notes that the ELF's focus on loose unification around the goal of independence left open the possibility of dialogue about what it meant to be Eritrean, an openness not found in the EPLF's expectation of adherence to ideological orthodoxy. The benefit of this more fluid and open-minded form of nationalism was that it accommodated difference. The down side was that it remained open to the influence of sub- or pre-national allegiances, loyalties, and commitments and thus remained unemancipated from society in key ways that ultimately proved problematic for the ELF.

Perhaps it is no surprise that the EPLF has been preoccupied with developing a sense of national unity, given both the challenges and importance of doing so elsewhere in Africa, one of the last regions of the world to be parceled out into discrete nation-states. African states were built on top of strong colonial states, but not states that were designed to unify or represent a national polity (Mamdani 1996). Meanwhile most African nations comprised diverse, varied, fluid cultural groups that often spanned national boundaries and resisted identification with the nations or, conversely, sought to co-opt the states by defining the nations based on their own particular ethnic, religious, or geographic affiliations (Dorman, Hammett, and

Nugent 2007).[2] Although the same could be said about many nations, particularly postcolonial nations, processes of nation-state formation in Africa have been particularly befuddled by the combination of strong, coherent non-national identities (for example, ethnic and religious identities) combined with the weakness of state institutions (Bayart 2009). Following a fleeting moment of patriotic, independence-era nationalism in the 1950s and 1960s, the process of creating a coherent sense of nationalism and viable states in most African countries floundered (Herbst 2000). New governments inherited state institutions from colonialism that were designed to consolidate political, economic, and military control in the hands of an elite ruling group (Rodney 1974). They also inherited little coherence, legitimacy, or loyalty around the idea of a nation among would-be national citizens (Davidson 1993). Elites in African nations often attempted to build legitimacy for these nations by creating national mythologies, origin stories, and sets of national heroes and symbols to fill this void and shore up the idea of these nations, but given the diversity of their populations, these symbols and myths often excluded and disenfranchised groups of citizens, galvanizing resistance to the governing elites and their ideas about the nations more than legitimizing them (Davidson 1993).

The EPLF thought of itself as trying to rectify the errors of both the ELF and other African nations by forging a unified nation and a strong state. The EPLF's nationalism, emerging as it did through war and defense of its sovereignty, has arguably required that Eritreans become a particular kind of national subject, one oriented toward sacrifice and service for the nation, one who will subsume other identities (religion, region, ethnicity) to nationalism. Despite the fact that the EPLF's notion of what an Eritrean should be is rather extreme—and, arguably, unsustainable now that The Struggle for independence is over—it has clung to this strict notion of Eritrean-ness. Because this is the form of official nationalism that has predominated in Eritrea until today, I now turn to a fuller discussion of the EPLF's version of nationalism and later evaluate the pitfalls inherent in promoting this type of national orthodoxy.

"Our Struggle and Its Goals"

The ongoing strategy of governance of the ruling PFDJ as well as the attributes of official formulations of Eritrean nationalism can find their roots in processes by which the EPLF consolidated control over the development of an Eritrean state and their particular nationalist ideology. Interestingly, the EPLF's efforts sought to quite intentionally fuse nation to state, simultaneously creating institutions to govern the country, instilling a sense of common national identity in its population, ensuring sovereignty over an independent national territory, and co-constructing both nation and state. In partial response to their contention that the ELF lacked an organizing ideology, in 1971, the EPLF authored the highly influential pamphlet "Our Struggle and Its Goals." In fact, it is speculated that Eritrea's president himself authored the pamphlet (Weldehaimanot and Taylor 2011). In the document, the EPLF outlines its version of the origins and history of The Struggle. This version of the history emphasizes the overwhelming support among Eritreans of all religions, regions, and ethnicities for Eritrean independence at the time of the BMA; the alliance of Ethiopia with foreign powers to ensure that Eritrea was federated with Ethiopia; political repression and manipulation on the part of Ethiopia, which dissolved the federation and led to the annexation of Eritrean by Ethiopia and the beginning of The Struggle in 1961; and, finally, the failings of the ELF to adequately organize or unify the country (Weldehaimanot and Taylor 2011). The 1971 document distinguishes the EPLF and its ideology from that of the ELF as well as from that of Ethiopia, historically details the origins of The Struggle for independence, and outlines a sketch of the nationalist goals, which are further developed in documents produced by the EPLF in 1977 and 1994 (EPLF 1977, 1994). One of the EPLF's projects was to define Eritrea as an independent nation, differentiated from Ethiopia but also from the Arab world, with which the ELF had aligned. The pamphlet clearly notes that Eritrea shares with the Arabs a stance against colonialism, imperialism, and Zionism, but it differentiates Eritreans from Arabs, a distinction that the EPLF believed the ELF had not made (Weldehaimanot and Taylor 2011).

The EPLF's nationalist language was heavily inflected by anti-imperial and anticolonial sentiments, all of which were propagated through an aggressive series of political education campaigns. These focused on class, instilling in Eritreans a sense that their history was a history of struggle against imperial forces including, but not limited to, Ethiopia (Pool 2001; Weldehaimanot and Taylor 2011). Political education was also combined with development efforts, which included access to education, veterinary services, and health care in the liberated areas (Hepner 2009b; Pool 2001). Literacy campaigns and education were also a vital part of the EPLF's struggle, both for fighters and for civilians (Gottesman 1998).

In addition to its orientation toward development and progress and its anti-imperial stance, creating a sense of national unity among Eritrea's diverse people was an essential part of the EPLF's nationalist program. "Our Struggle and Its Goals" details the multicultural origins of Eritrea and celebrates the diversity of its people (Weldehaimanot and Taylor 2011). The EPLF set out to create a common culture by studying livelihoods and lifestyles of its various regions and ethnic groups (Pool 2001). The party, at least initially, had a very strong sense of needing to not only learn from the people it was liberating but also educate them. The EPLF also attempted to pull together elements of different cultures to create a sense of fused Eritrean culture, something that has been continued by the PFDJ (Hepner 2009b). Organizationally, unlike the ELF, it merged fighters from different parts of the country into heterogeneous groupings. It also refused to declare a national language and set about establishing a program to promote indigenous language education in addition to using Arabic as a working language among the lowland populations (Bereketeab 2010; Hailemariam, Sjaak, and Walters 1999; Woldemikael 1993).

Another key element of the EPLF's revolutionary nationalism related to gender roles. Partly out of a pragmatic need to expand its fighting force, the EPLF actively encouraged women to serve as fighters (Bernal 2000; Müller 2005; Wilson 1991). It later incorporated gender-based reforms into its land policies and political education program where possible, although following the war for independence, many of these reforms were hard to continue (Hepner 2009b; Pool 2001). While equality for women was core to the party's revolutionary ideology, encouraging the participation of women in leadership roles was a key component of the way it formed governance structures in the liberated areas. Thus the PFDJ's approach to gender was central to both its nation- and state-building agendas (Müller 2005).

One of the ways that ideology was disseminated was through various forms of mass organization, which gathered particular segments of the population—women, youth, workers, and peasants—into associations (Hepner 2009b; Pool 2001). These efforts were remarkably successful in transforming the EPLF into a popular front, reflective of its name and its nickname, *Shaebia,* which translates as "popular." These organizations allowed members, initially in Eritrea and later in the diaspora as well, to participate in broader political processes. Additionally, through these organizations development was fused with political education, and fighters were able to engage with civilians around issues related to membership within these groups. Thus, Eritreans engaged with the front, and the nation, by joining an organization that represented their identities as youth, women, peasants, or workers, categories that cut across broader swathes of Eritrea.

The EPLF had a very strong state-building agenda. One of the factors that made the EPLF successful was that it began to act like a state even before liberation, organizing the civilian population, blending them with the fighters, and very effectively disseminating its national ideology in a way that built on sentiments that saw independence as an answer to experiences of repression under Ethiopian rule. The party's approach to nation building was not to work through existing organizational and institutional structures but to create its own and then to ensure that these new organizational structures, their ideology, and their symbolism were part of people's daily lives. With this in mind, where possible the party replaced traditional governance structures, which it thought of as co-opted by Ethiopian rule, with its own administrators (Pool 2001: 118). Arguably, at independence, Eritrea's leadership had already done a great deal of quite effective nation-building and state-making work, enabled by several factors. The EPLF's centralized governance structure, extensive organizational capacity, and vision of unified national identity meant that a coherent nation-building project was already well underway by independence. But while this was remarkably successful in many ways, it also required intensive discipline and strict ideological orthodoxy among the fighters.

Like other socialist or communist revolutions, the EPLF was inspired by both Marxism/Leninism and Maoism and sought to create an egalitarian socialist society, to reeducate the masses through the auspices of political education campaigns, and to instill a strong organizational structure throughout society that would maintain discipline (Pool 2001). The EPLF was particularly effective at instilling discipline and political consciousness within the front itself, and in some areas it was quite successful at organizing the masses and inculcating political identities, although doing so among civilian populations was notably more difficult than it was in the army. Nonetheless, uplifting the masses from various forms of oppression, be they economic or colonial, was at the core of the EPLF's doctrines. The expression *awet n' hafash* (victory to the masses) is a "signature slogan" (Pool 2001: 105) of the EPLF and continues to be used prevalently in the regime. In fact, all official communiqués are signed *awet n'hafash*. As the front tried to extend its influence to civilian populations, it reached out especially to peasants, the urban working class, women, and youth. Land reform throughout the liberated areas of Eritrea was particularly concerned with dismantling long-standing class hierarchies and building class solidarities (Pool 2001). Other policies were also aimed at building solidarity among the poor and working class and ensuring the business classes did not have access to disproportionate wealth.

The EPLF drew on anti-imperial, anticolonial ideologies to argue for Eritrean independence, but its nation-building project also sought to transform Eritrean society and enacted an intensive ideological as well as organizational campaign to do so. Much of the literature on Eritrea has detailed the ideological content of EPLF nationalism and its strong social organization of both the party and the masses. The EPLF has narrated the nation and its national origins in a very particular way. Following independence, the EPLF attempted to fuse nationalism with quotidian experiences of Eritreans by making experiences of the nation a core part of individual memories and everyday lives.

Massification, Militarization, and Quotidian Nationalism

It is important to note that while the PFDJ/EPLF was quite adept at producing a cohering, revolutionary national ideology; building state institutions to disseminate it; and constructing the symbolic and ritual means to socialize Eritreans into this sense of national personhood, Eritrean nationalism is not merely a party construct. In large part, what has lent it emotional heft is the way in which it draws on the experiences of Eritreans, particularly during The Struggle, and in so doing transforms experiences of suffering into valorous sacrifices and quintessential attributes of being Eritrean. The party narrates the nation in a way that connects with Eritreans' everyday lives and their recent, personal historical memories. In this sense, it has made its version of nationalism quotidian—a routine part of life. The following story about wanting to join the fighters told to me by one of my research subjects presents a narrative that is reproduced in various forms of popular media and aptly illustrates the ways in which lived experiences are appropriated by the party's national narrative.

Growing up close to the front line during the war for independence, the war deeply and personally influenced Isaac, particularly when the Ethiopian government imprisoned Isaac's father for revolutionary activities. Although the war ended before Isaac was old enough to join the fighters, he imagined that he would become a fighter and prioritized Eritrea's independence over his own education or future, thus epitomizing the ethos of sacrifice for the nation:

> The war was in the area surrounding [our village]. We could listen to the sound of the war. Our thinking was totally towards the war. Our brothers and sisters were at the front. We thought, "Why are we going to school here in the village? We should go to fight." I didn't have any goal or objective. But I did have a very long-term plan—when we got liberation, I would have good education—

better than under Ethiopia. This was my thinking. But we didn't have any plan. My plan was just to be an Eritrean soldier. All the surrounding area was covered by Ethiopian soldiers. It was very difficult. Some of us found ways to go to join the Eritrean forces, but I couldn't get to them. In 1989, Eritrean forces attacked my village, and then we tried to go with them, but when we went to this forest area to meet the fighters, they told us they were going a very long distance. They said, "We will come back again, so it is better to stay in your house. Stay here and go to school, and next time you will come with us."

Although Isaac speaks of this in terms of "not having a plan," the sentiment here is that his entire orientation was focused on the liberation of his country and becoming a fighter to bring this about. He could not have a plan because of the conditions his country was in. His story is an expression of willingness to sacrifice but also of the lack of options that war brings. Like many Eritrean young people growing up in Eritrea during the war for independence, early in Isaac's life he was willing to sacrifice everything to become a fighter to liberate Eritrea. Many Eritreans in Isaac's generation did join the fighters, and many others expressed the desire to do so. Even Eritreans who grew up in Ethiopia told me that their parents confessed that they did not tell them about The Struggle for fear that it would fill them with such a strong desire to join the front that they would run away from home and travel to Eritrea to join the fighters.

A young person "running away" to join the fighters is a common motif in Eritrean public nationalist discourse. Short plays that are either televised or performed live on public holidays often portray parents trying to convince their child not to leave home and then ultimately accepting the decision and sacrificing the personal need to keep their child alive for the good of the nation. These dramas link highly personal and emotional memories of the war for independence, desires to liberate the country, and fear of personal loss with public performances of what it means to be Eritrean. In these dramas, a parent, often crying, typically tries to prevent the child (often a girl) from running away, but the dramas always end up with the child succeeding in running away and joining the fighters and the parent recognizing that love for country must take precedence over love for one's child. This sends the message that everyone must be willing to make the ultimate sacrifice.

I would like to highlight two points that emerge from this narrative of running away to join The Struggle. First, any Eritrean could be, or imagine him- or herself as, a fighter. The "fighter" (*tegadalai/tegadalit*) is simultaneously an Eritrean icon and everyman/everywoman. Fighters (*tegadelti*) are pictured on postage stamps, murals, and posters and in documentaries and music videos on Eritrean state-run television. The image of the fighter is everywhere. However, the fighter is not a distant figure but every Eritrean, literally and metaphorically. Many people joined The Struggle when they were young, tried to join The Struggle as Isaac did, or supported the fighters in some other way. When Eritreans who grew up during The Struggle described their understanding of being Eritrean, it was often equated with a sense of wanting to personally help the country, particularly by helping the fighters, emulating the fighters, or becoming a fighter. Peggy Hoyle's (1999) survey of university students provides evidence of the kind of national symbol fighters are—a heroic everyman. When asked who is "the greatest hero of Eritrea," most students answered, "all fighters," "all martyrs," or "all Eritreans" (1999: 407). Although there are specific Eritrean heroes and heroines from the long war for liberation, what was striking in Eritrea was that in the post-independence years, Eritreans regarded all who fought, suffered, and died to liberate the country as heroic (Hoyle 1999). This is indicative of the fact that, in the post-independence years, many Eritreans bought into the idea that *all* Eritreans were heroic and had worked together to liberate themselves by virtue of the national characteristics of fortitude, self-sufficiency, and willingness to sacrifice.

In an interesting inversion, just as the fighter is everyone, those who might be put on (or put themselves on) a pedestal as heroes from The Struggle for liberation instead behave as ordinary people. Eritrea's leaders, including the president, take pride in being common people, something that Eritreans often comment on. They are not thought of as being above others, and, to this day, there is little cult of personality around the president himself. Ministers typically wear fairly casual clothes and drive ordinary cars. The party's political culture does not require those with power to acquire visible adornments of affluence. In the years immediately following independence, President Isaias could often be seen driving himself around Asmara in a small, modest car. It was also a common experience for Eritreans in Asmara to look up in a bar and find he was standing next to them watching a football game or enjoying a beer. These were not heroes put on a pedestal to hover over people and be revered by them; rather, they were thought of as ordinary Eritreans, just like everyone else.

Another idea emerging from narratives of young people running away to join The Struggle is the theme of sacrificing oneself and one's family members for the nation. A unit on patriotism in the national civics curriculum illustrates this theme. The unit begins with a story of a grandfather and his grandson being apprehended by Ethiopian soldiers. A group of Derg (Ethiopian) soldiers was lost without food and water in the Eritrean countryside. They came across a man named Omar Mohamed near the town of Afabet, pulled out their guns, and demanded that he take them to water and food and show them the way to Keren. Omar refused, and the soldiers threatened to kill both him and his grandson who was accompanying him. Omar then said that he would show the soldiers where they could find food and water if they let his grandson go. The soldiers suspected that after they let his grandson go, he would then refuse to take them to food and water. They said they would kill both of them. The man then said that they should kill his grandson in front of him before they kill him. The Derg soldiers were confused and wondered why this man wanted to have his grandson killed first. Then, fortunately, the EPLF showed up, freed the man and his grandson, did not harm the soldiers, fed them, and took them to prison. The conclusion of the story then reiterates that the man had no intention of showing the soldiers where food and water were. He was thinking, the curriculum notes, that he would tell them to kill him after they freed his grandson. The curriculum also notes that he did not want to leave his grandson with "these cruel enemy soldiers," but when it became clear that he could not save his grandson, he began to fear that if he died first, his grandson would show the soldiers to food and water, his focus shifting to protecting the nation by *not* showing the soldiers where the food and water were. The commentary on the story concludes: "Even this innocent child has to be sacrificed for the safety of his people and his country. There is a lot of this type of incidents in the Eritrean's struggle for liberation. It is the highest stage of patriotism" (Ministry of Education, Moral and Civil Education Grade 6, unpublished document). Clearly this definition equates patriotism with willingness to sacrifice not only oneself but also one's loved ones.

The celebration of martyrs and martyrdom extends the theme of valorizing, validating, and nationalizing suffering and sacrifice. Martyrs Day is a public state celebration, but one that penetrates the intimate realm of the home and the family. The events of Martyrs Day are choreographed not only to produce a particular affective climate oriented around loss but also to vindicate these losses, to give them purpose and claim them for the good of the nation. Indeed, sacrifice for the nation is at the core of government-produced definitions of what it means to be Eritrean (Bernal 2014). Through the commemoration of martyrdom, the government also subsumes personal memories of loss into the public commemoration of martyrs. Very personal experiences of grief and mourning are claimed by the state and given meaning. Martyrs are both an intimate part of Eritreans' everyday lives and key national figures who embody the national value of sacrifice. Few Eritrean families did not lose someone to The Struggle, and each family who lost someone is given a certificate, which is often displayed prominently in people's homes. That person's name is seldom mentioned without noting that he or she was "martyred" (e.g., "my uncle, the one who was martyred"). The martyr is a key national symbol and emblematic of the core national tenet of sacrifice (Hepner 2009b). As an ideal type of citizen, the martyr illuminates the ideal of willingness to sacrifice everything for the nation above all else. Being martyred, or being related to a martyr, thus demarcates the experience of being Eritrean, both identifying martyrs and their families as the ideal sacrificial citizens and locating the experience of mourning and loss within the national space.

In Eritrea, Martyrs Day has always been a somber occasion on which Eritreans grieve those they have lost in The Struggle. Unlike the more raucous Independence Day celebrations, there is no drinking or dancing on Martyrs Day. Bars are closed, their lights dimmed. Throughout the country, Eritreans walk or stand quietly, holding candles in vigil. Martyrs Day in 2001 was particularly poignant. On June 13, 2001, approximately one year after fighting in a three-year border war with Ethiopia had ended, the government announced the names of nineteen thousand people who had died in the border war. It was, literally, a day of public, mass mourning. Red-eyed and tearful, people cried as they walked down streets and traveled on public buses moving from home to home where thousands of mourning ceremonies were simultaneously being held.[3]

Official versions of Eritrean nationalism are oriented around sacrifice, and patriotism is inherently linked with sacrifice. The necessity of sacrifice in the face of the brutality of enemies is a theme that shows up in various places in the national curriculum, typically when recounting the atrocities of Ethiopian rule. English texts, history texts, civics texts, as well as movies and television programs depict the horrors experienced under Ethiopian rule. A reading in a grade 10 English book goes into detail about the conditions in a jail for Eritrean dissidents in Asmara by describing the processes of being interrogated and tortured. It also describes the sympathy that other prisoners had for those who had been tortured and notes the patriotism of those being executed: "As prisoners heard their names, they started walking out, shouting slogans: 'Long live the EPLF! Victory to the masses!'" (Ministry of Education, CRDI 1993: 21). This statement reflects a common theme that is also present in a passage on fortitude and other passages on atrocities under Ethiopian rule—that suffering can be transcended through patriotism.

Building on narratives depicting common experiences of oppression and atrocity during the war and the period of Ethiopian rule, the civics text describes "fortitude" as the ultimate Eritrean national character trait. The text notes that "fortitude is one of the moral values which our forefathers cherished" and that "a person with this characteristic can endure any pain or difficulty." It goes on to state that "he or she is dedicated to what he or she believes or stands for to the extent of death." The text defines fortitude as the willingness to sacrifice oneself for a cause, as the Eritrean fighters did when fighting for freedom for thirty years. Furthermore, it notes that this characteristic "has a deep root in the blood of every Eritrean" and describes those who lack fortitude as a burden on society. The segment on fortitude concludes by noting that "every Eritrean has inherited this behavior as a culture and this was witnessed in the very long and bitter war for independence.... There is no doubt that this moral value will also be inherited by all our young generation as a good culture of our forefathers" (Ministry of Education, Moral and Civic Education Grade 6, Unit 1, Fortitude, pp. 23–24, unpublished document). This sense of national character is rooted in the notion that all Eritreans possess inherent fortitude in the face of difficulty. The text depicts the fighters who liberated the country as embodying this characteristic; however, all Eritreans, the text suggests, have "inherited" this characteristic from their "forefathers." Fortitude, the passage above suggests, leads not only to personal success but also to the success of the nation, as the person with fortitude works hard, is patient, and is willing to sacrifice him- or herself for higher ideals.

In addition to the nationalization of personal experiences of loss and suffering, and the valorization of sacrifice and suffering for the nation, the party has also engaged in an ongoing, overt project of making the nation a core part of everyday life. As I noted above, the EPLF intentionally sought to produce a coherent, singular notion of what it meant to be Eritrean and a personal attachment between Eritreans, the party, and its revolutionary ideology. The EPLF, and later the PFDJ, utilized a variety of quotidian strategies to insert these values in Eritreans' everyday lives.

One quotidian strategy was the government's use of rhetoric and symbols to nationalize ordinary, everyday experiences and objects. The valorization of the *shida*, which I discussed in the beginning of the chapter, is one example of the nationalization of the everyday. The *shida* is one of several quotidian nationalist symbols that enable Eritrea's ruling party to imbue Eritreans' daily lives with nationalism. Values that are core to The Struggle, such as fortitude and making due with local resources, can be read in the *shida* and in other symbols. Similarly, the camel, another somewhat unusual national symbol, which appears on the national seal, references endurance and self-reliance. The use of camels to transport weapons and supplies through the dry terrain has been celebrated as an example of utilizing local resources to win the war. Camels have been particularly important in Eritrea's predominantly Muslim lowland areas, where people have commonly used them to transport goods. The camel's elevation to a very public national symbol thus referenced the fusion of lowland and highland peoples and ways of life in the Eritrean nation (see Hoyle 1999 for a discussion of camels as well as other national symbols). Additionally, the very use of the word "struggle" to describe the war for liberation may be seen as a quotidian rhetorical strategy. While "war" depicts events that are both geographically and emotionally distant and temporal (wars start and end), "struggle" is more intimate and continuous. Indeed The Struggle is depicted as the responsibility of all Eritreans. Like "revolution," the term "The Struggle" seamlessly extends from armed combat to other struggles against oppression, poverty, underdevelopment, ignorance, or whatever the regime pinpoints as in need of being struggled against. Struggle is a word that galvanizes on an ongoing, personal level.

Another quotidian strategy of nation making was to create routine, ritualized experiences for Eritreans that socialized them into what it meant to be Eritrean. National Service has been, of course, the quintessential process of socializing Eritreans into the values and experiences of being a fighter—the ideal Eritrean everyman/everywoman—but National Service was certainly not the only way to make Eritrean nationalism understood and felt to be part of everyone's everyday lives. Additionally, throughout my fieldwork, there were a variety of everyday national routines. In major towns and cities, at the beginning and end of the workday, flags were raised and lowered. All pedestrians and traffic were expected to stop when a whistle sounded. Pedestrians then stood in silence to salute the flag while it was lowered and continued moving only after the whistle sounded again. It was a striking experience to be walking down the street and suddenly find everyone standing still while gazing up at a nearby flag.

Similar to National Service, after independence, the government initiated a series of programs designed to ensure that this identification with the experiences of the fighter would transfer to subsequent generations. These programs initially built on desires to serve the country but over time turned mandatory. In the immediate postwar years, Eritreans willingly talked about the need to make sacrifices for the nation. This ethos of sacrifice, as recounted to me in interviews, often translated into a willingness to do whatever and go wherever the government said to. Aspiring students were told to be patient and volunteer while they waited for schools to get started. Civil servants and high-level officials all found themselves being told to make sacrifices as their salaries were furloughed, raises that were long overdue were delayed even longer, or they were transferred to postings they did not want (Hoyle 1999). Eritreans were told that their labor was badly needed, enabling the new government to allocate workers where they needed them and to use a degree of coercion to tell people where to go and what to do. The legacy of loyalty and obedience gleaned from the disciplined military culture created during The Struggle and the strong sentiments of pride in the new nation made sacrifices for the nation in the immediate post-independence years seem like an inevitable part of being Eritrean.

The government yoked the rhetoric of sacrifice to several homegrown development-oriented projects, which enabled successive generations of Eritreans to experience the legacy of The Struggle and have experiences that approximated those of the fighters. Most notable in this regard was Eritrea's National Service program. Initially, trainees spent several months on foot trekking through Eritrea's rugged terrain much as the fighters had, something that many civilians complained was overly harsh. In addition, they received political education and were ultimately put to work on development projects. Effectively, National Service was thought to transform all Eritreans into *tegadelti* (fighters). Citizens' participation in the various forms of service intentionally simulated the service and sacrifice of those who fought in The Struggle (Hepner 2009b; Müller 2008). National service thus was both a disciplinary practice that organized a labor force for development and defense and an ideological one intended to fuse the values of The Struggle into the population.

In the same vein, short-term service projects recruited high school students, university students, women, or, sometimes, members of the population at large into a variety of civic and service activities that might last anywhere from an afternoon to several months. Other mass service projects took on different forms, many of which simulated the developmentalist projects that brought civilians and fighters together during The Struggle. Community-wide cleanup days required all members of a community to clean their town or village. Summer service programs (*ma'atot*) sent high school and university students to different parts of the country to plant trees, terrace hillsides, or engage in other development projects. The goals of National Service and shorter-term service projects were to inculcate in citizens the value of service to the nation and to forge an attachment to the nation among all of its regionally diverse peoples through the common experience of service (Kibreab 2009b; Müller 2008). High school summer work projects also required moving teachers and students to different regions where they would mix with others.

The spectacle of those serving the nation also generated mass euphoria in the population at large. As in many other nations, in Eritrea, national loyalty is inscribed through bodily practices; ideally, as citizens viscerally feel the nation in their bodies, they imagine the state as the benevolent keeper of the national vision. Tekle Woldemikael (2009: 4) notes the importance of Independence Day celebrations to "produc[ing] docile bodies, subjects who fit into the ruling party's image of nationhood." Similarly, students traveling to National Service or summer work programs were often paraded through large towns, waving from buses with horns honking.

By the end of The Struggle, being Eritrean had become a lived experience due to the prevalence of the war and the sense that the fighters were one with the Eritrean people. In the immediate postwar era, the euphoria of independence led to a continuation of the desire to serve and sacrifice for the country. In the decades that followed, the PFDJ has continued to merge nationalism with people's lived experiences by creating a series of experiences whereby Eritreans viscerally and bodily experience the nation in their everyday lives. This happens through programs of mass socialization (National Service), everyday rituals (flag ceremonies), and the celebration of everyday, ordinary symbols that are both national and a part of everyone's lives (the *shida*). However, quotidian nationalism has faced challenges to its legitimacy in the years following the border war.

Contradictions of Revolutionary Nationalism in Post-Independence Eritrea

Revolutionary movements face particular challenges in sustaining their revolutionary ideals when the fighting is over. In part due to their military legacy and in part due to their ideological purity, regimes that come to power through armed insurgency tend to require adherence to an ideological orthodoxy and demand loyalty (or the performance of loyalty). They are also intolerant of internal cleavages, rifts, and dissent (Dorman 2006). But this adherence to ideological orthodoxy and absolute loyalty can prove to be unsustainable in the absence of a clear enemy. Postliberation or revolutionary regimes merge a progressive and developmental vision for societal transformation with a kind of coercive and intolerant politics that, as I show in the next chapter, winds up eroding the legitimacy that enabled the revolution in the first place. Thus, revolutionary movements can lead to political hierarchies and a particularly closed political climate; in their efforts to produce a society that is revolutionary, they also emphasize controlling the population over producing positive emotional attachments to the nation, all of which has been the case in Eritrea (Connell 2011; Dorman 2005).

Post-independence, the government showed itself to be intent on shoring up centralized state control. Shortly after independence, Eritrea reorganized the country administratively, creating five new administrative zones that bifurcated historic ones to ensure that no single ethnic group dominated any one geographical area. Also following independence, the government asserted administrative control at the local levels. While officially leaving traditional forms of governance intact, it also appointed to each village or municipality a centrally appointed administrator who, in practice, was more powerful than traditional leaders. Following the border war, these administrators were more often than not military personnel who had a great deal of power but little legitimacy (Dorman 2005, 2006).

The government also showed itself to be increasingly intolerant of all forms of dissent. From early on, the EPLF/PFDJ leadership cracked down harshly on any who opposed it, most notably in 1973, with the Menka'a incident in which a group of mainly former students protested the EPLF's lack of democratic decision making (Connell 2001, 2005, 2011; Pool 2001). The movement was swiftly put down and its five leaders executed. After that, the EPLF devised severe punishments for anyone who criticized its leadership. A similar incident in 1976 also met with swift brutality (Hepner 2009b). The EPLF was known for expecting loyalty to its vision for the nation, demanding strict discipline from its fighters, and enacting harsh punishments on anyone who disobeyed. This strict orthodoxy has been difficult to maintain in the postliberation years.

Since independence and particularly since 2001, any attempts to voice dissent have been cracked down on equally harshly. The summer and fall of 2001, only months after the cessation of hostilities agreement was signed with Ethiopia to end fighting between the two countries, was a time of unprecedented political debate. Letters drafted to the president from party elites raised questions about the management of the border war as well as the implementation of the constitution and the overall trajectory of the country. A group of diaspora intellectuals now known as the G-13 first attempted to engage Eritrea's leadership in critical discussions about how the country was being managed. Their efforts did not lead to the widespread debate they had hoped for but resulted in the country's leadership questioning the group's integrity (Hepner 2009b: 191–194). The G-13 was followed by a group that came to be known as the G-15, which authored "An Open Letter to Members of the PFDJ." The open letter made many similar points previously made by the G-13, but this letter was written by long-time members of the party's inner circle and leaders within the government itself, including ministers and ambassadors (Hepner 2009b: 194–196). In July 2001, student union president Semere Kesete was arrested following a controversial speech he gave at the University of Asmara. His speech voiced long-time concerns that university students held about voluntary service during their school breaks. Students who protested his arrest were subsequently detained and sent to work camps in the desert later that summer. In mid-September 2001, eleven of the fifteen members of the G-15 were arrested and have not been heard from since. Three were exiled, and one rejoined the government. Private presses were shut down at the same time and remain shut down to this day. Journalists were arrested or went into exile. Scores of others suspected of political involvement and activism were also arrested (Tronvoll and Mekonnen 2014). Since 2001, any attempts to organize and mobilize politically have been dealt with harshly; indeed, there has been little political resistance in Eritrea since 2001. In January 2013, this pattern was broken when a group of soldiers briefly occupied the Ministry of Information and aired part of a statement demanding the release of political prisoners. Opposition websites report that participants in these events have been arrested along with military commanders suspected of inciting this mutiny.

Service and sacrifice have long been the core tenets of Eritrean nationalism (Bernal 2014; Hepner 2009b; Kibreab 2009b). While initially there was support for service projects, increasingly, people's comments about government demands for service and control over citizens began to reflect increasing disillusionment with the government. This occurred against the backdrop of a broader critique of the government's failure to hold elections, implement the constitution, and institute democratic reforms. Whereas during The Struggle for liberation and in the early independence years people had faith in the ideal of service as well as, and perhaps even more significantly, faith in the government's capacity to manage manpower and care for citizens in service, later on service projects began to "lose their luster as more and more young people found their lives dictated by the government's demands for labor and defense as part of its self-reliant development strategy" (Hepner 2009b: 65–66). Throughout my fieldwork, I often heard the assertion, "We still love our country. We still love our country and we would defend it." But in the postwar years, these assertions of willingness to defend were usually a preamble to a bitter critique of all that was going wrong, particularly with National Service. Service to the country, it seemed, had become a punishment, not a national duty.

2

"It Seemed like a Punishment"

Coercive State Effects and the Maddening State

"In *Carcele*; Be Back in Fifteen Minutes"

In July 2002, my husband and I were staying in central Asmara. Much of my husband's time that summer was devoted to finding a rental house for his family, who had been living in one room in a "suburb" of Asmara that lacked running water and latrines. One morning, my husband had gone off to pursue this task, and, as I sat peacefully trying to write, the phone rang. A voice that I did not recognize on the other end told me in a combination of broken English and Italian that my husband was "in *carcele*" and that he would "be back in fifteen minutes." Confused, I tried to ask more questions, and then the line went dead. Initially, I shrugged off the odd phone call, assumed he would be back in fifteen minutes, and went on with my work. I knew *carcele* meant "jail," but why would he be in jail?

Fifteen minutes passed, and I started to watch the clock, which hovered on top of a street map of Asmara hanging on the wall. The word *carcele* repeated itself in my head despite my attempts to mentally brush it away. But after half an hour passed, the word reverberated even more insistently. *Carcele, carcele, carcele.* I started to wonder about the meaning of *carcele* and stood up to look at the map to see whether there was a neighborhood called Carcele, perhaps located near a prison, where he might have gone to look at a house. I started to feel a tingling in my limbs, blood swimming behind my eyes, the hot-cold tightening of the scalp that accompanies the onset of panic. I took a deep breath and berated myself for being paranoid. Why would he be in jail? Why would he be back in fifteen minutes if he was in jail?

After an hour and still no sign of him, the deep breaths that I forced myself to take could not stave off the onset of terror. My eyes teared up, and I felt that there was no space in my chest for breath. I could not concentrate on my work. The words in the sentences I tried to write refused to stay in order. I paced. I sat on the bed and sobbed. I thought about leaving the house, but where would I go? I thought about calling someone, but who would I call? Desperate thoughts collided with each other. What would I do if he did not come back? Who would help me? The U.S. Embassy that could not even gain the release of its own employees, who had been in jail for more than a year?[1] The Eritrean government? Whom was I connected to? Whom could I trust? Was I the reason he got arrested? Would I make more problems if I tried to fix things?

As quickly as I had worked myself up, I talked myself down. Things run late here. He is just running late. Everything runs late. He is not in jail. Why would he be in jail? He will be back. Carcele must be a neighborhood near a jail. He has found a house and is renting it. Fifteen minutes can mean two hours. I made some coffee and played a game of spider solitaire on my computer to distract myself, glancing at the phone, hoping it would ring, listening for the sound of his knock on the front gate.

I oscillated, several times, between tearful hysteria and calmly berating myself for being silly and paranoid. You have seen too many movies sensationalizing dictatorships and disappearances, I told myself. This is not a movie. This is just Eritrea. This does not happen to ordinary people here.

When he appeared almost two hours later, he was furious. "They abducted me," he said. The story unfolded. *They,* the government, were "abducting" any young man who appeared to be of military age, a process that came to be known as *gifa*.[2] Military personnel were posted on street corners, demanding to see ID cards. When an ID was presented, inevitably they were unsatisfied with it and required everyone to climb on a truck waiting to take people to one of the many detention centers set up for this purpose. Once in "jail," paperwork was more thoroughly checked, and some people were released after several hours. Those who were unable to produce satisfactory paperwork had to wait until a supervisor came to prove that they were not supposed to be on active military duty. Some remained in detention for several days. Some were returned to military units where they might be detained further, assigned to hard labor or possibly tortured.

When I heard that he had been in jail, my reaction was complex. Clearly, I was relieved that he had made it back safely, and partly I felt vindicated that my worry did not stem from mere paranoia. He had, indeed, been in jail. My hysteria was a reasonable reaction. But simultaneously I was horrified that what I had always feared—the latent capacity for the government to detain with impunity—had become real. Were there limits on its use of force?

The statement "in *carcele*; be back in fifteen minutes" is reflective of an ambivalence that Begoña Aretxaga (2003) aptly captures in the phrase "maddening states." That maddening state[3] refers to the profound ambivalence citizens feel as they are trapped between their desire for the "good" paternalistic state, a desire so strong that it produces its own evidence that the state *is* benevolent, and utter fear of what the "bad" coercive state—the state that has turned against its people—can and will do. The desire for the paternalistic state is strong; it enables citizens to stubbornly cling to their illusion that the state cares about its people even amid tangible evidence to the contrary.

The first statement, "in jail," inevitably raises alarm. Detention by authorities who have no cause, who are known to have the capacity to behave capriciously and without concern for individual well-being, as is the case in Eritrea, is distressing at best, terrifying at worst. A year earlier, in 2001, the Eritrean government arrested journalists and members of the inner circle of the ruling party who had openly spoken out against the government. As of 2002, the political purge of the previous year had not targeted ordinary citizens, but the potential for it to do so existed. Some Eritreans had experienced being detained by authorities, although a project on the mass scale of *gifa* had never taken place. Furthermore, many remembered the brutality of the Ethiopian officials prior to independence and were all too familiar with practices of arbitrary detention. People were alarmed that government personnel took it upon themselves to round up what seemed like everyone who was eligible for military service and put them in jail. There was clear evidence that the state was turning against its people.

But what do we make of the second half of the statement, "be back in fifteen minutes"? It sounds so ordinary, as if one had simply run out to the store for some eggs. It conveys that there is no cause for alarm, that all is well and normal. It conveys an assumption that detention is but a mere inconvenience. The statement is also intended to pacify. Indeed, my husband clearly intended to pacify me. It normalized the experience of arbitrary detention without cause. Citizens' faith that the state would not harm them and would protect them enabled this process of normalization. Citizens believed that government officials might detain without cause, they might inconvenience people, but they would not hurt them, because the state, at some level, was benevolent. Depicting mass detention as routine and normal was a means for Eritreans to retain and maintain the sense that everything was normal and that the state still cared about its people.

"Be back in fifteen minutes." This rather ordinary statement created a sense of affective dissonance. It said, "It's okay, but nothing is okay." This interplay between what was an extraordinary degree of coercion and control over citizen bodies on the part of the state and what was portrayed as "ordinary" and, therefore, nothing to worry about became a key part of the normalization of life in Eritrea from that time on. That afternoon in Asmara, my encounter with the capacity of the Eritrean state to detain with impunity, set against lingering imaginaries that characterized Eritrea as the kind of place where *this did not happen*, produced my own maddening state—a state of such psychological contradiction that I still struggle to make sense of the conflicting emotions that I experienced that day.

The dissonance that I felt that day is a common characteristic of life in Eritrea. Underlying the maddeningly uncertain climate were questions: Did the state care about us or did it want to kill us? Was it fundamentally paternalistic or violent? In Eritrea, these questions had a deep emotional resonance, as what was at stake during the course of my fieldwork and what came to a critical juncture during the *gifa* of 2002 was an uncertainty as to the nature of the Eritrean state. *Gifa* befuddled the assumptions of many that the state fundamentally cared about them. Some, of course, had already had coercive, or even violent, encounters with the state in previous years. In contrast, others would continue to believe that the state cared for them long after. But the 2002 *gifa* was a turning point. It affected everyone in urban areas; thus, once the government started using widespread *gifa*, most Eritreans could no longer deny the coerciveness of the state, and yet many still wanted to believe, needed to believe at some level, in a state that would take care of its people, a state that had a plan. Yet experiences of *gifa* were evidence to many Eritreans that they were living in a punishing state, something that many still did not completely want to believe.

The central argument of this chapter is that despite tenacious beliefs in a caretaking state, punishment has become a key modality through which the state is imagined in Eritrea. Imagining the state as punishing, thinking of oneself as being punished by the state, and responding to that perception of being punished are state effects of coercion. However, actually knowing whether, when, or why one is being punished is almost impossible, and, because of the maddening nature of the state, imaginaries of the punishing state always coexist with other explanations that rationalize the state's use of force.

Theories of state effects are ways to understand that while the state is not "a thing," it has the capacity to make people think, believe, and act in particular and specific ways. Timothy Mitchell (2006) notes that the state constructs its own "structural effect" whereby people come to believe that the state is an institutional reality. Although coercion is not often considered as a state effect in its own right but instead as a means to bring about other state effects, I suggest that exploring coercion as a state effect is essential to understand everyday life in Eritrea and elsewhere. Scholars have specified a number of state effects, including an individuating effect, a totalizing effect, an identification effect, a spatialization effect, and a legibility effect, all of which are a means to understand how state power manifests itself in the lives of state subjects without suggesting that the state is an actual thing (Corrigan and Sayer 1985; Mitchell 1991, 2006; Scott 1998; Trouillot 2001). Framed by Michel Foucault's (1990) work on governmentality, the focus on state effects explores the ways in which state power acts internally within subjects to produce ways of being, imagining, and thinking rather than externally (and emanating from particular actors) to constrain or promote particular actions (Mitchell 1991, 2006). State effects order individuals' experiences of being state subjects through language (that is, by telling people who they are and how they are supposed to behave as a member of that polity) and by disciplining bodies. They categorize, organize, and order subjects in space and time and thereby enable people to think of themselves as attached to a nation *and* a state and as having particular positions within that nation and state. Studies of state effects seldom view coercion as a state effect in its own right. In contrast, I show that coercive power produces distinctive imaginaries of state coherence/incoherence, understandings of state subjectivity, and behaviors. Coercion is adept at creating an appearance of actual state power but not particularly effective at producing many other state effects. Indeed, the coercive state effects alter other state effects because being coerced makes it harder for subjects to identify in positive ways with the nation, national territory, and the population. A coerced subject has a harder time thinking of him- or herself as a loyal, docile national subject, yet, ironically, the experience of coercion simultaneously forges a powerful imaginary of the state—in this case, one that revolved around being punished by the state.

Through discourse about being punished, Eritreans scaled up from everyday encounters with state actors at the local level to the upper levels of government. In a similar vein, Akhil Gupta (2012) notes that in India discourse and practices of corruption were the means through which people discursively constructed the state. Commentary about corruption in public media, people's routine experiences of corruption, and their remarks about corruption reveal citizen imaginaries of the state and tie together the local, interpersonal level with the "upper" echelons of the state. Like the discourse of corruption in India, discourses of punishment enable an imaginative scaling of the state in Eritrea. Elsewhere, I have argued that this sense of being a punished subject in large part replaced notions that the government had the legitimate right to demand service and sacrifice from its subjects (Riggan 2013b). Here, I emphasize how Eritreans linked experiences of being coerced, or forced to do something, with a sense of "being punished" and, furthermore, extended this sense of being coerced and punished to the condition of being Eritrean more broadly. At times, people knew that the government *was* actually punishing them, but Eritreans used the language of state punishment to describe their frequent experiences of being forced to do things, including instances where this was not actually a punishment or instances in which it was unclear whether punishment was involved.

Punishments were often arbitrary and unpredictable, and this unpredictability is a key component of the coercive state effect. The arbitrary sense that one could be punished at any time is better understood when we consider that Eritrea is a country aptly characterized by Giorgio Agamben's (2005: 39) notion of a "state of exception" in which "there is the force of law without the rule of law" (for discussions of state of exception in Eritrea, see International Crisis Group 2014; Riggan 2013a; Woldemikael 2013). Under a state of exception, rules become permanently suspended such that the exceptional (and extralegal) treatment of part of the population (and in the Eritrean case, a very large part) becomes the norm. Citizens under such conditions can seldom rely on having their "rights" protected. An expression I often heard during fieldwork that aptly sums up this sense of ambiguity and uncertainty is that the government "writes in pencil." This expression could refer to a range of government decisions, from whether teachers would be allowed to travel to Asmara for semester break to National Service eligibility. It reflected widespread sentiments that there was no rule of law in Eritrea or clear policy making and implementation. Eritreans were susceptible to the potential for a state actor, at any level, to use his or her power to force people to do things. In this context, force is more salient than written laws or policies, and state actors have the capability to utilize force in often unchecked ways; thus, no one knows where the state ends and the whims and opinions of individuals with the power to act on citizen bodies begin. The phrase "written in pencil" depicted the ephemerality of state mandates as well as their susceptibility to being interpreted by anyone with power at the moment. This makes encounters with the state very personal but also ambiguous—it is never fully known whether one is being treated a particular way because of a policy or because of an individual's decisions. Thus it was fundamentally unclear whether or when one was actually being punished, but such uncertainty enabled Eritreans to imagine themselves as punished subjects.

This chapter explores three facets of coercive state effects to argue not only that punishment has become a key modality through which the state is imagined in Eritrea but also that this imaginary has played a key role in delegitimizing the current government's vision of the nation. First, as I noted above, the discourse of punishment enables the scaling of imaginaries of the state by linking experiences of being coerced that resulted directly from state "policy" (decisions made by top state actors) with more quotidian experiences of coercion (experiences that may not have been the result of these top-down decisions). I explore this first by examining instances of state coercion and then by looking at how discourses of punishment were used to describe them. This imaginative reworking of the state as punishing partially replaced narratives of serving and defending the country but also led to a climate of impotence and evasion, which brings me to the second facet of coercion: Eritreans responded to this sense of being punished with tactics of evasion. Evasion, avoidance, or escape from experiences of being punished is the logical response to being forced to do things one does not want to do, but, more significantly, the state subject evading state punishment is a radical departure from the national subject who willingly serves and sacrifices. Evasion thus hollows out these national ideals, leaving them empty and "impotent" (Mbembe 2001). Finally, I return to the concept of the maddening state to show that imagining the state as punishing is always nebulous—one does not know whether coercive actions are actually punishments in large part because of lingering notions of the caretaking state—the maddening condition in which the desire for a "good state" coexists with evidence of a "bad state." One way in which desires for a good state manifested themselves was through attempting to find a rationale for the government's coercive actions. The government's ongoing efforts to construct a sense of heightened siege by reminding the population of various security threats contributed to the sense that the government was taking care of its people by resorting to extreme measures necessitated by a state of emergency.

Everyday Life in the Prison State: Citizen Bodies and Coercive State Effects

Eritreans often directly or indirectly referred to their country as a "prison" throughout my fieldwork. This phrase has been picked up by journalists and human rights organizations, which often utilize the term "prison state" to evoke the level of repression present in Eritrea (see, for example, International Crisis Group 2010). However, while journalists increasingly utilized the term "prison state" to reference an alleged network of "underground prisons" throughout Eritrea, Eritreans' depiction of Eritrea as a prison referred instead to the sensation of living in a place where they did not have control over their lives, their livelihoods, and, most importantly, their ability to leave the country. For Eritreans, the commonly voiced sentiment that the country is "like a prison" referenced the ubiquity of experiences of being forced to do things—for example, conscription, endless National Service, arbitrary transfers of civil servants, service projects, controls over people's movements—the sense of constant surveillance, and the prohibition on leaving the country. Talking about life in the prison state thus directly reflects the experience of state coercion.

By coercion, I mean actual instances in which people are forced to engage in a particular form of labor in a particular place, something that could occur literally at the point of a gun or through a similar threat of violence or through other coercive mechanisms. *Gifa* was an example of the former, but there was also a wide array of other ways in which the state could locate and relocate its subjects. The government in Eritrea forced a large number of Eritreans to live in particular places and do particular labor, either short term or long term. The government also coerced students to engage in various forms of service, civil servants to work in locations of the government's choosing, and civilians at large to do particular forms of "voluntary" work for the state by using a variety of other types of coercive mechanisms, such as docking pay, withholding transcripts, denying leave, and threatening people with various punishments. Eritreans were "forced" to do things and, more specifically, to be in places they did not want to be. I argue that these forms of coercion constitute a state effect that alters other state effects—individuating effects, totalizing effects, identification effects, and spatialization effects—and thereby recalibrates the relationship between state subject and identification with the nation.

Although the 2002 *gifa* was the first time round-ups had been carried out on such a large scale, *gifa*-like round-ups were not unfamiliar to Eritreans prior to that. During the war, there were quite a few accounts of arbitrary round-ups by the military and military commanders commandeering civilian bodies. One group of teachers told me a particularly alarming story. On their way home late one evening in 1998, they were pulled aside by soldiers who forced them to climb on a truck. Several waiting trucks drove them a long way into the desert. Terrified, they realized that they were heading toward the front line of the war that was then actively being fought. At the front, they were told to collect the bodies of wounded soldiers, work that would typically be assigned to military personnel. Other friends and acquaintances also recounted being rounded up to have their identity documents checked during this time. The experience of being arbitrarily detained or having one's labor commandeered was a ubiquitous one in Eritrea. While not all of these experiences were terrifying, all gave citizens the sense that their time and their bodies were not entirely under their own control. Furthermore, the government officials' willingness to arbitrarily round up civilians, load them onto the backs of trucks, and require them to perform dangerous tasks, such as collecting the bodies of wounded soldiers, reflects an assumption that any Eritrean was available to serve the government in whatever capacity a local official deemed necessary. As a result, civilians believed they were not safe in war time, not only because an enemy bomb might drop but also because their own government—or, more specifically, an individual with unchecked power—might place them in danger.

The constraints on citizen bodies were nowhere more apparent than in the de facto prohibition on leaving the country. Emigration was effectively illegal in Eritrea at the time of my fieldwork. Exit visas were required to leave the country, and completion of national/military service was a prerequisite to receive an exit visa or a passport (GoE 1995). Receiving an exit visa was premised on completion of National Service; however, since the border war with Ethiopia (1998–2000), very few had been released from National Service, and most recruited into National Service came to believe they would be serving indefinitely (Bozzini 2011; Kibreab 2009b; O'Kane and Hepner 2009; Reid 2009). Furthermore, during my fieldwork, exit visas were almost impossible to acquire even for those who had been released from or were exempt from National Service. Additionally, the border was heavily policed, and those who attempted to leave ran the risk of imprisonment, torture, being shot at the border, or being kidnapped by traffickers (Human Rights Watch 2009).

Preventing people from leaving the country transforms Eritreans' attitudes toward the national space, thereby altering the state spatialization effect. What Michel-Rolph Trouillot (2001) calls the spatialization effect is a means of producing an attachment between state subjects and their distinct national territory. Symbols such as the map, awareness of borders, and anything that produces an understanding of belonging to national space constitute this effect in Eritrea and elsewhere. Eritreans were profoundly aware of the nation as a bounded, territorial entity; however, the coerciveness with which prohibitions on leaving kept Eritreans *in* produced negative attachments between citizens and national space. The country felt like a prison, and its citizens seemed to have the desire, above all else, to escape. This phenomenon continues to be evident in the large numbers of Eritreans who flee the country despite the significant risks they face in doing so. Thus, state spatialization in Eritrea has bound Eritreans to the national territory by making them feel imprisoned by it, but the fact that such large numbers of Eritreans are fleeing the country suggests that this feeling of being made captive is at least in part responsible for producing the desire to escape (Poole 2013; Riggan 2013a).

National Service also produces spatialization effects, because it locates Eritreans across the country, but it simultaneously produces two other state effects—identification and totalization. Identification effects link individual identities with the nation, while totalization effects make them feel part of a larger collective—in this case, the military. One of the key ways in which identification and totalization effects are produced is through the disciplining of time, space, and the body such that subjects come to order their individual lives in ways that align with the expectations of the totality. The experience of being in the military simultaneously produces a particular type of individuated subject and a larger collective (Mitchell 1991, 2006). National Service is, first and foremost, an experience of becoming an individual military subject, an extreme form of subjugation in which one's entire being is subsumed to total discipline, as space, time, and the body are significantly regimented (Foucault 1995).[4] Military discipline (in the Foucauldian sense), in Eritrea and elsewhere, also produces totalizing effects whereby the effect of a collective military body to defend the nation is produced (Mitchell 1991, 2006).[5] National Service is supposed to inculcate the values of The Struggle, make Eritreans feel national, and incorporate individuals into a military whole. However, the coercive state effects prevalent in National Service mean that while it did produce identification and totalization effects, these came to have negative connotations, just as attachments to space did. Eritreans saw themselves not as docile, loyal individuals and not as proud members of a militarized core but as coerced subjects, forced to serve. Service denoted a collective experience of hardship at the hands of the state.[6] Furthermore, coerciveness in the military was experienced through the arbitrary and unpredictable nature of military discipline. The arbitrariness and unpredictability made it easy for conscripts to believe that they were at the mercy of their superiors and imagine themselves as being punished subjects. One of the ways this occurred was through the lack of a predictable schedule while in training. Time for military trainees was both intensively managed and unpredictable, making it totally oriented toward the will of commanding officers. Recruits were expected to live moment to moment and submit their entire beings obediently to their officers. Additionally, recruits were literally punished if they did not follow orders. I discuss punishments in more detail in the next section.

The coercive effects of National Service were well illustrated by a commonly heard phrase, "in Sawa," which appeared frequently in both public, official media and everyday conversations among Eritreans. The town of Sawa is the site of the nation's military training facility (and also the site of the newly created boarding school for all grade 12 students), but the commonly used phrase "in Sawa" had broad and complex meanings. In its most descriptive sense, "in Sawa" meant that someone was in service, and the phrase could refer to either going through military training, serving in the military, or serving in a civil capacity. The military training facility at Sawa is celebrated and glorified in public, government-controlled media and patriotic songs. The government hosts an annual youth festival at Sawa. Additionally, it sponsored trips to Sawa for diaspora youth, where they have experiences that are distinct from military conscripts and include musical entertainment. Sawa thus produces a spatial effect as it constructs an imaginary of a particular place and an identification effect with particular national narratives. However, for most Eritreans, mention of going to Sawa evokes fear and anxiety and is emblematic of the hardships, and coerciveness, of military training. The phrase "in Sawa" merges references to an actual place that has negative connotations associated with the hardships of military training with negative sentiments about service more generally. When most Eritreans commented that someone was "in Sawa" (a phrase heard almost daily), it referenced a sense of being subservient, and vulnerable to, the government. For example, teachers who were completing their National Service as teachers often referred to themselves or were referred to as being "in Sawa" a condition that was typically pitied. Senior teachers expressed worry about being sent "to Sawa," which evoked their concerns about having their salary and freedom taken away. Through the phrase "in Sawa," Eritreans drew together experiences of military and civil service and linked both to an experience of hardship, referencing an imaginary that equated service, military training, and state-induced suffering. Eritreans tended to think of military training, National Service, and military service as part of the same process. For Eritrea's leaders, this was supposed to produce an equalizing, nationalizing experience of service; however, for most Eritreans, the phrase "in Sawa" reflected an imaginary of a state that demanded service in a place that epitomized hardship.

One of the reasons service came to have negative connotations is that it became indefinite. Being a military subject is typically a temporary and limited experience. The vast majority of soldiers submit to that kind of intense, total subjugation for a specific amount of time. While militarization produces fairly common state effects, I suggest that coercive effects were created by policies that forced people to stay in National Service indefinitely, transforming what should have been willing subjects into coerced ones. The Warsai Yikaalo Development Campaign (WYDC) is the main vehicle through which military service was extended indefinitely (Hepner 2009b; Müller 2008; O'Kane and Hepner 2009). Under the auspices of galvanizing National Service conscripts to work on development projects, the WYDC, introduced in 2002, enabled the government to avoid mass demobilization after the border war concluded and effectively extend National Service. But given that there has been no significant fighting with Ethiopia since 2000, the ongoing mobilization of such a large proportion of the population is generally seen as illegitimate and outside the scope of Eritrean law; thus the common assertion among Eritreans, scholars of Eritrea, and human rights organizations is that National Service is indefinite or permanent.

Gifa during summer 2002 occurred at the same time that the WYDC was announced, further reinforcing the notion that service was now something Eritreans had to be forced to do. That summer many people, typically men who appeared to be under the age of forty-five, were detained multiple times. In most cases, they were released within a few hours, although in some cases, they were detained overnight or even for a few days. As others have noted, there was a sense among the population of being under siege not by external enemies but by the Eritrean government itself (Bozzini 2011). *Gifa* illuminated the effects of a coercive state to move and detain citizen bodies. The Eritrean state has always had this capacity, as, indeed, all states do; however, when widespread, mass *gifa* was enacted in 2002, it indicated that the government was willing to use this capacity on a scale that had previously been used only during the war to mobilize reserve troops and new military recruits for the defense of the country.

The capacity for the government to control the lives and labor of its citizens through indefinite National Service, prohibitions on leaving the country, mass round-ups, and arbitrarily commandeered citizen labor forms the fabric of ordinary life in Eritrea. Encounters with government officials, who were willing, empowered, or ordered to coerce citizen bodies in these ways, were ubiquitous; it would be hard to find an Eritrean, particularly an Eritrean adult man, living in Eritrea at this time who has not had one or more coercive encounters with someone representing the state.

Additionally, coercive state effects were felt in other, less anxiety-provoking but equally routine ways. Various types of service projects that could take anywhere from a few hours to a few months provide good examples of less extreme forms of state control. As early as 1995, the government set up summer service projects that took high school–aged youth to various parts of the country to terrace hillsides or plant trees. Similar forms of summer service exist for university students as well (and, indeed, conditions of these university service projects proved to be a political flashpoint in 2001). At the community level, mandatory cleanup days were required of entire towns several times a year. All of these projects were efforts to require citizens en masse to provide service to the government. Both National Service and other mass service projects create an individuating effect by producing subjects who think of themselves as service-providing subjects, but they also have a totalizing effect, as those in service became a highly visible corps.

The extreme and ubiquitous levels of control over bodies, space, and time in Eritrea resemble what Katherine Verdery (1996) refers to in her research on Romania as the etatization of time. Time is etatized when the state usurps people's time, compelling them to expend their time on state projects.[7] Eritreans' time was certainly etatized. In military service, Eritreans report that the microscopic detail of when (and where) to eat, sleep, study, run, walk, dance, and play was dictated by superiors, but because National Service was indefinite, Eritreans' time over the long haul was also controlled by the government. Entire lives were etatized because Eritreans were giving a life of servitude to the government. Eritreans complain that they could not go on to higher levels of education, get married, choose where to live, or have control over their lives because of the mandate that they serve, and in many cases serve indefinitely, either in the military or in civil service. Large numbers of Eritreans were located far from their own families and communities, giving the government direct control over when they could return home. This was true of not only military conscripts but also civil servants and even students. In all of these cases, few or no policies and procedures were in place to allocate leave in the case of a wedding, illness, death of a family member or vacation to visit family. Similarly, there was seldom a policy to determine when a civil servant or military conscript merited transfer.

Any attempt to move physically around the country necessitated an intense, interpersonal negotiation with low- and mid-level state functionaries, who thus had a great deal of power over individual lives. Eritreans describe these negotiations over leave and transfers as being based on their supervisors' highly personal feelings, which could be positive and sympathetic to personal circumstances or negative. Supervisors were often described as making certain decisions to punish those under their command. In these instances, the discourse of punishment brought the intimate and interpersonal state into alignment with the larger "government." Below, I explore the ways in which these experiences were depicted as punishments even when they were not necessarily actual punishments.

"It Seemed like a Punishment": Imagining Everyday Encounters with the State

In the wake of everyday experiences with coercion, many Eritreans started talking about themselves not only as living in a prison state but also as *being punished*. Discourse of the state as punishing is one mode of imagining the coercive state. Through talk about punishments, Eritreans link encounters with everyday coercion, such as those I describe above, to a sense of constantly being susceptible to punishment. Punishment here becomes a means of commenting on and interpreting state coercion and enables linkages to be made between a variety of types of experiences of the state, both those that individuals experience directly and narratives that circulate broadly in conversations and rumors. Eritreans interpreted the actions of supervisors and superiors as punishing but then, based on that experience of "being punished," imagined the state itself as punishing. This perception came from evidence that the government, in fact, had begun to punish people. While the motive to punish was clear in some cases, in other cases it was anything but, yet the widely circulating discourse around punishments constructed an imaginary of the state as punishing.

While they were in National Service itself, conscripts described being constantly at risk of being punished. Indeed, according to human rights reports, a culture of violence and punishment has taken hold in the military (see, for example, Human Rights Watch 2011). Teachers and others recounted to me from their experiences in military training that if they were not in the right place at the right time, if they could not perform tasks as requested, or even if they were caught purchasing food other than what was issued to them, they could be punished. Punishments that teachers described to me from their experience in National Service varied from minor forms of corporal punishment, such as being asked to hop like a frog or roll in the dirt, to more extreme forms of punishment, such as being beaten and tied in stress positions. Accounts from those who are still serving in the military are far more severe, with depictions of torture. Interestingly, in many of these accounts of military punishment, the land itself is used as a means to punish people. Both civil servants and National Service conscripts are sent to parts of the country with the harshest heat as punishment. A common form of corporal punishment in the military is to tie someone up and leave him or her in the hot sun in a desert area. (This too produces a particular spatialization effect—the Eritrean earth and climate are punishing.) Perhaps most importantly, these accounts all reflect the fact that conscripts are susceptible to the whims of their commanders and superiors. The lack of rule of law means that punishments are arbitrary and highly interpersonal. Furthermore, family members have been detained or fined in what has been referred to as "collective punishment" if a conscript escapes (Human Rights Watch 2011). In the military, by all accounts, there is a culture of violence, coercion, and punishment. As I have described above, punishments within National Service were common at the time of my fieldwork (and, by all accounts, still are). However, talk about punishment was also common, even when it was unclear whether one was truly being punished.

Being sent to National Service itself has been used as a punishment for civil servants and others. One incident in particular signaled to Eritreans that service itself could be used as a punishment (Müller 2008; Treiber 2009). In summer 2001, Semere Kesete, the head of the University of Asmara student union and valedictorian of the senior class, was arrested for publicly protesting the conditions of service. University students subsequently protested his arrest and were themselves arrested, detained in the city's soccer stadium, and sent to work on a summer service project in the town of Wi'a, one of the most remote and hot parts of the North Red Sea zone. It was common knowledge that students were sent to Wi'a as a punishment, a sentiment that circulated broadly in conversations among Eritreans and that the government did not seem to deny. Two students died of heatstroke there.

Another instance of using service as punishment affected a group of teachers whom I knew personally. After the evacuation of Assab, upon arrival in Massawa, every able-bodied man of military age was conscripted. When the teachers arrived in Massawa, the precise date on which they would begin their military training was unclear. Officials in Massawa gave the teachers and other evacuees from Assab permission to make a brief trip to the capital, Asmara, where most had relatives, to drop off their belongings. Officials told them to return to Massawa on a particular date, but because the teachers were not sure when exactly military training would begin and knew that the government was notorious for starting things late, several of them decided to spend some extra time with relatives in Asmara. They planned to return to Massawa when they heard that training would start rather than on the appointed date. Another small number of teachers who were long-time residents of Assab actually stayed in Assab instead of evacuating. They received word that they had been called up for military service quite late and then had to figure out how to make the two-day journey to Massawa. The entire group of teachers from Assab who came late to military service—both those who had decided to spend more time with their families in Asmara and those who decided not to evacuate from Assab—were subsequently punished with the addition of a period of several months to their time in military training. While other teachers were released after their military training ended, these latecomers were required to stay in service to perform an additional two months of hard labor in the western lowlands even though the war had ended by that point. Making conscripts perform additional labor and denying them release time to visit family were common punishments in National Service and often had the effect of making sure that people reported for military duty and complied with government mandates.

In addition to what appears to be a culture of punishment within the military and the utilization of service itself as a punishment, civil servants believed they were constantly susceptible to being punished by their superiors and described actions that their supervisors took against them as punishing even when it was unclear whether they actually were being punished. There was a general sense that when it came to conscripting older, educated, professional people, such as civil servants and teachers, being called up for National Service itself was often used as a punishment. In perpetuating this belief, older civil servants discursively linked their experience/perception of being punished to narratives of national punishments, such as the incident at Wi'a and the generalized sense that soldiers were punished people. Like those in the military describing being punished by superiors, many teachers described their transfers as reflective of highly personal grudges, jealousies, and emotions. In fact, any time a teacher was transferred to a remote location, he or she assumed that someone did not like him or her. There were several cases among teachers I interviewed in which a teacher was offered a much coveted and rare opportunity to attend Eritrea's sole university or to leave the country to get a master's degree, only to hear a few weeks later that he or she had also been called up to report to Sawa for military training and National Service. These teachers inevitably assumed that some particular individual was jealous of their receiving an opportunity to further their education and was instead routing them to service.

Teacher Elias recounts one such experience. He was selected to work on a master's degree partially at the University of Asmara and partially abroad. While working on his degree, he was assigned as an administrator in the central Ministry of Education office:

> My boss at that time was not good. From the day I came here [to the Ministry of Education Office], I was treated not well. They thought I was new and could be treated how they wanted. He was not a real boss. He deliberately sent me to Sawa. He sent my name to them. So, anyway, I had to go, and I told them that I have to complete my education, but the Ministry of Defense didn't care.

Stories like Elias's were quite common. Two points are key here. First, Sawa is depicted as a form of punishment or mistreatment. Second, Elias blames his boss's personality, claiming that his boss was "not good" and "was not a real boss" because he behaved jealously rather than fairly. Indeed, I heard that teachers had been simultaneously selected for higher education and National Service frequently enough to believe that these were not coincidences. Teachers often cited these types of stories as evidence that the power of immediate supervisors was often utilized intimately, maliciously, and based on personal emotions, such as jealousy.

Casting individuals with power as malicious and jealous set against the backdrop of the state known to be punishing reveals a scaling up from an individual encounter with a jealous superior to an imaginary of the punishing state as a whole. Elias blames his boss for "sending his name to them" but then becomes a victim of the uncaring Ministry of Defense and ultimately is susceptible to being sent "to Sawa." The jealous punishing boss sets him on a path of state punishment and thus has two faces, and an encounter with the state through this boss has two meanings—on the one hand, the supervisor is an individual using his power punitively and capriciously, but at the same time, he represents the punishing nature of a state that operates on the basis of these personal jealousies. This is similar to what Walter Benjamin (1978) and Aretxaga (2003) think of as the "double body" of the state.

Elsewhere, I have detailed the nature and variation of these types of imaginaries of the punishing, jealous state (Riggan 2013b). For example, younger service teachers might more quickly imagine all Ministry of Education officials as punishing, while more experienced professional teachers might distinguish between those who are bad and not bad. In all of these instances, however, power is experienced as "close to the skin" and then interpreted, imagined, and scaled up, on the basis of its closeness, to reflect a broader imaginary of the "bad" state, or the government turned against its people (Aretxaga 2003).

Similarly, teachers in the South Red Sea zone experienced being transferred to teach in remote locations in the Danakil desert not as part of a broader nation-building project but as a form of punishment. In doing so, teachers often cast blame on the punishing nature of their supervisors who, like Elias's bad boss, often made decisions based on jealousy. Especially after the Wi'a incident, teachers increasingly commented that anyone who made trouble, complained, or spoke out might be *sent to the desert* as a punishment. There was some evidence for this belief that being transferred to the desert was a punishment. Teacher Ezekiel, who was transferred to Tio in 2000 at a time when many of his peers were being transferred to Asmara, was chair of his department and a highly regarded teacher. Ministry of Education officials argued that they needed strong, well-trained teachers in villages such as Tio, where a new Junior Secondary School had recently been opened, but Ezekiel insisted that his transfer was a punishment for being too outspoken. He often complained openly about problems with the school and policies of the local Ministry of Education office. He believed that he was a direct threat to the then regional director of the Ministry of Education and that he was transferred accordingly. Another teacher also transferred to Tio claimed that his transfer was a punishment as well and cast blame on the punishing nature of his supervisors rather than on his own actions when discussing the situation with me:

> Jennifer: Tell me about your transfer to Tio.
> Gebreselasie: [My transfer to Tio] seemed like a punishment. If you look at the soldiers, there are so many ways to punish them, but there is no way to punish teachers. Because we are National Service [and not earning salaries], they cannot take our salary. The only thing they can do is send us to Tio.
> J: So what did you do to make them punish you?
> G: I don't think I did anything. As I told you, I was given some months' rest, and I was in Asmara for about six months.
> J: Did they send you [to Tio] for coming late to school?
> G: They gave so many reasons for this.

I would like to highlight several points revealed by Gebreselasie's comments. First, while Gebreselasie may have deserved to be disciplined for arriving late—and, indeed, he was something of a bane to his supervisors—it is key to note that they had no means to discipline him because he was in National Service. National Service, which was the very mechanism set up to manage the population and transform the entire populace into a particular type of national subject, made it impossible to discipline and hold individual teachers accountable. Prior to summer 2001, at which time the vast majority of teachers were recruited into National Service, supervisors and school directors punished teachers by docking their salary. However, when teachers no longer received a salary because of National Service, there was suddenly no way to hold them accountable. Several supervisors and school directors expressed great frustration to me that there was no way to discipline teachers and often noted that if they were soldiers, there would be ways to "punish them." (This is an example of the inefficiency of coercion and the ensuing impotence of the state, which I elaborate on in the next section.)

Second, and even more importantly, it is significant that Gebreselasie, like other teachers, believed that his being sent to a remote area was a punishment, and, furthermore, asserted that he had done nothing to deserve this punishment. When I asked Gebreselasie if the government transferred him because he showed up several weeks late for the school year, he waived his hand dismissively and said with disgust, "They gave so many reasons for this"—or, in other words, it had no good reason for this. Gebreselasie did not believe that this punishment/transfer was merited by any particular action on his part. Instead, he believed that it was characteristic of the state's desire to punish.

Perhaps most importantly, Gebreselasie's comment that "there are so many ways to punish soldiers" recasts the soldier from national symbol to punished figure. It is telling that in discussions that evoked teacher transfers as punishments, comparisons between teachers and soldiers often came up. These comments typically built on the idea that soldiers *could* be punished. In making this comparison, Gebreselasie and others who made similar comments undermined the symbolic value of a pivotal and much celebrated national figure—the *tegadalai/tegadalit*, or fighter. As noted in the previous chapter, the quintessential Eritrean is the fighter in the struggle for liberation. The fighter embodies nationalist values of personal sacrifice and willingness to defend or develop the nation. In contrast to the heroic revolutionary fighter, the punished soldier is cast as a victim of demands for endless service. The word "soldier" in Tigrinya tends to refer to professional soldiers, a category that many Eritreans argue does not exist in Eritrea. The occupational group described by the English word "soldier" was referred to by participants in my study using two different terms in Tigrinya: When describing former fighters, Eritreans used the word *tegadelti*, but in contrast, those in military service tended to refer to themselves simply as *agelglot* (service), emphasizing their servitude (Bozzini 2013). When using the English word for soldiers, Eritreans described a group of people to be pitied because they were highly disciplined, were often punished, and had little control over their lives. Their bodies were totally at the mercy of the state. But even as teachers differentiated themselves from soldiers in their talks with me, they also believed that they were like soldiers. Like soldiers, teachers felt controlled by their supervisors and the state itself, but unlike soldiers, teachers' supervisors and directors did not control them as intensely as military authorities controlled soldiers. Teachers had much more freedom in their everyday lives.

Michael Herzfeld's (1997) notion of social poetics is useful here as a means to explore the interplay of official symbols and narratives with everyday discourses that reinterpret and rewrite official symbols and narratives. As Herzfeld (1997: 25) notes, social poetics "links the little poetics of everyday interaction with the grand dramas of official pomp and historiography in order to break down illusions of scale." If we understand Gebreselasie's commentary on soldiers as one such instance of these "little poetics of everyday interaction," we can see how this commentary reworks the "grand drama" of Eritrean nationalism, a drama that casts the figure of the soldier as the quintessential sacrificing, serving Eritrean. Rather, the soldier is symbolically evoked as a victim of a punishing state. Thus the state not only is characterized as inherently punishing but also, in characterizing soldiers as victims of punishment, engages and alters the symbolism of the nation itself.

Eritreans playfully engaged the idiom of the fighter/soldier. Ironically, as the Eritrean government has developed increasingly coercive mechanisms to shuttle all Eritreans into service, Eritreans have come to identify with being fighters/soldiers, but in the process the fighter, an icon of willing service, has been transformed into the soldier, a specter of punishment. Just as "in Sawa" has come to have negative connotations, the soldier has come to be used as an index of how the state "controls" its citizens in various forms of service. Casting "service," in its various forms, as a punishment delegitimizes the government's ability to require service from its citizens. In the absence of a widespread sentiment that people should serve the country, the government has had to resort to increasing levels of force to pull people into service. In turn, the people themselves have begun to find more ways to evade and avoid being caught by the government.

"Sleeping Late and Making a Wide Turn": Evasive Maneuvers and Impotence

During the course of summer 2002, the house where we were staying was often turned into a safe haven of sorts. We would hear a knock on the door and a friend or relative—a man of military age—would duck in, usually smiling and joking, making a quick escape from the authorities. Located in central Asmara, we were well positioned for that summer's events. At times, it felt like a rolling party in our house. At other times, parties we had planned fell flat because everyone stayed home to avoid *gifa*. It was not uncommon to see young men duck into shops when walking the main streets. More common was for young men to avoid the main streets altogether. *Gifa* had the capacity to change ordinary, daily life events and reorder time in highly unpredictable ways. Coercive state effects not only "etatized" time but also politicized the ordinary actions of everyday life, commanding citizens' bodies, time, and public spaces (Bayat 2010; Verdery 1996).

Coercion produces a vicious cycle. The regime was increasingly not imagined as the benevolent, caretaking state. It could no longer legitimately command Eritreans to do their national duty; it could only coerce them to do so. As Eritrea's leadership became more and more reliant on using force to command Eritreans to do their "duty" as citizens, civil servants, and students and, specifically, to conscript them, the state became more illegitimate and impotent. When a regime must rely on force to govern, it strips itself of legitimacy, thereby further necessitating a reliance on force.

The concept of impotence, which I borrow from Achille Mbembe (2001), illuminates the effects of state coercion. Mbembe notes that authoritarian regimes produce a condition of impotence as they attempt to command subjects who are subtly but persistently resistant to their commands but never capable of overturning them. What I call coercion is in many respects similar to Mbembe's notion of the *commandement*. As I have noted, according to Mbembe, when state subjects perceive that the state has the capacity to absolutely command (coerce) them—to tell them when, how, and where to walk, stand, dance, talk, work, fight, and so on, they will comply, but only to the extent that they are forced. Mbembe notes that as the *commandement* is enacted, symbolic and disciplinary realms join to produce docility and obedience, but they never quite produce complete compliance among citizens, and thus the seeds of transgression may emerge in subtle ways as symbols are transformed, rituals subverted, and narratives quietly rewritten.[8] Subjects simultaneously evade or resist the state *commandement* and ridicule those in power with all sorts of humorous and vulgar displays that delegitimize their power. This process of evasion and ridicule leads to what he calls impotence. Impotence is not resistance to power but a condition of mutual disempowerment—an effect of coercion. Mbembe (2001: 111) argues that the subtle inversion of the signs and symbols of officialdom, rather than undoing official power, "produces a situation of disempowerment . . . for both ruled and rulers"; it erodes official power but fails to produce effective resistance, resulting in what he calls "mutual zombification." Ruler and ruled are caught in a sort of bizarre, grotesque dance that leaves them both sapped as impotence profanes the sacred symbols of nation and state and also lays the groundwork for the evasion of state *commandements*.

Gifa created unofficial categories of people—those who were safe from prolonged detention and punishment and those who remained vulnerable to imprisonment, conscription, and further punishment. These categories did not necessarily reflect who was actually avoiding service and who was not. People with high positions in the ministries, who tended to be released quickly as soon as they were identified, were inconvenienced by *gifa* but not endangered by it. Civil servants who were doing essential jobs, such as doctors and nurses, tended to be released within a few hours. Teachers, who were on leave for the summer, might languish in detention for several hours or even days before a supervisor got around to getting them released. And those who were self-employed or business owners, and therefore not under the control of the government, might have a very difficult time being released unless they happened to have a close contact among the country's leadership. Thus, those more essential to the state were relatively safer in times of *gifa*, while those who were not essential were in relatively more danger of being ignored, forgotten, and released only after a great deal of effort, or perhaps not at all.

The unpredictability produced by this time of intense *gifa* led not only to anxieties about being detained but also to tremendous inefficiencies. When people were detained for hours or days, they could not work. Because the net of *gifa* was cast so widely, even officials, administrators, and supervisors were detained. Initially when the 2002 *gifa* began, the only people qualified to secure the release of the detained were those who were very highly placed—in some cases, the minister or the minister's deputy. This meant that during times of *gifa*, high officials were spending a great deal of time negotiating the release of their employees rather than attending to other tasks. Furthermore, *gifa* encouraged people to hide at home, leaving government offices and businesses understaffed. During *gifa*, young men's friends, family members, and even supervisors advised them not to go out on the street, even if it meant not coming to work. During one particularly challenging week in summer 2002, I had conversations with several teachers who had business to complete in the central Ministry of Education office and complained that they were unable to do their business because they were arrested every time they left their house. They were advised by Ministry of Education officials to stay home. Magnus Treiber (2009) also notes that one of his informants was told to leave work and go home, where he would be safe, because he did not have the correct paperwork. Employers and supervisors apparently thought it was easier to send people home to hide than to get people out of detention. Productivity slowed.

Through *gifa*, everyday life was politicized because everyone became potentially suspect of avoiding service. Ironically, this coercive politicization of everyday life rendered the functioning of the government itself completely inefficient, as Eritreans responded to this politicization of everyday life with evasion, something Asef Bayat (2010) notes is common under conditions of authoritarian rule. If the round-ups themselves were described as evidence of the mean-spirited nature of the government as a whole, the individuals carrying out the round-ups were described as ineffective tools in the hands of that mean-spirited government. Many Eritreans commented that the military police doing the round-ups were illiterate, did not recognize all forms of identification, and were from remote (read: less developed) parts of the country.

The Eritrean state had a strong need for a means to catch those evading National Service, but a limited technical capability to monitor the population (Bozzini 2011). Until about 2004, civil servants typically did not have papers that denoted that they had completed National Service, which made it difficult to ascertain who was and was not evading it (Bozzini 2011). Because so many people were in National Service, the government lacked clear mechanisms to show who should be in a military unit and who should not. Furthermore, a wide array of documentation could be used to show that someone was not required to be in National Service. Student IDs and ID cards awarded by an individual's employing ministry typically served this purpose. But rather than actually proving completion of military service, these cards showed only that the individual was temporarily ineligible for service or had been ineligible at some point in the recent past. This plethora of forms of identification and documentation required that police or military personnel make determinations about their validity (Bozzini 2011). *Gifa* created a massive net intended to catch all who were evading military service, but in the absence of a clear means of identifying evaders, the mechanism proved clumsy and coercive. *Gifa* was a blunt object in the hands of a government that wanted to exert tight control over its entire population but lacked the technology to do so. As more and more people started trying to evade service, this lack of technological capability became clear, leading the government to turn to force and creating a manifestation of the vicious cycle of impotence.

What evolved during summer 2002 was a series of techniques of evasion and a general sense of good-humored solidarity around how to best avoid *gifa*. By evasion, I refer to tactics to avoid being punished by the state (or avoiding coercion perceived to be punishment). When passing each other on the street, strangers would warn each other about which way to walk to avoid the soldiers. Rumors would circulate as to which days *gifa* would happen, and people would avoid going to work that day. One friend of mine articulated a strategy to evade *gifa* that I think is emblematic of the condition of impotence that marked this time period. Because *gifa* typically occurred during the hours when people were commuting to work and soldiers tended to be located on the busiest street corners, his strategy was to "sleep late" (meaning leave for work late) and to "make a wide turn" (meaning walk to work down side streets). His comment that he could avoid *gifa* by sleeping late and making a wide turn highlighted the absurdity of the situation and articulated the ethos of evasion that took hold that summer and came to demarcate Eritreans' relationship with the state.

Jokes about *gifa*, such as my friend's comment about sleeping late and making a wide turn, revealed that the overall climate in summer 2002 was not one of fear, although fear was present, but of solidarity in evading the authorities. A culture of evasion was produced that resulted in many people "sleeping late" or avoiding work altogether to evade being rounded up. If practices of *gifa* made things inefficient, then solidarities formed around evasiveness, and jokes made about evasion rendered the state completely illegitimate, ridiculous, and impotent.

Solidarities created around evasion extended to other areas during the years of my fieldwork as well. Teachers avoided returning to schools at the start of the school year, making schools start weeks and at times months late (something I take up in more detail in Chapter 4). In some regions where teachers traveled back and forth to Asmara regularly, I heard from supervisors in the Ministry of Education that schools ran only three days a week because teachers were constantly traveling to Asmara, thereby evading work. Civil servants also dragged their feet and refused to go to posts at times.

Perhaps the clearest example of evasion is reflected in the extraordinarily large numbers of people who have fled the country. While the number of people fleeing Eritrea has always been high, a variety of reports suggest that there has been a surge in these numbers (Al Jazeera 2014; Gedab News

2014c; UN News Centre 2014).⁹ Eritreans continue to flee the country despite known, and increasing, dangers and risks of capture, kidnapping, or shipwreck in doing so. Recent accounts on opposition websites suggest that what we might think of as evasive tactics are becoming more widespread in other ways. These websites suggest that the army is operating at a fraction of its strength because so many have fled (Gedab News 2014b, 2014d). Awate notes that the army recently told returning recruits to stay home instead of returning to their units, and, taking advantage of a lapse in government control, many either fled or went into hiding to avoid being recalled to their units in the future (Gedab News 2014a).

I think it is also significant that evasion and avoidance are far more common that outright resistance in Eritrea. With a couple of notable exceptions, there have been no instances of outright, open, coordinated protest.¹⁰ Evasion, however, is highly political. It is a form of what James Scott (1985) would call a form of "foot dragging" and a "weapon of the weak." Typically, this type of resistance has an impact, as Scott argues, but it is not as effective at bringing about political change as more coordinated resistance. As I showed above, evasive maneuvers, such as sleeping late and making wide turns, make the functioning of the state inefficient but lack a coherent message or intention.

There are some interesting signs that more recently the tendency toward evasion has been galvanized and transformed into a more coordinated political message. In 2011, opposition groups inside Eritrea organized "Freedom Fridays." Freedom Fridays are a form of protest in which Eritreans are encouraged to stay home on Fridays rather than going out, to act by not acting—in short, to be evasive. As this book goes to press, accounts gleaned from opposition websites suggest that government tactics in the latter part of 2014 have oscillated between increased coercion and evidence of loss of government control. In light of this, there is even more evidence that what have been individual evasive tactics are being organized into coordinated resistance movements. Reports on Asmarino in October 2014 note that Freedom Friday urged Eritreans to refuse to report for National Service, calling on them to do, or rather not do, something that it appears many were already inclined not to do in the first place (Arbi Harnet 2014a, 2014b, 2014c; Plaut 2014; Vincent 2014). Freedom Friday has "organized" people around refusal, or, in other words, organized people around a strategy they may have already been using to evade and avoid becoming a punished subject. If evasion has functioned as a spontaneous and logical response to state coercion, Freedom Fridays might be seen as an effort to coordinate and politicize this natural, everyday form of resistance. In short, Freedom

Fridays ascribe a political message to evasion and encourage Eritreans to oppose the regime by being evasive.

The government's loss of control in part comes from the sheer difficulty of managing the large numbers of people evading government control. If accounts of the military (and the civil service) operating at a fraction of its strength are true, it is no wonder that the government can no longer engage the population coercively. I can think of nothing that makes Mbembe's (2001) notion of impotence clearer—a government that cannot control its people because it has chased so many of them away by being too coercive, a government that has been so coercive and punishing that it no longer has the capacity to coerce and punish. The vicious cycle of coercion and evasion, which for so long has resulted in impotence—mutual disempowerment—may finally have run its course, ending the impotent stalemate between coercive state and subjects seeking to avoid punishment. Or, as many speculate, the government could return to even greater use of force to limit the capacity for escape from being a punished subject.

It is, perhaps, curious that, in a regime renowned for its long-term armed struggle for independence, evasion is the predominant form that resistance to the regime seems to be taking. I think there are a few reasons for this. First, it is very likely that many, if not most, Eritreans are afraid of outright resistance, something that is not surprising given what has happened to those who have attempted to resist the regime over the years. A number of writers have discussed the state's construction of fear (Feldman 1991; Green 1995; Skidmore 2004; Sluka 2000). However, an affective tone of fear is complex. The climate produced in Eritrea by the state's coercive effect at the time of my fieldwork reflected fear mixed with a number of other powerful emotions, such as anger at being coerced and solidarities formed around evasion. Fear was tempered by frustration and disappointment in the way things had turned out. The affective tone with which *gifa* was described reflected a sense of righteous anger at being denied rights and a sense of being entitled to certain freedoms. Additionally, fear was often accompanied by humor and shared strategies of evasion. People made jokes about the government's strategies of rounding people up not working very well. People were fearful enough that they tended not to resist in any coordinated fashion, but they often refused to comply with government mandates, citing all kinds of excuses or simply sleeping late and making wide turns. Second, beliefs in the caretaking state still coexisted with coerciveness. It is hard to mount outright resistance to a state that has delivered so much historically—independence and its promises. There were lingering beliefs that the government was using force only because extreme measures were needed to protect its citizens from an ongoing threat—the return to war. The palpable sense of siege cultivated by the government and the ways in which a sense of siege continued to render the state maddeningly ambiguous are addressed in the next section.

State of Emergency or State of Exception? Rumors, Rationale, and "the Last *Gifa*"

I arrived in Asmara from Assab to lecture at the university on November 15, 2004. A tension that encompassed the country as a whole was palpable in the capital city. The government had announced that everyone who had served in the military and was not currently working as a civil servant, including students over eighteen, was to report to his or her former military units. This order evoked memories from just prior to the war in 1998, when all reserve units were called up in a similar manner. It elicited a sense of fear of renewed war and of being on alert. In Asmara, fighter jets buzzed over the city every night for several weeks.

Around the same time (about ten days before I arrived in Asmara), an incident occurred that has come to be known as the Adi Abeto incident. Earlier that November, the government began rounding people up in the capital in what some of my interlocutors referred to as "a massive *gifa*." Rumors about Adi Abeto not only had spread through Asmara but had already reached Assab. In fact, we heard that one of our colleagues, a teacher in the Senior Secondary School, had been arrested in this round of widesweeping *gifa*. When I arrived in Asmara, I was able to piece together what happened and recorded the following account from one of my interlocutors in my field notes:

> My friend was there, and so I can tell you what happened. They [the people who were detained] were being held and got frustrated. They realized they could push down a wall, and they did. Two soldiers on the other side were crushed to death. Other soldiers started to fire. Prisoners, especially those without an ID, started stampeding to get out. Many died or were wounded either from the soldiers' fire or from being stampeded.

The Adi Abeto incident, like *gifa* and the government's coercion of civilian populations more broadly, poignantly reveals the maddening state of Eritrea during these years. Clearly Adi Abeto was an extreme manifestation of state violence, but it occurred amid an attempt by the government to galvanize its defense capabilities. Conversations about Adi Abeto reflected struggles with questions about whether the state was good or bad. Was the violence of Adi Abeto an unfortunate side effect of necessary processes of calling up reserves, reconscripting anyone who could fight, and placing the country on war footing? Was it a necessary measure to protect the country from the threat of renewed war? Was the threat of war legitimate? Or were efforts to place the country on war footing a charade to create an illusion of danger and thereby justify these extreme uses of force? Was the government mandating brutality because it was brutal? What is maddening about the coercive state is that citizens can never quite know whether the state is using force for protective, and therefore benevolent, ends or malevolent ends.

Another way to think through this maddening condition in which the benevolence/malevolence of the state is ambiguous is to understand the blurry distinction between the state of emergency and the state of exception (Agamben 2005). By evoking states of emergency, something states often do in wartime or other crises, states claim exceptional powers, particularly the use of force. Agamben's (2005: 39) notion of the state of exception allows us to see how the state of emergency becomes normalized and operates as an ordinary technology of the state. Like the state of emergency, the state of exception derives from the perception or reality of being constantly under siege, or, in other words, from concerns about security. Indeed, Eritrea has been described as "a siege state," a place where exceptional measures are taken to reorganize society around the need to defend against perceived external threats to the nation (International Crisis Group 2010; Müller 2012a; Tronvoll and Mekonnen 2014). Siege gave a rationale to state coercion during the war, but after the war the sense of siege was more nebulous and no longer fully legitimated the use of force. In the years following the border war, this wartime state of emergency has been indefinitely extended. As the state of siege extends there are ever-expanding gray areas where written law becomes secondary to governing practice, including practices that are experienced as coercive. Because *gifa* and other forms of state coercion emerged from a wartime state of emergency, there was always a maddening ambiguity regarding whether the state was trying to punish its people for disloyalty or trying, albeit sloppily, to bring order to and improve the country.

Wartime entangles experiences of being coerced by the state with beliefs in a caretaking state. In wartime, the state is supposed to take care of its people, and many citizens are willing to do their part to defend the nation. For this reason, under conditions of war, many citizens are willing to accept a state of emergency, which extends greater powers to state actors to address security concerns (Agamben 2005). In Eritrea, commentary on other instances of state violence also shows Eritreans' attempts to reconcile state violence with the perceptions of an ongoing state of emergency. The following story told to a group of us in the school cafeteria and recorded in my field notes captures the tension between experiences of coercion at that time and rationalization of why the government needed to use force:

> Iyasu told us a troubling story. He was at the front fighting during the third offensive during the border war. When he returned to Assab after the fighting stopped, he was rounded up. He remembered watching people who were resisting the soldiers. The soldiers were using a lot of force. He recounted that he saw people being handcuffed and tied around the neck. He saw people being beaten and yelled at. They tried to arrest him because the person he was with did not have an ID, but he convinced them to let him go because he had an ID. Iyasu in the end said, "This is a state of emergency, so the government has to do these things."

Despite these extremes of violence, Iyasu attempted to explain the government reactions by saying, "This is a state of emergency." The question of whether Eritrea is in a state of emergency is key to making sense of the maddening state in Eritrea—if the country faces a legitimate threat, then the government, according to some, may use exceptional powers, even against its own people, to keep the country safe. But if the threat is no longer legitimate, then the government's use of coercion against its own people is malevolent and punishing, not benevolent and protective.

When the border war began in 1998, citizens were forced into the military and thus began to feel even more coerced and punished, but, until fighting ended in 2000, they also believed that what the government did was in the interest of defending the nation. Although a state of emergency was never formally declared in Eritrea, various government actions indicated that something approaching a state of emergency was in place. In 1998, just prior to the outbreak of war, everyone who had been trained in the military was recalled to his or her unit. Thus the wartime state of emergency allowed the government to extend the time-limited contract of National Service (a contract that allocates eighteen months of citizens' lives to the government) indefinitely. Under conditions of "war and mobilization," the National Service Proclamation states, "Anyone in active National Service is under the obligation of remaining beyond the prescribed period" (GoE 1995, Article 21). This is not particularly unusual in times of war, but during the war in Eritrea, the government also conscripted a much larger proportion of the population. Therefore, wartime not only extended military discipline across a longer span of time for those recalled to National Service; it also expanded the number of people who came under military discipline. Eritreans were all directly affected by the war. Although there was still a sense that the government itself was dangerous, unpredictable, and could harm its citizens, there was also a sense that it was appropriate to mobilize citizens to defend the nation and that if the government needed to use force to do so, that force was justified. Not surprisingly, the desire for a state that could be thought of as benevolent, protective, and paternalistic coexisted with these fears. People understood that wartime produced a state of emergency, which might lead to extreme measures. Most who were headed off to the front lines during the war went willingly. The state was charged with defending the nation, and during the war there was an understanding that people needed to participate in this defense, but even at that point, using civilians, not military personnel to do so, created a sense of fear in the state, leading to the "maddening state" of tension between imaginaries of a paternalistic state and a coercive state (Aretxaga 2003).

After the war, the ongoing use of force was increasingly delegitimized through the discourse of punishment and solidarities formed around evasion of state coercion. In closing this chapter, I return to the maddening state to argue that, despite increased state illegitimacy, uncertainties about whether the state continued to be a caretaking, protective entity lingered in the imaginations of Eritreans. If imagining the punishing state is a way of interpreting state coercion as evidence that the state is malevolent, seeking out a rationale for the state's use of coercion is a lingering attempt to imagine the benevolence in the caretaking, protective state.

Rumors that circulated in 2002 in an attempt to explain why the government was using *gifa* provide particular insight into attempts to make sense of being a coerced subject at this maddening time, during which the line between emergency and exception blurred. Many of these rumors attempted to ascribe a motivation to the government's efforts to round people up. Some tried to ascribe a protective role to the government. Most were highly ambivalent. One rumor that was particularly common during summer 2002 (one of the most intensive periods of *gifa*) was that the government was not really trying to catch draft dodgers but was using *gifa* as a pretense to round up hidden political dissidents. These rumors suggested that *gifa* was effectively a cover for catching a small, limited number of individuals and that mass round-ups were a pretense for making isolated arrests. This rumor tried to distinguish between "bad" people who might actually be undermining the security of the country and other "good" Eritreans. By evoking this rumor, Eritreans cast themselves as "good" and the government as attempting, albeit clumsily, to protect the country. Other rumors suggested that those detained during round-ups were suspected of producing counterfeit ID cards. Indeed, mass round-ups placed new importance on having a valid ID card and created a great deal of confusion about which ID cards were acceptable because they were not standardized. The fact that there were no standardized ID cards created a healthy market for counterfeit identification. Understandably, at this time, the government had great anxieties about the counterfeiting of ID cards, which would only make the population harder to manage and control, but like rumors that suggested that the government lacked the means to catch those who were opposing it, rumors about counterfeiting also revealed the weakness of the state.

In 2004, following the Adi Abeto incident, rumors took a different tone. Amid speculation about whether the nation was actually at risk of returning to war or the government was simply rattling the war drums to legitimize its use of force, many people suggested that, following the deaths at Adi Abeto, the government would cease using *gifa* as a technique because it would recognize the limits on its use of force. Adi Abeto was talked about as a sort of "last *gifa*," and comments on it suggested that the government realized that things had gone too far. (Although, as David Bozzini [2011] notes in his work, *gifa* certainly did not end after the Adi Abeto incident, there was a sense that that was the last *gifa* for a while). Like rumors that sought to ascribe rationale to round-ups, rumors about "the last *gifa*" were also an attempt to find benevolence in the state. Commentary on "the last *gifa*" reflected the hope that state actors know when they have gone too far. These rumors suggested that the state knew its limits, alluding to the fact that while the government may have deemed some force necessary, it could be held accountable for the use of extreme force. All of this suggested an imaginary of state power in which the state was characterized as ultimately concerned for its people, if flawed and at times violent.

Rumors that suggest there is a reason for and a limit to state violence run counter to imaginaries of the punishing state. Ascribing a rationale to state violence reflects lingering desires for the paternalistic state—the state that would take care of its people—and recasts *gifa*, which was an experience of being a target of state coercion, as an experience of being accidentally caught up in the state's attempt at protecting the population from various threats, such as counterfeiters, dissidents, and others. Imaginaries of being punished do the opposite—they delegitimize state violence and instead focus on experiences of being a coerced subject.

It is also important to note that the particular rumors about *gifa*, both in 2002 and 2004, demonstrated a popular awareness of state impotence. While these rumors ascribed a rationale and a limit to state violence, they also depicted the state as somewhat incompetent in these efforts. Rumors of counterfeiting reflected an imaginary of a state that could not keep the lid on illegal activity. Rumors of government attempts to catch someone elusive through *gifa* provided evidence of a government that had to resort to the sweeping, blunt instrument of mass round-ups to catch a small number of people. These rumors that tried to make sense of *gifa* thus revealed both a desire for a paternalistic state and a frustration with its ineptness. Rumors about counterfeiting, government dissidents, and "the last *gifa*" were simultaneously commentaries on the state's preoccupation with control and an evaluation of its lack of capacity.

States can never control their populations solely through force. The demands that the Eritrean state placed on citizen bodies, particularly National Service, lost their legitimacy after the war, meaning that the government had to rely increasingly on coercion to conscript its citizens. But coercion produces a vicious cycle of force and evasion—increasing reliance on force renders that force less and less legitimate, leading increasing numbers of citizens to evade coercion, which in turn leads to increasing reliance on force. Additionally, as more and more citizens have to be forced into service, the state capacity to do so becomes weakened, making the state impotent both symbolically and in terms of its actual capacity to control its population.

State coercion is seldom legitimate, but it is always maddening. It results in subjects who commonly comment on being punished, forge imaginaries of the punishing state, evade, form solidarities around evasion tactics, and ridicule the state's efforts at controlling them even as they fear the consequences of coercion and violence. And yet citizens' desires for a benevolent state produce an attempt to rationalize its use of force, to make state actors out to be rational. However, even these rationales reveal the state's weaknesses and impotent condition. The state cannot control without force, yet force can never be legitimate and only leads to further evasion. The ultimate state effect of coercion, thus, is impotence. This interplay of impotence and coercion played out in multiple spheres of Eritrean life, most notably in schools.

3

Students or Soldiers?

Troubled State Technologies and the Imagined Future of Educated Eritrea

Cowboy Hats and New Curriculum

A couple of days after I arrived in Eritrea in August 2003, I ran into two friends who were elementary school teachers. With a grin they asked me, "Jenni, have you heard? They are going to give us horses and cowboy hats when we teach!" We shared a hearty laugh about that. They were referencing the workshop they were attending on what teachers dubbed the "new curriculum." Teachers who were in Asmara to attend end-of-summer teacher training sessions were under the impression that they were being trained to implement a curriculum based on Texas's standards-based curriculum,[1] although no one knew exactly what that meant or what was Texan about the curriculum. No one was taking it seriously. I heard a version of this same joke repeated over the coming weeks and even months later.

But after that summer, no one mentioned Texas. Several months later, when I conducted interviews with Ministry of Education officials and specifically asked about Texas, they refused to acknowledge that it was more than a passing influence. And yet teachers were aware enough of it that they made jokes about cowboy hats. In fact, prior to my arrival in Eritrea, I had seen several e-mails calling for consultants who could adapt Eritrea's curriculum to the Texas standards. I never did find out what happened to Texas, but once the school year started, it turned out to be irrelevant.

Teachers were accustomed to new policies being introduced and then either sluggishly implemented or never fully implemented at all. Educational policies, it was often said, like laws in Eritrea more generally, were "written in pencil." They were reflective of someone's *idea* of what education should be but so disconnected from the material reality of overcrowded classrooms, teacher shortages, and lack of materials that they were impossible to implement. The jokes about cowboy hats, on one level, were a commentary on the lack of capacity to implement new policies and the misfits between these policies and the lack of resources in schools.

However, while certain components of the policies introduced in 2003 were weakly implemented, other components were anything but. These policies were far more comprehensive than any previous policy reforms—they applied to all subjects, all grade levels, and even the system of higher education as a whole. They were intended to radically change curriculum, course offerings, pedagogy, and promotion policies. They restructured secondary and tertiary education. Indeed, these policies did radically change the education system, but not in the ways denoted by policy documents. This chapter explores these 2003 policy reforms, the differences between policy reforms on paper and in practice, and how these radical policy changes revealed competing visions of the ideal Eritrean citizen. Teachers struggled to make sense of these new policies and reconcile them with long-held beliefs about the meaning of education and its potential to bring about a bright future for the nation. What was revealed in this process was the complex micropolitics of making meaning out of education. As technologies of the state shifted away from teachers' disciplinary focus on producing a small cohort of educated, elite individuals and toward the government's biopolitical emphasis on producing a nationwide mass of student-soldiers, inconsistencies emerged. Teachers and students continued to assert their own beliefs about what education meant and to argue that changing educational priorities would result in profound consequences for the nation.

A Bright Future?

The education reforms had many facets, but the most radical was to seamlessly integrate the education system with military training and National Service by requiring all grade 12 students to attend school at a boarding facility in Sawa, the location of the military training center, where they would complete the first part of military training prior to their final year of high school. Students would enlist in National Service prior to grade 12, by virtue of moving to Sawa and beginning military training. Prior to the implementation of the 2003 policies, students were required only to go to Sawa for military training and enter National Service after they either turned eighteen or completed the highest year of education for which they qualified, whichever came last. Previously, students entered into secondary school, were promoted each year of secondary school, and then qualified for university by passing rigorous exams. Under the new policies, students took a selective exam to enter into secondary schools, but after that all students were mass promoted through each year and went to Sawa for their final year of high school. From there, they were given exams to qualify for higher education; those who did not pass seamlessly entered the military, while those who did were assigned to National Service as teachers or civil servants when they completed their education.

It is well known that schools either directly or indirectly, officially or unofficially, by design or by default, prepare students for particular economic, political, and social roles once they complete their schooling (Bourdieu and Passeron 1990; Foucault 1995; Levinson and Holland 1996).[2] The 2003 reforms changed the ways in which educated Eritreans were prepared for these roles in two ways. First, the reforms made military service a prerequisite for completing secondary school and moving on to higher education. Second, military service effectively became a direct consequence for students' failure to qualify for tertiary education. This altered both the imagined and actual life course of educated people and had implications for how the nation, national duty, and state were imagined.

There are inherent tensions between the "bright future" of being an educated person and the bleak future of being a military subject, which we can better understand by examining how educated persons are culturally produced, particularly in the developing world, where education is available to very few and educated people tend to see themselves as a somewhat exceptional, valued, and valuable elite. Educational development and expansion are integral to developmentalist aspirations at both the personal and national levels. In much of the postcolonial world, schooling—particularly secondary and tertiary schooling—is a scarce resource, accessible to very few and oriented toward producing not just a national subject but a national elite who comes to think of him- or herself as an educated person destined to play a particular role in developing the nation (Levinson 2001; Stambach 2000).[3] In Eritrea, educated people were thought to not only possess particular skills but also be endowed with particular moral attributes that would enable them to lead society. The perceived superiority of educated people in terms of skills, morality, and responsibility is a key part of how the educated national subject is constituted in much of the developing world, and it is a traditionally prevalent view in Ethiopia and Eritrea.

Education produces a teleological imaginary of the nation—an imagined past but also an imagined, aspirant future and, most importantly, a sense of the role of educated people in bringing this future into being (Kaplan 2006; Stambach 2000). The hopes for progress and prosperity in the future of the nation are cultivated through education and the processes of producing educated subjects. Students are, in theory, endowed with particular skills and knowledge to provide the human capital to bring this imagined future into being, but they are also taught to think of themselves as doing this for the nation (Benei 2008; Kaplan 2006; Levinson 2001).

In contrast, the military is the instrument of sovereignty, defense, and violence. If one of the key roles of educational institutions is to produce national subjects who can imagine a brighter future for the nation and help bring that future into being, one of the key roles of military institutions is to produce a sense of the might and power of the nation and national subjects willing to kill or die to defend the nation. The military is responsible for protecting and defending the territorial state, the people within it, and the values that the nation is imagined to stand for. Soldiers, the national subjects produced through processes of militarized nationalism, are symbolic of the state, responsible for its defense, and victims of state violence (Bickford 2011; Macleish 2013). As symbols, they represent the state's protective, paternalistic capacity and its capacity for violence. They represent patriotism at the height of its passions—the willingness to kill, hurt, and die for the highest ideals of the nation. But the lived experience of *being* a soldier is often at odds with what the soldier symbolizes. Being a soldier is often marked by the trauma associated with suffering or perpetrating violence, harsh living conditions, a lack of control over one's daily existence, and the general invisibility of soldiers to society overall (Macleish 2013). Somewhat ironically, while soldiers as symbols are celebrated and venerated, soldiers as people are disposable (Macleish 2013)—bare life, in Giorgio Agamben's (1998) terms. They are allowed to die to defend the nation. But soldiers are also sovereign in Carl Schmitt's ([1922] 2005) and Agamben's (1998) sense that the sovereign is the one who "decides on the exception" or decides when to apply violence and to what extent.

The teleological orientation of education thus clashes with the sacrificial orientation of the soldier. In Eritrea, government employees, bureaucrats, and officials themselves seemed aware of the fact that while both were essential for nation-state making, experiences of being militarized and being educated were radically different. Citizens in Eritrea and elsewhere imagine education as bringing promise, while the military brings pain. Educated subjects think of themselves as having power to shape the nation, while militarized subjects must think of themselves as giving up power over their own survival in the name of the nation.

This student-soldier was a very different kind of national subject than the educated citizen imagined by teachers and students. These educated people thought that the attributes, character, and life trajectory of a student subject should be distinct from that of a soldier. This is not to say that teachers and students believed that educated people should be free of responsibilities to defend the country or fulfill their duty in National Service. Indeed, most teachers had either fought or trained to fight during the border war, and most would argue that it was their duty to defend the country in times of crisis. But in peacetime, the outlook of these educated people was that the student subject must be able to envision an imagined future distinct from that of the soldier.

As I discuss in more detail below, when I asked teachers what was wrong with the new educational policies, they repeatedly said that students no longer had a "bright future" and asserted that a "bright future" was necessary to motivate them to work hard and do well in school. Exploring the way teachers imagined this bright future, and perceived that it was endangered, helps explain how the relationship between the nation and the state was recalibrated at this particularly complex time for Eritrean schools. For Eritrean teachers, "bright future" referenced a particular way of imagining the future of the nation *and* of the individual students, and it depicted a particular relationship between national subjects and the nation. Teachers believed that for the future of the nation to be bright, the future of the students had to be bright, and vice versa. In this particular moment, the future for educated people seemed bleak rather than bright.

The Rapid Transformation of Eritrean Education

The official rationale for new policies in Eritrea was to increase the overall level of education, with level defined as the number of students who had *completed* high school. Other elements of the reforms emphasized more pragmatic education with an emphasis on skill building. But ultimately, in its moment of transition, the new package of policies implemented in 2003 created an entirely new pathway through which students were channeled into the military while they were still students, replacing the imagined "bright future" of being educated with the bleakness of a military future. The main aims of the reforms are summarized in the draft document outlining the "Rapid Transformation of the Eritrean Education System" (Ministry of Education 2002a):

> Now the time is ripe for the Eritrean government to make all the necessary changes and reforms it needs to make so that the Eritrean educational system would measure up to the needs of the country to produce manpower necessary to propel it forward as a viable and vivacious nation of the twenty-first century. The reforms that should be introduced must achieve the following:
>
> a) All wastage of manpower, resources, effort and time in the educational system must be abolished in as much as it is humanly possible.
> b) All doors and opportunities must be open to Eritreans of all ages to develop to their full potential both professionally and personally.
> c) Education must be employment oriented such that at the end of any level of education any person can find gainful employment commensurate with the person's level of education or training.
> d) The standards and quality of education and training in the educational system must be high enough such that products of the educational system would have a high degree of acceptability in the international arena of education and employment.

To meet these goals and make the Eritrean education system simultaneously efficient, pragmatic, internationally competitive, and high quality, a plan detailed the following changes. The overall emphasis of these changes was twofold—to make education more oriented toward job skills and to expand access to education. Education would become job oriented through the addition of certain subjects, such as IT and home economics, and by emphasizing learner-centered pedagogies. Over the course of the coming fifteen years, Eritrea planned to build more schools at all levels, develop regional vocational colleges, and implement new curricula in all grades and subjects (Ministry of Education 2002b). Additionally, at the tertiary level, there were plans to build six new colleges. Finally, the new policy changes also radically changed the structure of secondary education and promotion policies. Grade 12 was added as the final year of Senior Secondary School, but, as I have noted before, it was offered only at a boarding facility in Sawa. Elementary schools continued to teach grades 1–5, and Junior Secondary Schools continued to teach grades 6–8. All Senior Secondary Schools around the country offered grades 9–11. And all students went to Sawa for grade 12.

Before and after the reforms, education was, in theory, open to everyone up to grade 8, although Junior Secondary Schools were not available in all areas and some students chose to withdraw from school before grade 8, usually for financial or family reasons. In grade 8, students would take an exam to determine whether they qualified for Senior Secondary School. Promotion levels between grades in Junior Secondary School and between Junior and Senior Secondary Schools remained largely unchanged. Admission to Senior Secondary Schools had always been extremely competitive, but there was also intense competition between grades. Many students flunked out between grades, and many others did not make it to university. In 2000, only 9 percent of Eritrea's Senior Secondary School–aged youth attended school at that level, only 55 percent of students who entered Senior Secondary School had the opportunity to sit for the matriculation exam, and only 10 to 15 percent of those had the chance to go on to some form of higher education (Ministry of Education 2002a).

New promotion policies sought to ensure that once students passed the grade 8 exam and entered into Senior Secondary School, they would complete grade 12. They would begin military training in the summer before grade 12, complete grade 12 in Sawa, and take the matriculation exam. If they passed the matriculation exam, they would gain admittance into one of the new colleges and then complete National Service after their schooling in a professional capacity. If they did not score well on the matriculation exam, they would go into National Service immediately and would likely serve in the military.

Despite the fact that the military component of the new policies was the most strongly implemented, it is largely unarticulated in policy documents, where the merging of military training gets only a brief mention. The Ministry of Education policy document that outlines the change in educational policies mentions the integration of summer service and National Service with secondary education only briefly toward the end (Ministry of Education 2002b):

> According to the new recommended education system, the students start to branch out into different fields of study starting from Senior Secondary School. This allows for students to take military training as electives. So, most or all of the six months' training of

the National Service that Eritreans have to undertake can be incorporated into the Senior Secondary School education program. For example, students can take military training as elective courses during the school year when they are in the eleventh and twelfth grades. This combined with field training during two summers at the end of their eleventh and twelfth grade school years should enable them to complete all the military training they are supposed to get in the National Service. Actually, the training they acquire this way should be much better because they would have more time for theoretical military training in the classroom and they have a longer time in general to seep in their training both physically and mentally. Some Senior Secondary Schools in the USA actually have such programs.

Interestingly, while this clearly states the ideal of merging military training with secondary education, such as exists elsewhere, it suggests that this is an elective, an option, painting quite a different picture of how the military would be embedded in secondary education. In contrast, military training was a required component of education and was experienced as being forced on students.

There is a striking difference between the policy priorities stated in documents and the way these policies were actually implemented. As with previous policy changes, many remained changes on paper only, or changes weakly implemented. Meanwhile, other components of the policy were not just implemented but expanded.

New courses and the promotion of learner-centered pedagogies were never fully put into practice. The Ministry of Education introduced new curriculum in select grades, and a selection of teachers from all grades were trained in learner-centered pedagogies; however, the new textbooks were not available in any of the subjects in the Junior and Senior Secondary Schools by the time I completed fieldwork in 2005. Teachers generally disliked and distrusted the oversimplified content of the new curriculum. Furthermore, they balked at what was communicated to them as a prohibition on lecturing. "They told us we are forbidden to lecture," one teacher complained to me. Initially teachers blamed the adoption of a "foreign" curriculum for the policies' ineffectiveness and commented that what worked in Texas would not necessarily work in Eritrea. Teachers were also concerned because it seemed that, in the absence of textbooks, there actually was no curriculum; instead, there was a set of vague guidelines that they were told were loosely based on the Texas standards. A train-the-trainer model was implemented whereby a few teachers were trained in the capital and then would give similar training to the rest of the teachers in their schools; however, these training sessions tended to be poorly attended. While teachers were given a stipend to attend the train-the-trainer training in Asmara, the local training sessions carried no such stipend. The fact that teachers were paid very little if at all meant that there was much bitterness and jealousy about who got to attend training in Asmara. In fact, teachers spoke of training as a chance to earn much-needed extra income rather than as a chance to gain professional skills. This meant that training sessions in Asmara were much coveted, while training sessions in local sites stirred up resentment. Additionally, teaching materials required for learner-centered pedagogy, such as lab equipment, manipulables, and even library books, were often nonexistent or in short supply, making many new subjects and new activities impossible to implement. Despite these limitations, many teachers experimented with learner-centered pedagogies. I witnessed some very creative attempts to do lab experiments and science demonstrations with large classes and few materials. I also observed history, geography, and English teachers engaging students in debates and discussion activities with some interesting results. But overall, there was no mechanism to enforce the implementation of these "new" methods, and teachers tended to teach in ways that were familiar, comfortable, and effective given the constraints of class size and resource scarcity.

The teaching of new subjects did not fare any better than the attempt to change pedagogy. The situation in the Senior Secondary School in Assab was typical for many such schools. Memos would come through mandating that schools offer new subjects, such as IT and home economics. The director would diligently change the weekly schedule to incorporate the new subjects, but then no teachers arrived to teach those subjects. Existing teachers were then assigned to teach the subjects, but they lacked materials and training to do so. The teacher assigned to teach IT barely knew how to use a computer himself and had only one computer to wheel to class with him. One teacher, whom the students commonly regarded as a buffoon, taught the home economics class infrequently and irregularly. After an unqualified teacher had been attempting to teach a new subject for a few weeks, inevitably another memo would arrive cancelling the subject. One semester, the director had to change the roster four times as he dutifully tried to comply with mandates for which he had no resources. Eventually the Ministry of Education agreed that schools did not have the resources and retroactively advised them to cancel the new subjects. By the end of each school year, only the traditional subjects were taught. As a result, students never took new subjects seriously. These classes were poorly attended, and students who did attend were even more poorly behaved.

In contrast, several elements of the new policy were stringently implemented. First, the government opened the Warsai Yikaalo School in Sawa immediately. The first class of high school–aged students in that school completed grade 11 in spring 2004. Almost immediately after the 2003–2004 school year ended, the government arranged for buses to take students to Sawa to begin military training, and, despite a somewhat-delayed start to the school year, they began grade 12 the following fall.

Second, the tertiary education system was also overhauled, although popular perception of these changes differed significantly from the rationale for the redesign of the system. There was a common belief that the government was trying to destroy the University of Asmara. Many believed that this was out of anger toward the students who had protested in 2002. Beginning in 2003 and going until each class had graduated, the university did not enroll new first-year students. At the same time, in 2002, a new college in Mai Nefhi was opened, and in the years that followed, other colleges were opened around the country. Once all students had graduated from the University of Asmara, it was temporarily closed and then reopened to house one of these new colleges, but this college was one of a network of colleges and did not have the same symbolic significance as the national university had. Although the university was not immediately or officially closed, the failure to admit new students to the university was generally believed to be the beginning of the end of the university and all that it represented. At the time, there was little faith that these new colleges could equal the University of Asmara in quality or stature. Many Eritreans believed that this new higher-education structure was a government effort to destroy the national university. Subsequently, teachers and students believed that the role of Senior Secondary Schools was fundamentally altered. Senior Secondary Schools would no longer funnel students into the university, once the pinnacle of the education system, but instead into Sawa. As of 2015, seven colleges exist around the country, and students who pass the matriculation exam currently move from the Warsai Yikaalo School in Sawa into these various colleges, thereby integrating the military/National Service system with the education system (NOKUT 2013). Students moving into tertiary education have to do so via Sawa and military training. They then move from tertiary education into National Service.

Finally, the policy of "avoiding wastage" by changing promotion policies was implemented very seriously, although with complex results. The policies implemented in 2003 mandated that all Senior Secondary School students should be promoted from grade to grade, and all should be given the chance to sit for the matriculation exam. By the end of the 2003–2004 school year,

Senior Secondary School teachers understood that students should not fail. Almost all grade 11 students passed to grade 12; this was accomplished by simplifying the curriculum but also by changing the role of the teacher. Teachers who previously created competitive conditions designed to weed out large numbers of students were now responsible for enabling students to pass.

Subtle and not-so-subtle messages made it clear to teachers that they were to ensure that their students were promoted. The new policies mandated limited student failures; however, initially teachers and school administrators were confused as to how to pass students. Prior to 2003, students who "failed" for the year would repeat the grade the following year. Students who failed a second time had to withdraw from school.[4] Following the policy changes, teachers and students were initially told that students who failed would be required to take a summer make-up class (for which they would pay) and to pass a "re-sit" exam before being promoted to the next grade. However, during the two years of my fieldwork, the school did not offer a make-up class, few students took the re-sit exam, and all of those who did, passed to the next grade.

Despite the initial confusion, it quickly became clear that the government was serious about enforcing the policy intended to promote students. To ensure that students would not fail, in spring 2004 the Ministry of Education dropped the grade necessary to pass from 60 percent to 50 percent, and again in spring 2005 from 50 percent to 40 percent, meaning that almost all students passed. Because mass promotion coincided with sending grade 11 students to Sawa, teachers, parents, and students interpreted dropping the promotion grade as a government technique to enlist as many students as possible in National Service.

Meanwhile, in grade 8, many students actually feared passing, because failure in the Junior Secondary School was a means to avoid being sent to Sawa. As I noted above, education was open to everyone through the Junior Secondary School level (grade 8). At the end of grade 8, students took a national examination to determine whether they would be promoted to Senior Secondary School. However, there was no uniformly implemented policy that determined how many times grades could be repeated in the Junior Secondary School. In the absence of a clear policy regarding promotion at this level of education, increasingly large numbers of students, particularly students who knew they would not be promoted to Senior Secondary School, were failing and repeating grades year after year as a means to avoid entering into National Service. These students, according to teachers, were not interested in learning or being students but merely using schooling as a means to evade service.

Taken together, these three policy changes—the change in promotion policies, the changes to tertiary education, and the addition of grade 12 in Sawa—altered the way schools prepared students for the future and transformed the future for which students were being prepared. It was difficult for teachers to understand why the government would undermine what they saw as a functioning education system by simplifying the curriculum and promoting most students. The fact that everyone was sent to Sawa for military training made teachers even more skeptical of the government's "real" motivations in changing promotion policies. Although some teachers understood and supported the logic of helping weaker students and avoiding wastage by making sure all students learned, most believed that this clashed with their educational values of rigor and competition and undermined their primary role of cultivating elite students for participation in university. The University of Asmara was effectively being closed and students were simultaneously being mass promoted via the grade 12 boarding school in Sawa into the military, which meant that teachers became even more skeptical of the government's motivations. They questioned whether the government really cared about education. The fact that certain components of the reforms were weakly implemented (new textbooks for the new curriculum, an adequate number of teachers, substantial teacher training, and materials for the new subjects were not provided) while those most closely affiliated with militarization were strongly implemented further fueled mistrust in the government's motivations. As I illustrate below, it was generally perceived that what motivated the government to "avoid wastage" and institute policies of mass promotion was its desire to enlist all educated people more efficiently in National Service. Schooling had been reduced to a conduit for producing soldiers.

Students or Soldiers?

Eritrean teachers and students were quick to assume that the government's implementation of new educational policies was merely about producing soldiers. The Eritrean People's Liberation Front/People's Front for Democracy and Justice (EPLF/PFDJ) has a long history of subsuming education into the military. During the struggle for liberation, education as a strategy of nation building went hand in hand with fighting to defend the nation (Gottesman 1998). The EPLF always prioritized education, and as soon as resources were available it ensured that recruits in the liberation forces were literate (Gottesman 1998; Müller 2005, 2007; Pool 2001). Additionally, it implemented literacy campaigns in liberated areas and set up schools (Gottesman 1998). In

Chapters 1 and 2, I showed how pivotal military identities were to a sense of being Eritrean, but these military identities meant something quite different for Eritrea's leaders, most of whom were fighters in the struggle for liberation, and for ordinary Eritreans, especially educated Eritreans.

The revolutionary front's ideal of merging "fighting and learning," to borrow Les Gottesman's (1998) term, never quite took hold in the post-independence years. During this time, many Eritreans revered and celebrated the figure of the fighter as liberator of the country, but these same Eritreans were not necessarily keen to become that revered figure. As I discussed in the last chapter, once the government started forcing everyone into indefinite terms of National Service, the meaning of being a fighter changed. Fighters no longer represented the national value of sacrifice but were instead seen as punished figures. While Eritreans might have venerated fighters in the postliberation years, they now experienced being a soldier as a punishment. At the same time, the inevitability of almost everyone becoming a fighter/soldier threatened educated people, because this was the antithesis to a "bright future" for both the individual and for the nation. Being a fighter indicated a future of endless sacrifice as one waited, ever ready to defend a country that might be plunged into conflict at any moment.

For teachers, who had always tried to help students imagine a bright future for themselves and the nation, the policies signaled an attack on what they thought of as their nation-building work—to produce a motivated, educated person who would build the nation through example, by having a nice life, and by contributing to society by virtue of being educated. Educated people believed that the government regarded them as a threat. The president in particular developed a reputation for being "anti-education." On several occasions, I heard teachers complain that the president never attended a graduation ceremony at the University of Asmara, yet he never failed to attend the graduation of each group of recruits at Sawa. Another subtle but reoccurring critique that I often heard throughout my fieldwork was that the country was being run not by educated people but by fighters who had gotten their education in the field. Teachers often questioned the legitimacy of educational administrators who had received their education in one of the many schools set up for fighters during The Struggle. This challenge to the legitimacy of fighters, whom teachers regarded as uneducated, set up a contrast between two forms of education—that of soldiers and that of formally educated people.

As I noted earlier, the dominant, official version of Eritrean nationalism asserted that being Eritrean was defined through the values inherited from the struggle for liberation, values that were to be embodied by the lived experiences of all Eritreans, particularly through National Service. Those who fought in The Struggle, and particularly those who were in leadership positions, would argue that Eritrea's indigenous education originated in The Struggle. The director general of General Education emphasized the importance of teaching these values to produce students willing to defend the country:

> This [new policy] is modern. At the same time, it has some elements of the *indigenous situation*. In general, we are transforming the education system in terms of content, and at the same time this transformation takes place in the attitude of the child. . . . Let me give you an example [of] modernity: We have to introduce information technology. This is one of the aspects of the modern. *At the same time, we also have our own values that we should give to the society. These values are inherited from the armed struggle.* We want to build on that so this will be one of the subjects incorporated into civics education. (Interview, Director General of General Education; emphasis added)

Teaching the values of The Struggle was seen as an essential component of producing an Eritrean student who was willing to defend his or her country and make sacrifices for it. In the following quotation from the director of Quality Management, an Eritrean's love for his or her country is characterized primarily through a willingness to defend and sacrifice for the country:

> We want to make students who love their country, who love work, who love their people, and who are willing to defend their country. . . . And the whole idea behind civics education is about doing this. We provide civics education, we provide [the] history of Eritrea, we provide [the] geography of Eritrea, we teach about the liberation struggle, and we bombard the child from all sides, and the whole idea is to produce a student who loves their country, who is ready to defend their country, who is willing to sacrifice. (Interview, Director of Quality Management Division, Ministry of Education)

The merging of love of country, love of work, willingness to defend the country, and values of The Struggle, as articulated by the director of the Quality Management Division in the Ministry of Education—himself a former fighter—mirrored the rationale for National Service itself. As Gaim Kibreab (2009b) notes in his discussion of National Service, the institution was set up not only to defend the country but also to instill in youth a "love of work" and the values of National Service. In fact, Kibreab (2009b) quotes President Isaias Afewerki in the *Eritrean Profile* in 1994, when National Service was instituted, as using the phrase "love of work." Furthermore, as Kibreab notes, the proclamation that set up National Service outlines its key goals, including (1) establish a defense force; (2) pass on the "courage, resoluteness and heroic episodes of the last thirty years"; (3) "create a new generation characterized by love of work"; and (4) promote economic development and national unity (GoE 1995). The ideal Eritrean citizen, as defined by officials in the Ministry of Education, directly mirrored this language in the National Service charter and also resonated with other official accounts of what it means to be Eritrean.

In contrast, for teachers, the ideal citizen revolved around notions of morality, knowledge, and respect. Teachers' discussions of their role in making students into citizens focused less on helping students develop a willingness to sacrifice for and defend their country and more on having "a great responsibility to make citizens, to make them knowledgeable and respectful of society" (Interview, Yakob). Being a good citizen was equated with morality. As another teacher reflected, "The teacher should try to mold the students as a good citizen of the nation. How do they become a good citizen to the nation? We have to introduce some moral values into the minds of the students" (Interview, Estifanos). Teachers saw themselves as shaping students to make the nation a better place:

> When I started teaching, I got very much interested. I found that it's a very noble profession, and a desire in me started—I should produce better children for our nation. . . . You see, to build a nation, it's in the hands of the teacher, so we can produce such children for the nation. Those [children] themselves *are* the nation. I think the teacher is the luckiest person, whose work is to shape a child. We know what is good and what is bad. We just concentrate on the good things, not only teaching what is there in the lesson. The teacher has in his hand the development of the child. He is like a potter. If he shapes it in his hands, he makes its shape. He decides if he wants it to be narrow or round. The teacher is very lucky to have this chance. If I teach two plus two is five, he learns five. If I say it is four, he believes four. It is in the hands of the teacher. (Interview, Arvind)

These were common sentiments among all teachers: The student was a moral blank slate, an unformed lump of clay who needed to be taught to distinguish right from wrong. Rather than being prepared to sacrifice for the nation, children "[were] the nation." Thus, for the nation to be good, the child had to be made good. The notion that the students were the nation reflected the ideal, common among educated people, that the future of the nation was reflected in the future of its educated people. This posed a direct contrast with notions of soldier-citizenship, in which the future was sacrificed for the nation. As another teacher noted:

> When the teacher gives advice [to students], their behavior becomes good. If they give respect for school or learning, then they help the society. This is a young generation. When they have a family, they will become good parents for their students. The teacher tells them about their future. Otherwise, if the teacher doesn't care about behavior, they become bad students. (Interview, Isaac)

The belief that there was a continuum between school and the society was apparent. If students developed well in school and learned right from wrong, they would be good parents and good members of society. Respect for school helped society. Learning to be a good student made them a good parent. Focusing on the future would make them good citizens. Teachers' beliefs about the moral worth of schooling itself was evident in this and other quotations, as was the moral worth of the educated person to society as a whole.

Additionally, teachers' vision of the ideal educated citizen was someone who was characterized by the motivation to do well in school and had the discipline to accomplish this goal. Ideas of respect for authority and society were embedded in this vision of the disciplined student. Respect was specifically exemplified by the idea that students should follow the rules, adhere to schedules, be neat, and observe particular spatial boundaries. Ideally, teachers in Eritrean schools expected students to follow schedules, arrive in school at the appointed time, sit in class in an orderly way, remain in the classroom throughout school hours, and generally comport themselves "as students should." As one teacher told me, ideal students "follow the rules and regulations of the school. They should attend the flag ceremony and the class properly. They should go out only at the time of break time. They know all these things" (Interview, Vijay).

Teacher Iyob fleshed out this notion of the morality of the educated person and rooted it in Eritrean traditions. He spoke specifically about what motivated people toward education and the importance of rewards:

The value of education in Eritrea goes back to the old generation. They [our parents] have that idea. The person who has studied and learned has a better life and also more money. That [idea] comes from the old generation and also from how the educated people are acting in the society. Even when I was a child, I didn't like to go to school, and I remember how my mother was encouraging me by giving me some sweets or some chewing gum to encourage me to go to school. . . . They [our parents] used to also say as a proverb, "Those who didn't learn cannot save you from anything." This is an old proverb. . . . They can see the society and how educated people are leading the country and working in different departments. And they think, hopefully, their sons and daughters will accomplish that. Even to be a priest, a religious leader, they have to read, they have to write. So on the basis of this, they have this interest [in education]. (Interview, Iyob)

I would like to highlight two points about the value of education and the role of the educated person that emerge from Iyob's words. First, he outlined the role that educated people should play in leading the country and society and bringing about change. The belief that only educated people could help society was commonly held among students and teachers; in fact, some version of this was repeated in almost every interview I did and in many of my informal conversations with students and teachers. Iyob's reference to the proverb stating that "those who didn't learn cannot save you from anything" reflected the sentiment that educated people were special.

Second, Iyob linked being educated with personal improvement—higher levels of education should bring with them "more money" and thus a "better life." As I noted earlier, educated people were supposed to have a bright future. But it is also interesting to note that Iyob suggested that his mother had to bribe him with sweets to do well in school. The emphasis here was on using something sweet to create positive associations with education. Sweets were given to students because the rewards of education were to be sweet, he suggested. The way Iyob's mother talked about sweets was similar to the way teachers talked about giving students a bright future. Children were to be motivated by sweets, while high school students were to be motivated by the promise of a bright future. The message here was that education is hard, so there should be rewards for those who engage in this hard work.

Many teachers depicted having a bright future as essential to motivating students to do well in school and thereby become the ideal educated citizen.

The University of Asmara played a key role in framing how students imagined their future. As the only university in Eritrea, it was what secondary students ideally strove for and the goal for which all teachers prepared their top students. It was the pinnacle of the competitive education system. The university also functioned symbolically to determine the aspirations and define the imagined future of educated persons.

Such universities as Addis Ababa University in Ethiopia and the University of Asmara are inherently elite, competitive institutions. Addis Ababa University in Ethiopia was at the top of the education system and the most prestigious university in Ethiopia. Prior to independence, the University of Asmara functioned as a satellite site of Addis Ababa University. The vast majority of all university-educated people, including the Eritrean secondary school teachers of the older generation in my study, were educated at Addis Ababa University. One gained admittance to the university through successfully competing one's way through eleven or twelve years of education. A quotation from Emperor Haile Selassie's ([1961] 1965: 306) speech at the inauguration of Addis Ababa University in 1961 acknowledges the elite nature of the university: "The educational process cannot be a narrow column; it must be in the shape of a pyramid and broadly based." While universities were for the elite at the top of the pyramid, they in theory relied on competition among those who wished to become the educated elite—a broad base for the top of the pyramid to rest on. In African countries, where the demand for university education far exceeded the capacity, this competition was especially exacerbated. Since Eritrea had been part of Ethiopia in the memory of most teachers at this time period, Addis Ababa University was seen as the pinnacle of educational accomplishments, highly competitive but worthy in part because of this competition.

In the early days of independence in many African nations, universities were charged with not only developing nations by creating skilled manpower but also cultivating the social, cultural, and spiritual development of the nation. With words that resonated with many teachers' beliefs about educated people, Emperor Haile Selassie ([1961] 1965: 305) spoke to the highly nationalistic and profoundly symbolic role that the university played and the value of university educated people: "A university taken in all its aspects is essentially a spiritual enterprise which, along with the knowledge it imparts, leads students into wiser living and a greater sensitivity to life's true values and rewards." These words in many ways resonate with the comments made by teachers in the emphasis placed on moral "wise living," knowledge, and rewards. The quality and existence of institutions of higher education, the competitive nature of the university, the wisdom and morality of educated people, the rewards they would reap, and the future of the nation were tightly linked. The university thus symbolically embodied the potential of the nation to have a bright future and represented the pathway through which educated people would develop the nation.

Teachers' vision of producing educated citizens hinged on challenging students, making them work hard, and encouraging competition. Teachers believed that the move to mass promotion indicated to students that they did not have to challenge themselves educationally and that if students were assured of passing, they would not see the value in working hard and striving for educational success. In the following quotation, Teacher Kessete explains how facing challenges in one's education was essential for learning to face life and to develop the country:

> Life itself is difficult. We are teaching students to cope with life. . . . We need to give them challenges. If we forget the difficult things in life, how are we thinking that students are going to develop the culture? If we make things simple, how are they going to solve their problems? For everything, we have to fight. Even for grades. There is now a very big difference between [the new policies] and the real life. (Interview, Kessete)

For teachers, it followed that this shift to mass promotion undermined the rigor of the education system and, by extension, the quality of the educated manpower that was needed to lead and develop the nation.

A very particular notion of self is apparent in these ideas about what it meant to be an educated person—the educated subject is seen as having a special role in the future of the nation. For this reason, the educated subject needed to be a cultivated self, cared for and nourished not only with good moral lessons and knowledge but also with the material rewards promised by the sweetness of a "bright future." In contrast, the military subject, as I showed above, was supposed to be willing to sacrifice his or her time, aspirations, freedom, and, if need be, life for the nation. The educated citizen was prepared for rewards. The military citizen was prepared for sacrifice.

Teachers saw that requiring students to go to Sawa was incompatible with cultivating the educated subject. It was the opposite of giving them a bright future. Teacher Fitwi linked the idea of making things easy on students through the policy of "avoiding wastage" with the government's intention of forcibly recruiting more students into Sawa for military training:

This new policy says that there should be no wastage, so this makes the students not work hard. They are thinking that the government is going to take them to Sawa and, because the government wants to send them to Sawa, there is no chance for them to repeat grades. (Interview, Fitwi)

Fitwi suggested that students saw no point in working hard if they would be sent to Sawa regardless of how hard they worked. Repeating grades indicated having a second chance to work for university admission. Without the chance to repeat grades, students could not move on with their education. Instead, with the policy of avoiding wastage, becoming a soldier became the inevitable outcome of being a student, regardless of how individual students performed in school. Teacher Fitwi continued:

The thing I always think is that the curriculum should make the students have a bright future. It should make them have a bright future. It should encourage them. How do you encourage them? This National Service, going to Sawa, in my opinion, should be voluntary. We should not push all people to go there. Those who have done service should have government advantage and privileges. By having those privileges, you can push other students to go there. Now students are discouraged to go there. So it should be voluntary. Then the students would have bright futures. So the students would try to compete in the classroom for opportunities. (Interview, Fitwi)

Fitwi argued that if Sawa were voluntary and based on rewarding the students who went, students would be more motivated. Students could not see a "bright future" if their education was leading them into the punishing conditions of Sawa rather than the reward of attending university.

Teacher Vijay also reflected the sentiment that Sawa should be voluntary and that its being mandatory was damaging the good students:

Now at this time, when they complete 11th grade, they are all going to Sawa. I don't know, going to Sawa, they are afraid of it. When they go to Sawa, they are going to do some work. They are going to delay what they do in grade 11. Earlier it was not like that; when they completed their matriculation exam, some would go to Sawa and some to university, but now all the students will go to Sawa. Of course, the students were needed to do some work, but they should not be forced to do it like this. Even in India, the students are doing some National Service. Those who are interested to join will join. But here, it is not like that. They are forcing the students to these things. All the students are forced to go to Sawa. Before there were some brilliant students who were curious and asking many questions, and now they don't care; they will say, "We are going to Sawa." (Interview, Vijay)

Other teachers noted that a large part of the problem was that National Service had become permanent. Embedded in these complaints about the length of time that the military took was a complaint about the nature of suffering in military training as well. One teacher explained to me why Sawa was incompatible with having a bright vision:

Tomas: Students aren't motivated. In order to motivate them, they must have a vision. A bright vision, but they don't see it. Without that vision, they are not ready to learn, so that's why they don't go to school on time, they don't follow rules, they don't care if you send them out or not. So they don't care; they don't expect a bright future. I'm afraid of it.
Jennifer: The future?
T: Yeah. The near future.
J: What makes you afraid?
T: Students do not have vision. Unless they learn and have the positive vision, who are we? They are not ready for education.
J: There is a whole generation who is lacking vision.
T: I'm sure of this.
J: What could be done to improve or correct the situation?
T: The policy of the government should be changed.
J: Which parts?
T: The military training. The way they are handling it.
J: The length of time or the training itself?
T: Well, no length of time is good. You go there. You suffer. You serve five or seven years. The youngsters see it that way. So I think this is the case. It's the way they are handling the military training and the length of time they serve. I have my daughter there. She was nineteen, and now she is twenty-six, and she is still serving. So this is the problem, of course. (Interview, Tomas)

Again, here we see commentary on the belief that suffering inhibited the bright future of both students and the nation. Military training, indefinitely imposed on students, prevented the nation and individuals from having a bright future.

None of this is to say that teachers did not think it was their (and their students') duty to defend their nation, but rather that being a soldier was antithetical to being educated for the nation; thus, when the government forced students to become soldiers, their passion for National Service was dampened. Teacher Kessete complained to me that even his very clever students lacked motivation because "they just think they will be soldiers." This was a common refrain among teachers. In a conversation that appeared in my field notes, he contrasted the enthusiasm that young people had for going to Sawa when National Service was instituted in 1995 with the current situation. Whereas once they were excited to go to Sawa, he noted, "They think it [Sawa] is the worst place." But then he added at the end of his comments, as if to put all of this into context and remind me that Eritreans are patriotic, "We still love our country and would defend it." Teacher Kessete's and other teachers' comments revealed that teachers and students were critical of the state that forced them to serve but not of the nation itself, which they were still willing to defend.

Teachers also suggested that National Service had undermined their ability to motivate students' and society's respect for education. This was manifested by parents' lack of concern for their children's education:

> National Service has spoiled the teaching and learning process. Everyone here under forty is in National Service and cannot support himself and cannot have anything. So he has some [work] other than teaching. The way society thinks about teachers—they don't give respect for teaching. They send their kids to school but do not follow up because they think about other things. They send their students, but when they come home, no one follows up. There should be [a] connection between parents and teachers. So when students come home, parents will follow up [on] their behavior. At this time, there is not much relationship between parents and teachers. So we don't know what the society thinks about us. There should be a close relationship. If the society knew about the teaching and learning process, they would respect [it] and be responsible. National Service spoiled not only teaching but everything for everyone. Everyone in this country is trying to think of something else. We give respect for our country and are trying to protect our country from outside attackers, and we always try to develop our country socially, eco-

nomically, politically, but to do all these things, you should have something comfortable. (Interview, Isaac)

This quotation outlined the belief that National Service took away the hope of "something comfortable" for the future, which not only had eroded the teaching and learning process but also had led parents, society, and students to devalue education and teachers. The words "National Service spoiled . . . everything for everyone" are a powerful statement about the relationship between stalled progress, dashed hopes for the future, changed parental expectations, and radically altered educational processes, even though Eritreans still had a strong desire to defend and develop the country.

One argument teachers and students often made was that students should first be given the chance to finish school before joining National Service. As one teacher described, "Grade 12 is very military, and children at this age should be with their family. They are told when to study, when to work, when to eat, when to play. They have some military exercises. They don't like it" (Field notes, October 2004). Another teacher who was assigned to take the students to Sawa in summer 2004 recounted their fear upon getting off the bus. He told me that when the students arrived, military personnel immediately drilled them, something the students had never experienced and were terrified of. This teacher shook his head sadly and reflected the same sentiment stated above—that they were too young to go off to Sawa alone: "They should be with their family. They should be students" (Field notes, July 2004).

Anxieties about students being sent across the country to Sawa where they would be removed from families and communities and at the mercy of military commanders directly referenced an imaginary of the punishing state. "Family" was thought of as safety and security for students. In Eritrean culture, as elsewhere, family is supposed to protect young people and keep them free from harm and, even more importantly, from corrupting, immoral influences, an idea that I expand on in the next chapters. Comments that "students should be with their family" suggested that if they were removed from their families, students would be vulnerable because no one would be there to morally guide them and to protect them from potential abuses. Rumors of military trainees being abused by superior officers—and, in particular, women in service being sexually abused—heightened this sense that students were vulnerable. Adults' uncertainty about whether the government (and individual government actors) would behave in benevolent or abusive ways was key here. The fact that they had little faith that state actors in Sawa would take care of the students who were in their care reflected an imaginary of a state turned against its people rather than of a caretaking state that had legitimate rights to require service.

While educated people in Eritrea increasingly saw "student" and "soldier" as two radically opposed ways of being Eritrean, the imaginary of the state as punishing further amplified the disjuncture between the two national imaginaries. Embedded in the distinction between student and soldier was a very different notion of the national subject. In short, the military subject needed to be willing to subsume all parts of him- or herself to the nation, sacrificing any ability to choose or work toward his or her future. In contrast, the educated person was supposed to cultivate him- or herself with learning, good habits, and the promise of future rewards. The educated subject was produced through discipline—specifically, the competitive conditions of the national exam, the hard work needed to do well on the exam, and the rewards given if he or she succeeded. The educated subject was an elite who not only expressed love for the nation by striving, studying, and working hard for it but also embodied the hopes for the future of the nation and its capacity to move in new, "bright" directions. The military subject, in contrast, needed to be willing to obliterate him- or herself for the nation. A military subject's love for the nation was expressed through his or her willingness to sacrifice and die for it. Merging being a student with being a soldier, symbolically and literally, contradicted the role that the educated elite was envisioned as playing in developing the nation. This new and uniform military future in National Service directly contradicted the "vision" of a "bright future" that teachers believed students should have to perform well as students.

From Discipline to Biopolitics

Above, I suggested that when the promotion policies changed, there was a great deal of uncertainty as to whether schools were preparing students for a future as educated citizens or a future as soldier citizens. Previously, examinations were the sorting mechanism and also the orienting principle around which schooling was organized. Examinations determined which level of education each individual student would achieve. If a student failed a grade in Senior Secondary School twice or did not get a high-enough score on the matriculation exam, he or she would go into National Service; when finished, he or she would be eligible for a job, probably in one of the ministries. In Eritrea, secondary schooling was so competitive and there were so few secondary school students in the country that each grade completed in secondary schools added a level of stature and qualified students for better jobs and higher salaries. Although students feared examinations, which were very difficult to pass, teachers and students believed them to be fair. Teachers and students thought that the stringency of the examination put all students in the same field, emphasizing the commonality of the student experience even if that commonality ultimately landed students in different places.

As I outlined above, teachers believed that this rigorous and competitive system motivated students, but they also thought that students were motivated by their future ability to get a good job by virtue of having completed some secondary education:

> Earlier, before the war started, when a student completed secondary school, he thought he could become a worker in any office, and he knew his elder brother and sister would have the chance to be employed in the port or the refinery or the offices. So they knew they would have good futures, and they were encouraged to study in the school. And they were very much interested in studying and learning in the school. (Interview, Iyob)

Here Iyob, like many other teachers, linked students' motivation to do well in school with their understanding that working hard would lead to educational accomplishment, a job, and a "good future" even for those who did not matriculate to university.

All of this changed with the implementation of the new promotion policies, which effectively changed schools from institutions oriented toward rigorously preparing *individual* students for a tremendously selective and challenging matriculation exam to institutions oriented toward preparing *all* students in the nation for promotion. This transformation entailed a shift from disciplining individual students to managing the entire student body.

Michel Foucault's (1997, 2004) discussion of the transition from discipline to biopolitics as a technology of state power is particularly helpful to illuminate these shifts. Discipline focuses on the regulation of space, time, and the body to simultaneously train individual bodies to behave in appropriate ways and to normalize the rationale for doing so, such that disciplinary training comes to seem natural and inevitable. Biopolitics shares with discipline the capacity to produce norms but, in contrast, is concerned with the attributes of the population rather than the individual. Indeed, biopolitics is concerned with the population only as understood through a series of measures, statistics, and indicators and not at all with the individuals who make up that population. In Eritrea, the new educational policy was concerned with the entire student *population* completing high school rather than the quality of rigorously trained *individuals* who would pass into university. In this transition, teachers were told that they had to be concerned with promotion rates among the student population *as a whole* rather than with building the capacity of *individuals* who were capable of passing the matriculation exam.

Schools are extraordinarily adept as disciplinary institutions. They consist of rules and procedures that regulate time, space, activities, and behaviors. Systems of punishment keep these regulations in place. Schools are "observatories" in which surveillance and strict regulation of time, space, and the body instill in students "correct" attitudes and dispositions (Foucault 1995). In the process, schools not only train students to act appropriately but also define and normalize what appropriate student behavior is. The disciplinary nature of schooling thus is about not only disciplining individual bodies to comply with school rules but also making the rationale for discipline, an often taken-for-granted norm.

The changing meaning and use of examinations in Eritrea illuminate the shift from discipline to biopolitics and highlight why this change was so threatening to students and teachers. According to Foucault, in *Discipline and Punish* (1995), the examination is central to disciplinary power. Disciplinary power combines hierarchical observation and normalizing judgment, merging the two through practices of examination. Examinations simultaneously produce a sense of collective experience (everyone takes the exam and views it as a pivotal event in schooling) and differentiate among that collective (the examination determines different life outcomes).

In Eritrea, the collective experience of taking exams and the collective anxiety about this experience were key components of what it meant to be a student. In addition to the National Exam and the Matriculation Exam, which were the culminating events that students spent their years of education working toward, rigorous end-of-semester exams framed the student experience. Teachers shared the collective belief that this system of stringent selection examinations would ensure that the best and the brightest would move on to each level of education. Students became students through participation in this experience. Competition itself was disciplining; although not all students would pass, the disciplining effects of preparing for and orienting oneself toward that exam compelled disciplined behavior. As a technology of the state, these national examinations thus produced a common, national experience of being a student, but they also distinguished between good, bad, and mediocre students. And since there was limited money and space in higher levels of education, examinations determined whom the government would allocate these scarce resources toward.

In this highly selective and competitive system, the impetus was on students to be motivated and do the work needed to pass. Selective examinations disciplined students to act like students—to study hard and follow rules. The role of the teacher was to set a challenging examination rather than an examination that would enable students to pass. In fact, in conversations with many teachers, I learned that they intentionally put a certain number of challenging questions on their exams, even if they had not explicitly taught the material or skills to answer them, to distinguish the exceptional students.

The new promotion policies (and the fact that the Ministry of Education was very serious about making sure that these policies were being implemented), including the mandate that *all* students should pass, represented a decided shift toward biopolitical forms of management and away from disciplinary technologies as being the central role of examinations. Few documents were available from the Ministry of Education, but a quotation from the World Bank, which was working with the Eritrean government on these reforms, utilizes the language of biopolitics to explain what was increasingly seen as the "problem" with the Eritrean education system. This report describes what the World Bank, and, indeed, the Eritrean government, regarded as the "problem" of grade repetition, efficiency, and wastage prior to the implementation of the new policies:

> Internal efficiency indicators are unacceptably low. The repetition rate stands at about 20 percent for elementary and middle levels and 27 percent for secondary school. Repetition is encouraged by highly stringent selection examinations and the limited spaces as the learner progresses up the education ladder. In an attempt to improve their chances of qualifying for a place in the upper grades, learners repeat grades sometimes several times. . . . In addition to increasing the cost of education, high repetition rates deny other children an opportunity for schooling. It is estimated that at a ratio of 42 learners to a classroom, about 16,870 repeaters occupy 401 middle school classrooms and 11,627 repeaters take up 277 high school classrooms. (World Bank 2003)[5]

Interestingly, the World Bank document accurately assesses the education system as tremendously competitive due to few slots at each progressively higher level of education. However, what teachers valued as competitive and challenging for students is described in this document as an "unacceptably low" "efficiency indicator." For teachers, the fact that few students were promoted and many had to repeat grades had previously indicated that the system was working well, because it channeled the appropriate number of students into higher education; the World Bank, though, labels this as "inefficient," because too many students failed and repeaters were taking up classroom space. The shift in emphasis here was away from the quality of the educated individuals and their experience in school (for example, what they learned or became capable of as a result of their years in school). Additionally, what promotion, failure, and repetition meant to individual students was not taken into consideration. The focus instead was explicitly placed on indicators that reflected a concern for the system as a whole, such as the "percentage rate" of failure, promotion, and repetition, as well as an emphasis on the completion of each "level" of education.

The new promotion policies rewrote the goals of the education system and reinvented the norms on which the system was based. The "stringent selection examinations" that teachers valued as "competition" because they motivated and trained individuals, particularly the very talented, were now thought to hold down the overall percentage rate of students who completed each level of education. The meaning of "promotion" changed from a privilege for a few to something that was accessible to everyone. Meanwhile, promotion rates became a way to assess the country as a whole. Prior to the new policies, many students expected to fail. After the new policies were implemented, "failure" itself became not a norm for most students but an indication that schools were failing. Grade repetition was transformed from an opportunity that gave many a second chance to an indicator that the system was inefficient. The completion of each level of education suddenly became the normative expectation rather than a much-coveted reward for a select few.

New policies in Eritrea were concerned not with creating a carefully cultivated educated *individual* who possessed attributes of discipline but rather with creating an educated *population* of high school graduates. Like discipline, biopolitics aims to internalize power by naturalizing a particular set of behaviors; however, unlike discipline, which is concerned with producing norms and normalized behavior at the individual level, biopolitical technologies are much more concerned with management through statistical means and accountability measures designed to produce particular behaviors on a larger scale. For teachers, making this shift from participating in state technologies of discipline to being part of this biopolitical machinery was troubling.

Teachers as Troubled Technologists of the State

According to the new policies, there were to be limited failures among students; however, initially there was a great deal of confusion as to how this was to be accomplished. The transition between the disciplinary and biopolitical paradigms was not easy. This normative shift from discipline, with its focus on training individual bodies, to the biopolitical regulation of the population as a whole led to pressures on teachers to change the way they engaged with students. Teachers were told that they had to promote students; furthermore, they were quite suddenly held accountable for student performance in a way that they had not been previously. The system blamed teachers when students failed despite the fact that one year earlier, teachers, Ministry of Education officials, parents, and students themselves expected that many students would fail. However, as teachers predicted, students who were no longer challenged by a selective examination were simply not motivated to work. To make it even more complicated, many of the students themselves were purposely trying to fail to avoid or delay going to Sawa even though the system was reoriented to make them pass more easily.

Teachers were charged with the duty of following up with and helping "at-risk" students, a term first heard in Eritrean schools after the promotion policies changed. Prior to 2003, failing students were the majority. These students were not considered "at risk," because it was expected for large numbers of secondary school students to fail and there was nothing wrong with their doing so. Completing secondary school was not seen as a necessity for everyone, but a privilege for a few. The shift to labeling failing students "at risk" was confusing for teachers who saw these students as no more at risk than they had been prior to the implementation of these policies. The creation of the "at-risk" category was fundamentally a biopolitical technology that enabled failing students to be considered a problem (rather than an inevitability) and thereby enabled teachers to manage this problem. Previously, a teacher's job was to work within the system of stringent examinations to discipline students, enact rigorous training, and let the exam itself determine who would or would not pass. Under the new biopolitical dispensation, a teacher's job, in theory, was to manage the entire mass of students and ensure their promotion.

Teachers were instructed that they should also utilize a variety of techniques to enable students to pass. The school director made it clear that teachers were to contact students' families if they were doing poorly and offer extra help to these students. While some teachers had always been in touch with families and most teachers had always been willing to offer extra help, previously teachers had done these things out of a sense of kindness, community, or intellectual camaraderie. The mandate that they do so had a distinctly biopolitical tone. It was the teachers' duty to manage their students' lives by staying in touch with the families of at-risk students and recommending that these students get extra help if the teachers determined they needed it. Supervisors also advised teachers to use a rigorous system of record keeping to monitor students' progress.

Another strategy that teachers were instructed to use to help students pass was "continuous assessment," which involved giving students more frequent assignments and tests. Most teachers believed that this technique made it easier for students to pass. "The more tests, the more promotion," many teachers often repeated. Trainers urged teachers to "continuously assess" students and emphasized theories of assessment for formative and pedagogical rather than summative and evaluative purposes. A series of assessment "frequencies" mandated precisely the number of homework and classwork assignments, tests, quizzes, and projects teachers were to assign each semester. Under the previous disciplinary system that revolved around examinations, students themselves were responsible for their performances on the exam. Under the new system, teachers had to monitor students and help them pass. Continuous assessment was a means to do so.

Despite all these techniques, many students were still doing all they could to fail. In many cases, students were showing up for class infrequently or not at all, or they were not doing their work when they did show up. Teachers were not willing to simply pass these students, despite the mandate to do so, so they labeled large numbers of students "incomplete." This category had always existed but was seldom used and was typically reserved for a student who had a good reason for not completing his or her work during the semester—for example, a severe health issue. The large numbers of students labeled "incomplete" were in a holding pattern, a liminal space of sorts between the disciplinary paradigm, under which they would have failed based on their lack of hard work and attendance, and the biopolitical paradigm, which sought to include them among the statistics of those who were promoted. Teachers knew they were supposed to pass these students but could find no grounds on which to do so.

The increased usage of the category of "incomplete" revealed the troubled transition between the disciplinary and biopolitical systems. Teachers, caught uncomfortably between two paradigms of promotion, were troubled technologists of the state and from this position created a new category in which to fit students. The following excerpts from a description of a staff meeting, which occurred in February 2004, a few months after the new policies had been implemented, illuminate the troubled nature of teachers as technologists of the new biopolitical machinery. The debate during this staff meeting addressed the issue of incomplete students and the role of teachers in managing student promotion more broadly.

Henok, a new teacher who had been teaching for less than a semester, asked earnestly what to do about incomplete students. The director answered that first Henok should try to "make the student understand his problem." The director then said that homeroom teachers should have a record from all classes and asked whether Henok had such a record for his own homeroom class. Henok, growing frustrated, said he did. The director then asked whether Henok had given these students "moral advice," a sentiment that echoed older views of education as inculcating moral virtues rather than the biopolitical technique of mass managing the population. To this, Henok replied that he did not even know the students, because they had never come to his class. Effectively the director was suggesting that Henok utilize three different techniques to biopolitically manage the students so they would pass—informing the students of their progress, monitoring the students through record keeping, and advising the students about what they might do to avoid failure.

Ironically, Henok could utilize only one of these techniques—record keeping—because these students were not coming to class at all. They existed on paper only. Still, the blame for the failure of these techniques was placed on the teacher; the assumption of the director was that Henok was not using the tools at his disposal to appropriately monitor and promote his students. In the past, these students would have been categorized as school leavers and removed from the school's roster. However, because of the new policies of mass promotion, students were no longer allowed to be dismissed from school.

As the discussion continued, other teachers became involved in the conversation. A more senior teacher, Kessete, supported Henok by noting that many students were not attending classes. Another teacher then added that it was "not a teacher's work to do all of these things," meaning that it was not the teachers' responsibility to monitor students who refused to show up for classes.

The director then jumped back into the conversation and responded with frustration, saying that there was a common problem throughout the nation about the students' futures, but the school was still charged with a particular responsibility. He said, "So what shall we do? Kick them out of school? Or try to help them?" Interestingly, the director quite clearly articulated the problem and the mandate: He noted that the problem was a national one, implying that the problem was with National Service, but then he returned the conversation to the idea that teachers must try to help students.

Alem joined the discussion and argued that while teachers could better take measures to monitor students, they could not resolve this problem: "In my four sections, all of the teachers are doing this kind of counseling. The attending students didn't fail. But some students had to sign a disciplinary warning for absences and still they are absent. If they are doing that to me, what are they doing to the new teacher?"

The conversation concluded with Mahendra asserting angrily, "They should fail." This was the first and only acknowledgment in the conversation of the role of failure in maintaining a disciplined system.

There are a few points to highlight about this exchange and teacher responses to the new policies. First, no teacher suggested that teachers should not be monitoring students. Teachers accepted their biopolitical mandate to monitor students and facilitate promotion and adapted their techniques to the ethos of mass promotion. But while teachers seemed to have partially made the shift from their disciplinary roles to their biopolitical ones, most drew the line when it came to passing students who were simply not coming to class. They could not manage all of these students into passing, because the situation was out of their control.

The school never fully resolved the dilemma of what to do with incomplete students, who were doing all they could to fail while schools were mandated to pass them. Similar problems were occurring around the country. Eventually, a Ministry of Education mandate would make a much larger percentage of students pass by dropping the grade required to pass from 60 percent to 50 percent. These students would not do well enough to move on to higher education after military training, so when they were inevitably shuttled off to Sawa, they would find themselves endlessly trapped in National Service. Given that permanent National Service would be the end result of mass promotion for many students, we might view teachers' refusal to pass incomplete students as a refusal to take part in a system that wanted to transform schools into a biopolitical mechanism oriented toward militarizing students en masse. Teachers were, at least in part, willing to make the paradigm shift to manage and facilitate student promotion, but they chafed at the mandate that they promote students who they knew would be relegated to a life of National Service.

Conclusion

Teachers and students were mistrustful of the new policies from the beginning. These policies, introduced under the auspices of modernizing and improving the education system, were unevenly implemented. While weakly implemented policies were familiar to teachers and students, what made them mistrust these policies was the fact that the parts that were effectively implemented resulted in shuttling students into Sawa, dismantling the tertiary education system, and radically altering promotion policies. It looked like education was being embedded in the institutions of the military and National Service. As teachers and educational officials commented on these new policies, what was revealed were two radically different ideals of the kind of national subject to be produced by schools—an official, government-sponsored version of the soldier-subject revolved around sacrificing for and serving the nation, while an educated student-subject revolved around students' becoming a carefully cultivated elite who would set a good, moral example for society.

Simultaneously, the new promotion policies radically changed the techniques and technologies that teachers used and were mandated to use. Teachers' roles shifted from one oriented toward discipline to one oriented toward biopolitics, from a focus on disciplining and cultivating talented individuals to shepherding and managing a mass of students through a system of mass promotion. Many teachers were willing to make this shift, in part. They slowly embraced the biopolitical shift in their work as educators, but they were not willing to become part of a state technology that simply shuttled students into the military.

4

Educating Eritrea

Disorder, Disruption, and Remaking the Nation

A Ritual for the Nation

It was October 2003 in the Senior Secondary School in Assab at 7:20 in the morning, ten minutes *after* the flag ceremony was scheduled to begin. A teacher stood on the podium next to the flagpole, lecturing the hundred or so students who stood in scraggly rows in front of him. He complained that only 30 percent of the student body was regularly attending the flag ceremony. The students applauded in the middle of his speech, and a teacher standing beside me laughed and told me that meant they wanted him to stop talking. No one was in uniform.

Two teachers walked up and down the disorderly lines of students, saying, "You, go there. You, make the line straight." They pushed students into the correct positions. Students responded, good-naturedly but lazily, moving as directed but then jumping into a different line when the teacher was not looking. Another teacher walked in and out of classrooms, swishing a switch he had pulled from a tree through the air as he chased students hiding in the rooms into the schoolyard. Their playful shrieks and giggles distracted the students standing in front of the flag. Most of the teachers waited in the staff room for the ceremony to end.

A boy ascended the podium and tied the flag to its pole. The lead teacher instructed the students, "OK. When I say 'attention,' you have to stand like this." He demonstrated the proper attentive position, in an exaggerated manner, pinning his legs together, standing straight with his hands at his side, pushing his chest out. "When I say 'at ease,' go like this." He demonstrated for them. Then he drilled them. "Attention! At ease! Attention!" The students in the front followed his instructions as he chastised them to "do it right." The students in the back ignored him, slouching with their arms dangling at their sides, gazing down at the ground or up at the sky. The ones in the middle shuffled their feet back and forth in a vague imitation of the drill.

Giving up on having his instructions followed, the teacher continued, "OK, begin singing." The flag rose, and the sound of the students singing was so soft it could not be heard over the rushing wind. The teacher cried out, "Be loud!" The students' voices rose to a barely audible pitch.

Flag ceremonies, pledges of allegiance, or other rituals for the nation are present in schools around the world. They epitomize the process of inculcating the nation into students and, in doing so, creating a national citizenry (Rippberger and Staudt 2003). In Eritrea and elsewhere, students are inspected, lined up, drilled in military fashion, and required to sing the national anthem in unison. Theoretically, as individual student bodies are fused into a collective, national body and then marched off to class, a specific kind of educated national subject is produced (Foucault 1995; Luykx 1999). In this process, the nation becomes "embodied," or viscerally felt (Benei 2008). These ceremonies are also a routine part of everyday "banal" nationalism—nationalism that gets inside its subjects and normalizes itself there (Billig 1995). Flag ceremonies are indubitably one of the most salient means through which students come to know that they are national, but these rituals do not always make students *feel* national, at least not in the way the nation's leaders want them to.

As described above, in the Senior Secondary School, deviance and evasiveness occurred with such frequency during the morning flag ceremony that the ceremony became a mockery of itself. Students hid in classrooms or arrived late. Those present slouched, shuffled through the drills, and dragged their feet. They refused to sing. They lackadaisically went through the motions, not rejecting or opposing the ceremony outright but resisting through passivity, performing the ceremony, but not as they should. In the process, the symbols of the nation—anthem, flag, military-like drills—were hollowed of their meaning and no longer sacred. The authority figures ostensibly leading the ceremony—teachers—were either avoiding the ceremony or being laughed at by students.

More often than not throughout the time of my fieldwork, the flag ceremony in the Senior Secondary School was more a reflection of disorder and mockery than of discipline. The broader politics and power dynamics at play in Eritrea produced this dance of resistance and discipline and effectively reduced the quintessential ritual of the nation to a caricature of itself and a joke. National rituals provide a rich framework through which to understand how national subjects *feel* about the nation, and classroom-based rituals are a key means to produce affective ties to the nation and embodied sentiments of reverence and passion for it (Benei 2008). However, a particular kind of affective tie to the nation is produced through disorder; at the same time, disorderly performances of the nation are also a manifestation of the everyday politics of impotence.

Education embodies the hopes (and fears) for the future of the nation itself. As noted in the previous chapter, one teacher stated, "Children *are* the nation." Thus, perceptions of whether children will grow up well reflect imaginaries of the nation's future and the ability of the nation to develop as well. The way citizens think about the transformation of the educated young person into a productive adult is reflective of desires not just for young people to grow up well but also for the nation to grow up well. According to many—teachers, members of the government, and parents—the failed aspirations for a "bright future" both reflected and produced a crisis, not only for schools but also for the nation. Mockery of the flag ceremony was emblematic of the conditions of disorder present in schools across Eritrea following the implementation of new educational policies. I knew from conversations with teachers who worked elsewhere and educational administrators that Assab was not the only town experiencing such disorderly conditions. While some flag ceremonies in Assab and throughout the country were far more orderly than those that routinely occurred in Assab's Senior Secondary School, many schools repeatedly experienced conditions of chronic disorder.

These conditions of disorder in schools were a result of the vicious cycle of coercion and evasion that emerged in the years following the implementation of the Warsai Yikaalo Development Campaign (WYDC). As noted in Chapters 1 and 3, for the ruling party in Eritrea, learning to be national was equated with learning to be military—or, more specifically, adopting the ethos of the fighter. National Service was designed to be a transformative experience. It was supposed to ritually change students into national subjects who would emulate the values of the fighter. Given this, we might expect that as policies embedded schools into the military, everyday life in schools would become more ordered and disciplinary like the military and that teachers' roles would shift accordingly. Indeed, in other countries with a strong military ethos, schools have been militarized in this way. For example, in Turkey, schools and the army are both seen as training grounds for national subjects (Altinay 2005; Kaplan 2006). But in Eritrea, schools became a site of resistance to militarization. The widespread use of coercion to impose the military project on citizens resulted in evasiveness rather than buy-in. This chapter shows how this evasiveness played out in schools. Disorder was a manifestation of evasiveness, a means for teachers and students to enact their discontent with mass militarization, and a rare opportunity for critique of the government.

Schools in Eritrea and elsewhere are the key site through which educated young people learn to be national, and discipline and order are key means through which students become properly educated, national subjects, but the political implications of disorder in schools and its role in the production of national subjectivity are seldom examined and little understood. If order produces a disciplined, docile subject, disorder produces and is produced by a subject who is critical but also stuck in a liminal state, and therefore impotent. Disorder in Eritrean schools was produced through the tacit complicity of students and teachers as a political response to the implementation of life-changing policies, which they were powerless to protest. The first section of this chapter looks at schooling as a site of ritual transformation whereby children are turned into adult citizens within the context of mass militarization in Eritrea. I show that, in light of permanent National Service, students specifically and Eritreans more generally failed to "grow up" and instead got stuck in a permanently liminal condition. The following sections explore the implications and consequences of limitless liminality for schools, for relationships between students and teachers, and, ultimately, for the formation of affective ties to the nation. Educated subjects in Eritrea were produced through disorder, which, in turn, produced a climate in which a critical stance toward party versions of nationalism could emerge. Disorder in schools was a reflection of not only the broader national climate of evasiveness but also official struggles to legitimize the national project and the ensuing condition of impotence for both citizens and the state.

"A Teacher Is Someone Who Doesn't Grow Up": Education, National Service, and Limitless Liminality

In the modern era, schooling is a key rite of passage, a key means to grow up by acquiring status and stature. Formal education moves students from the life stage of child to adult and, in doing so, transforms them from uneducated to educated people.[1] This transformation involves not only growing up in age and maturity but also acquiring a higher status as an educated person and as a full, adult, national citizen. The years spent in school may be thought of as a liminal phase in a young person's life through which the young person moves from the dependency of childhood to the responsibilities of adulthood, which include duties to the nation. Liminality denotes a condition of being "betwixt and between" known social categories (Turner 1969).[2] So, too, students are liminally located between the dependency of childhood and the responsibilities of adulthood (Quantz 2011). The concept of liminality denotes a phase of ritual in which subjects retreat from society and go into seclusion to learn the sacred teachings of that society and reemerge, transformed and prepared to take on a new role as an adult or higher-status subject (Gennep 1960; Turner 1969).

Schooling is not the only means through which young people make this transformation to responsible adult subjects/citizens. Many countries utilize the military and national service to turn young people into full citizens (Gorham 1992). In Eritrea, National Service and military training were arguably the government's preferred method of ritually preparing its young for their roles as adult citizens in the nation. National Service, which was supposed to last for eighteen months, typically in a remote location, was arguably an intensive initiation into being Eritrean. While in National Service, the nation's young people had to submit absolutely to military authority, were indoctrinated and given political education by fighters who fought for the country's freedom, and were put through a series of rigorous physical exercises. The period of isolation from society, the submission to authority, the sacred teachings about the nation, and the physical rigors present in National Service were all reminiscent of initiation rites. By merging education with National Service, the two forms of ritual were fused, and one became fully Eritrean by becoming simultaneously educated and "like the fighters." If we see both education and National Service as liminal phases out of which a full-blown Eritrean adult emerged, fusing them suggests that the new policy reflected a move toward producing educated fighter-citizens rather than two distinct classes: educated citizens and fighter citizens.

By merging education and National Service and situating National Service at the end of students' secondary education, the government made it clear that Eritrean young people would not be allowed to become educated without also going into National Service, effectively combining the two liminal stages to produce an educated *and* militarized Eritrean man or woman. This merger by itself was problematic, given that many Eritreans tended to see the two classifications as distinct, but it was even more so because the liminal phase never ended. Liminality is, by definition, an in-between stage, and a *transition* from one phase to another. Clarity regarding what precedes and follows it is necessary to bound and give meaning to the nebulous "in-between-ness" of liminality. Increasingly, in Eritrea, it was unclear which stages Eritreans were *between*. When National Service became indefinite with the introduction of the WYDC, the in-between became the norm, but it did not ever seem to lead to another stage. When one entered National Service, one did not leave normal life to pass through a liminal phase and emerge as a military, national citizen. Instead, one left ordinary life and entered into an indefinite phase of limbo.

A key example of this endless "in-between-ness" is illustrated by the blurring of category distinctions among types of teachers. There were two roughly defined categories of teachers—service teachers and professional teachers.[3] (The latter were generally referred to simply as "teachers," but for clarity, I use the phrase "professional teachers.") Service teachers were assigned to teach as the unpaid, volunteer portion of National Service. In contrast, professional teachers were teachers who did not enter the teaching profession by way of National Service but instead had been teaching for some time. During the first five years or so after the National Service program was introduced in 1994, the lines between service teachers and professional teachers were quite distinct. But as time went on and more and more university graduates were assigned to the teaching profession upon completion of their service, these distinctions started to blur—service teachers eventually became professional teachers. When their voluntary service was over, they would begin to receive salary and, in many cases, would continue teaching in the same location. The border war and the WYDC blurred these status distinctions even more. Between 2000 and 2002, the majority of professional teachers were compelled to join National Service. Indeed, in 2001, as noted in the Introduction, all teachers around the country who had not previously completed military training were conscripted into military training.[4] Following their training, they continued their work as teachers but now worked for pocket money, like others in National Service. The WYDC then extended this eighteen-month National Service commitment indefinitely. Thus, almost all male teachers under forty-five could have been thought of as "service teachers," yet the professional teachers never completely thought of themselves in this way.

Despite this blurring of categories, there were still distinctions between types of teachers. Professional teachers continued to disparage the lack of maturity and commitment among some of their junior, "service" colleagues. Service teachers and professional teachers also had a different sense of the extent to which they were being coerced to teach by the government. Being "in service" made teachers feel as though they were being compelled to teach. Conversely, being released from service through demobilization would indicate to teachers that they had a modicum of free will, would begin receiving their salaries, and could choose their jobs. (In reality, demobilization meant that they were finished with their National Service commitment and would begin to receive their full salaries again, although they still had little choice about remaining in the teaching profession.) As of 2003, no teachers in Assab had been demobilized. All of them were disappointed, but professional and service teachers articulated these feelings differently. The professional teachers spoke as if it were just a matter of time. Indeed, within a few months of the start of my fieldwork, the professional teachers had been demobilized (at that point, this group of teachers had been in National Service for approximately two-and-a-half to three years). In contrast, the service teachers were frustrated, hopeless, and seemingly completely confused about their status vis-à-vis National Service. They had no faith that they would ever be released.

Service teachers and professional teachers shared the sense that their lives were commandeered by National Service, leaving them in limbo. This created a sense that teachers would never "grow up." While all teachers regarded teaching itself as a condition of being "stuck" and failing to "grow up," service teachers felt particularly stuck. The following is Paolo's story of how he came to be a teacher in Assab. It reflects this sense of being stuck. His story reveals his ambitions, his sense of lack of progress, and the role of both teaching and National Service in his failure to "grow up."

Paulo was a geography teacher in Assab with whom I always enjoyed talking a great deal. Like many of the teachers, he was good-humored and keenly analytical about his own circumstances and how they reflected the circumstances in the country as a whole. He was a service teacher. Neither of Paolo's parents had any formal education, and yet, like many, he placed great importance on education. His father was a small business owner, but his mother was illiterate. He had hoped to study business or accounting and become a business owner, but because he was working while in school, his exam results were not high enough to join the business program; instead, he was assigned to geography. As soon as he was assigned to geography, he knew he would be a teacher, because there was nothing else for a geography graduate to do. He told me that his first instinct was to leave the university and start a business on his own, but he knew if he did not stay in the university, he would be required to go into National Service, so he studied geography. When he finished his studies, Paolo completed his military training and then was assigned by lottery to do his service teaching in Assab. Most of the other teachers were assigned in the central highlands where they were from. "I was unlucky," he said with regard to his assignment to Assab. At first he did not like Assab, and at the time of our interview he still had mixed feelings about the town. He said that he was "afraid of the climate" because of the heat and worried because he did not know anyone. For a service teacher, who earned almost nothing, having relatives nearby was essential to survive.

From the beginning, Paolo treated teaching like a lower-status, undesirable career path that he took only because it represented an escape from the worse path of permanent conscription into the military. As a result, he noted that he had difficulty feeling like he was a teacher, especially because he was in National Service:

> Paolo: When I came to this school, I thought to myself, "I am a teacher, and I should be acting like the other teachers," and I was always trying to explain my knowledge to the students.
> Jennifer: What does it mean to act like a teacher?
> P: Outside the school, I don't feel like a teacher. Starting from the beginning, my interest was not in geography or in teaching, but because I didn't have good results, the university assigned me to be a teacher. So it is my duty to do everything that the teachers do, and I keep to my duty and try to think to myself, "Now I am a teacher and I should act like a teacher, and that is why I am trying to spread my knowledge." I have a duty, but when I am outside, I am different. I came to Assab as National Service and am still National Service.

Paolo cast himself as not really being a teacher but merely "acting" like a teacher. He equated teaching with National Service, a liminal phase that he clearly hoped to pass through.

Paolo felt stuck in not only teaching/National Service but also the town of Assab. He noted that over time he came to like the town of Assab but would never stay there voluntarily because it was a dead end: "There is no opportunity [in Assab]. I like the society, but I don't want to stay, because there is no opportunity. Not only for us [teachers] but for everyone in this city, there is no opportunity. It is a big military camp. I like the society; when you make relations, it is good, but there is no opportunity. Here we are young, so we have to grow up." Again, he equated being stuck with militarization. Since the evacuation in 2000, Assab was full of soldiers on leave from the front and people in National Service. Paolo's perception that the town was a "military camp" was a commentary on the everyday life of the town being commandeered by National Service, which eroded civilian life and the capacity for business development.

He also illustrated the low status of teachers and the consequences of his own failure to grow up by talking about a failed relationship with a woman whom he was trying to pursue:

> I was trying to make some relation with one lady, and I invited her to have a lunch, and the fourth or fifth time, she asked me about my job. So when she asks me about my job, I say I am a teacher, and she says, "Oh, Jesus." She was surprised and upset [and said], "Oh, teacher, I hate teacher." Because she knows about their economic background. So I became upset. So maybe what she says may be reflected and the society thinks in that way. They might think a teacher is someone who doesn't grow up and doesn't get opportunity, so how can you feel good? So it creates [a] certain pressure on me.

I asked Paolo what he meant when he said teachers never grow up, and he answered:

> Here the society gives respect for someone with good position and money. Teachers don't have power and money and status. So how can society give respect? So if you don't have those, you become careless. Then students don't do what their teachers say in class. So their parents' [attitudes] become influential for their students. And the students don't give respect for us, and this becomes really bad for the whole situation. Here the students are not motivated to learn, because no one has any opportunity. Everyone is involved in military service. Most of them have jobs, and they care more about their jobs than school. So there is some crisis in the idea about school.

Paolo's story, like the life narratives of many teachers, was marked by not only aspirations and hopes for a better future but also the belief that being educated should help him meet his goals but, given the current climate of mass military service, could not. Teachers and students believed that because they were educated, they should have the chance to grow up, or to acquire greater status and wealth, but instead, teachers believed that they were relegated to a permanently lower-class status. This feeling had material effects on their ability to get promotions and to be able to save enough money to attract and marry a spouse, both actions that are markers of being "grown up" in Eritrea. But, as Paolo noted, national/military service was central to the inability to grow up, and ongoing National Service led to "carelessness" among both teachers and students.

Paolo's story was reflective of the dreams of many Eritreans. It was also reflective of broader trends throughout the developing world, where education is seen as the means to change one's status but quite often never enables educated people to achieve this hoped-for status bump (Bolten 2015; Mains 2012). In Eritrea, teachers' dashed hopes were exacerbated because their lives were commandeered by demands for endless service. Arguably the telos of hope for a better future both gives meaning to being an educated person and is produced through aspirations for education. Conversely, the failures of teachers to "grow up" served as a perpetual reminder of the inability of education to help people achieve their aspirations and, thus, unraveled this telos of hope.

Another teacher, Isaac, had a similar story to Paolo's. Isaac, interestingly, was not a service teacher but instead had been an elementary school teacher who had been given the opportunity to get further training and, at the time of my research, was a Junior Secondary School teacher. He had achieved some professional mobility through teaching, but despite this, he believed that teaching was holding him back and keeping him in a low-status position:

> Isaac: We Eritreans, we always think about how to get money. We work. But the problem is this work—teaching—doesn't have any value. We can't pay for our houses. To tell you the truth, if you are a teacher, you are not going to get a wife. In this country, [being] a teacher means having a totally lower status. The teacher has full-time work, but when you ask to get a wife, it is a difficult.
>
> Jennifer: But you have a wife.
>
> I: Yes. It took a lot of time to convince her to marry me. I had to tell her I will leave education to find another job. In general, a teacher is very poor in our country. The construction worker is better than the teacher, because they make more money. We work hard, but no one cares about us.

According to Isaac, the markers of growth—money, a house, and a wife—were not possible for teachers. Effectively, teachers were stuck in a liminal place—no longer students, but also not having the stature expected of educated people.

This failure to grow up is a common theme in the literature on youth in Africa (see, for example, Argenti 2007). The category of "youth" in Africa more often than not refers to status rather than age. Indeed, official categories of youth often contain an age range that is wide. Although the category of "youth" in Eritrea was somewhat variable, it typically included people up to age thirty-five and often up to forty-five, the age at which one was no longer eligible for National Service. But many more attributes might determine whether someone could be categorized as youth. For example, if someone (male or female) was married and/or had children, he or she was likely no longer thought of as youth. Youth also reflected wealth, professional status, and birth order in families. Older siblings tended to be regarded as "grown up" more readily than younger siblings, but they also tended to be saddled with financial responsibilities for their families as well. Growing up in general was thought to reflect the ability to hold down a lucrative job and to save enough money to get married; however, everyone hoped to grow up even further and perhaps own property, start a business, or acquire further wealth and stature.

In many parts of Africa, one can grow old ("grow up" in Eritrean terminology) only by acquiring wealth and status (Argenti 2007; Bayart 2009). "Youth" itself is equated with powerlessness and lack of status, while "age" is linked with status and power (Bayart 2009). In many parts of the continent, youth growing up is linked with client-patron relationships and produces the permanent dependence of a large group of youth on a small number of wealthy and powerful "big men." However, in Eritrea, state institutions allocate power to leaders who are empowered through the centralized single-party system itself rather than to a more decentralized network of "big men."[5] As a result, in Eritrea, the failure to grow old/up was less about vulnerability as a result of permanent dependence on "big men" as it was elsewhere in Africa; however, perhaps ironically, youth were vulnerable because of government policies that placed them in a sort of clientilistic relationship with the party/government/state as a whole, rendering them effectively dependent on the state/party. The failure to grow up mainly manifested itself in dependence on the government, a condition that the government itself produced through conditions of National Service.

Isaac, Paolo, and others specifically noted the linkage between the failure of teachers to grow up and the ongoing condition of National Service. Later in my conversation with Isaac, he noted, "If someone works somewhere, he should have money. But we worked for four years in National Service without payment. We became fed up." Isaac complained that other civil servants doing National Service actually were better cared for than teachers. Although teaching was thought of as a low-status position to begin with, National Service even more severely flattened any stature that teachers once had.

Furthermore, there was a sense that being a teacher was somehow on par with being a soldier, but slightly better than being a soldier (a concept discussed in Chapter 2 and also illuminated in Paolo's comments). Paolo complained that Assab was like a big military camp, where there was no opportunity and everyone was in a common position of dependence on the government. And yet, while being a soldier was, in many respects, the Eritrean condition and equated with being a teacher, it was also seen as worse than being a teacher and something to be strategically avoided, as Paolo did when he chose to study geography rather than go into business. Another teacher, Gebre, told me, "I never wanted to be a teacher, because it is not a good job, but when we were in military training, we hoped to be teachers. Now, sometimes I become angry because I am a teacher, and then I start to think about the soldiers and the hardship they face, and it is better to be a teacher. I say thanks to God." Paolo, Gebre, Isaac, and others articulated a sentiment that both teachers and soldiers were stuck in a limitlessly liminal condition—they could not grow up—and yet being a teacher was preferable only because it involved less physical suffering and hardship.

Teachers were in a limitless liminal phase in several ways. Their profession itself inculcated in them the ideals of growing in status by virtue of one's education, but the relatively low status of teaching left them with aspirations they could never achieve. Furthermore, many of them believed that the government was complicit in depriving them of the opportunity to grow up. Many teachers stated that they were not allowed to quit teaching. Indeed, if they hoped to get another job, they would have to acquire a letter of release from the Ministry of Education, something that was hard to come by even if they had completed National Service. National Service, which blurred the categories of professional and service teacher, exacerbated this sense of being "stuck." While in National Service, teachers could not leave teaching or seek another job. They were unsure of when they would be released from service and had no money or ability to get married or change their status.

This failure for teachers, who were supposed to be in positions of authority, to "grow up" had a significant impact on relations between teachers and students. Those in the liminal phase are supposed to submit to the (often totalizing) ritualized authority of those in charge of their initiation— authority figures responsible for sacred teachings. In this case, teachers should have been those authority figures, but because of National Service, teachers were stuck in a liminal phase and could not fully take on their proper positions or roles of authority. Instead, students often saw teachers as being more like their equals, their friends. Initiates in a liminal phase forge an egalitarian and communal bond with each other, which Victor Turner (1969) calls "communitas." While teachers should have been the authority figure, because both teachers and students were in an endless "in between" together, they formed communitarian bonds of a sort with each other, blurring, but not erasing, notions of authority. This relationship had significant implications for creating order in the schools.

There was also the sense that because no one was growing up, the nation was not developing. This sense of being stuck played out at the macrolevel of the nation and the microlevel of schools. Previous nationwide "macrorituals" through which educated persons were supposed to move up to new status positions changed beyond recognition or ceased to exist. Examples of these macrorituals were selective national examinations, including the matriculation exam, and university graduation. Instead of taking these selective exams and moving on to university, as of 2003, students were to be unceremoniously shipped off to Sawa and then kept in service indefinitely, not unlike teachers. Peter McLaren's (1986) work on schools in the United States notes that macrorituals that demarcate status change align with everyday microrituals of schooling.[6] In Eritrea, just as these macrorituals, which were supposed to transform the status position of educated people, broke down, the microrituals that punctuated the school day and year were also disintegrating. This was most clearly illustrated in the fact that schools had a very difficult time actually getting started at the beginning of the school year. The sections that follow look at this breakdown of authority as well as microrituals of schooling.

Liminality, Disorder, and Schools That Never Really Started

Monday, October 6, 2003, was my first day of fieldwork in the Senior Secondary School and was supposed to be the first official day of school, according to the school director and signs posted around the school. At 7:15, I walked through the school compound in the blistering late summer morning sun toward the classrooms. Thinking I was late for a school day that began at 7:00, I rushed as much as I could in the heat with the wind pressing against me. Sweat dripped down my back. Crows cawed. I was struck by the emptiness around me. Where the shouts of students should have filled the air, I could hear only wind and crows. The wide playing field was an expanse of dust devils and blowing scraps of paper. I could even hear the sea, which lay some three or four hundred meters away, just out of sight on the other side of a concrete wall.

Reaching the end of the playing field, I turned a corner, and on the other side of the main office building, where there should have been hundreds of students, I saw the school director standing in front of a cluster of about twenty students. The director shook his head, said good morning, and mumbled, "No students. No teachers."

"Maybe they'll come in fifteen minutes?" I suggested weakly. I sat on a bench in front of the staff room, fanning myself with my notebook and watching as he oriented the students.

Teacher Fitwi was the first teacher to arrive. He joined me on the bench and raised his eyebrows in surprise when he saw so few students. "We have to start today," Fitwi told me earnestly. "We have to give them something to do, so they will tell the others to come."

Several other teachers arrived and pulled chairs out of the staff room into the breeze, gazing at the spectacle of the director and his two dozen students. One teacher started laughing as soon as he saw the students and joked, "Today we are going to teach students one on one!"

Around 7:45, the students trickled off to their classrooms, which were so full of dust that there was nowhere for them to sit. Swooshing noises ensued as students attempted to dust off their seats with scraps of paper that they had found on the classroom floors and clouds of brown dust billowed through the open windows. Teachers walked into the rooms with attendance lists but shortly after they took attendance, they returned to the staff room for a spontaneously called meeting. The students went home.

The first two weeks of school, I knew from my experience teaching at the school in previous years, were typically a sort of "warm-up" time, a liminal phase during which teachers and students adjusted to being teachers and students and prepared themselves to reenter the school year with its rigid routines and rituals. This warm-up period served as a transition between the no-school summer and the school year. As a liminal phase, it both was and was not school and, as such, was "betwixt and between" and marked by "anti-structure" (Turner 1969). Anti-structure is not an absence of structure but the spontaneous and unpredictable oscillation between kinds of structure—formal and informal (Turner 1969). In these spaces, social rules and hierarchies break down, and alternate types of relationships, marked by a more communal orientation, surface. In this space of anti-structure and disorder, new ways of thinking, imagining, and relating begin to emerge. Anti-structure also relates to categorical blurriness and is a key reason why those who cannot be clearly categorized (including those in a liminal phase) are often regarded as dangerous, taboo, or impure (Douglas [1966] 1984).

During this liminal period of "warm-up" school, students and teachers mingled and interacted in a relaxed manner and lackadaisically enacted routines. The few teachers and students who were present would go through the motions of the school routines, but schedules were not followed, little teaching or learning took place, and the school day was often abbreviated. Instead, teachers would casually drop into classrooms, write a few introductory notes on the board, and leave after a few minutes. Teachers spoke of "giving students something to do," meaning they would give them some information, usually in the form of notes written on the blackboard, so that they would go tell other students that school was beginning. "Giving them something to do" was a means of transition from the "summer state" to the "school state"; however, "giving them something to do" did not constitute "school" and was therefore a liminal, in-between, transition phase. No one expected things to go according to schedule or plan because teachers and students were performing the everyday rituals of schooling in a somewhat erratic way.

When a critical mass of students and teachers had arrived at the school, as if someone had given an invisible signal, a series of ritualized practices began that signaled that the school year was about to truly begin. At this point, teachers began to talk about "controlling" the students.[7] Controlling the students signaled a change in attitude and authority relations between teachers and students. The first practice that signaled control was making students clean the classrooms, in effect transforming the space of the classroom from chaotic to orderly. Control also consisted of homeroom teachers taking attendance, creating a rotation of students to clean the room on a daily basis, and appointing class monitors whose duties included, among other things, managing student behavior when the teachers were not in the room.[8] Once all of this had happened in the majority of classes, then all teachers would begin to follow the school's schedule, a bell would ring in between periods to demarcate specific times for specific periods, and the director would enforce rules around lateness for both students and teachers. The director would also, at this point, expect students and teachers to stay in their classrooms throughout the entire class period. Students who had uniforms would be expected to wear them. Teachers would begin to give tests and assignments for marks. All of these cues, which occurred tacitly, indicated the true beginning of the school year.

What was surprising about the start of the school year during the years of my fieldwork was that after the first two weeks went by, the school seemed no closer to starting than it had been two weeks earlier. A ritual demarcating the actual start of school should have followed the liminal phase, but that liminal warm-up phase seemed to take over. The transition from summer state to school state extended well beyond its typical length of a week or two. In fact, at several points throughout the year, it felt like schools would never really begin. Every semester when I conducted fieldwork between fall 2003 and spring 2005, it was not until about a third to halfway through each semester that school really got up and running. Additionally, examples of uncontrolled activity, such as chronic truancy, excessive lateness, and ongoing behavioral problems (issues that previously would have occurred at the beginning of the year or in isolated cases) continued throughout the entire semester. Just as teachers (and students) believed that they were increasingly stuck in a permanent state of "growing up" (never grown), schools seemed to be permanently poised to start but never quite did.

When I asked teachers and students why the school year was so late to start, teachers said they were not showing up to school because students were not showing up, and students said they were not showing up because teachers were not showing up. Teachers and students were tacitly complicit in producing this disorderly start to the school year, as their lateness influenced each other.[9] In fall 2003, I recall sitting around the bars and tea shops in Asmara, feeling anxious that I should be in Assab to start my fieldwork when, indeed, most of my interlocutors remained in Asmara, where most of them spent the summer visiting family. For weeks, Assab's teachers routinely met in Asmara and exchanged thoughts on when they would return. Their decisions hinged on speculating as to when the students would arrive for school, gauging how many teachers had returned, and knowing that as long as a critical mass of teachers remained in Asmara, there would be no consequences for their lateness. Occasionally, we would run into teachers from other remote regions who were having similar conversations. Around the country, everyone seemed to be waiting for a cue to start school that was slow to come.

There were several practical reasons for this extended foot dragging. Teachers, almost all of whom were now in National Service, were disgruntled; since they did not receive a salary, they knew they could not be penalized for late arrival, so they made it a point to return to Assab as late as possible. The Ministry of Education was also implicated in student lateness through some of its actions and lack of organization. For example, in 2004, the government-sponsored boarding school, a home for students whose families lived in the villages outside Assab, was not prepared with supplies and equipment, so approximately 50 percent of the Senior Secondary School students who lived in the boarding school could not come at the right time. Additionally, a shortage of seats on public buses to Assab meant that teachers had to wait to find a seat on a bus, and fuel shortages meant that private or government vehicles that teachers might catch a ride on were delayed in leaving Asmara. But the main reason for the late start of school was a collective lack of will to show up.

It is significant that just as National Service, which had recently been indefinitely extended, was merged with schooling, both teachers and students appeared to give up on maintaining the rituals that made schooling formal and formulaic. What was happening beginning in fall 2003 was an expansion of the liminal, until everyone existed in a permanent condition of "in-between-ness." Liminality, in the traditional sense of the liminal as a ritual stage, is supposed to be a contained, powerful, and volatile state. Although Turner (1969) has noted that liminality may be an extended state, I think it is important to explore some of the idiosyncrasies of permanent liminality. The late start of school was the clearest manifestation of these idiosyncrasies. During the "warm-up" weeks of school, rigidly hierarchical relationships between teachers and students tended to be more relaxed. This liminal phase at the beginning of the school year, with its more relaxed sociability and relationships between students and teachers, was supposed to end and give way to more structured schooling and relationships wherein students and teachers acted predictably and adhered to their proper roles, but this did not happen. As I explore in the next section, lines of authority and hierarchies in the classroom blurred as teachers and students increasingly started questioning the purposes of education. The rigidity of the categories of teacher and student became more flexible, contributing to a climate of disorder.

"Playing with Us": A Tale of Two Teachers

As the overarching "macrorituals" of schooling were changing (and being merged with the macroritual of becoming part of the military), the lines of authority between teachers and students began to blur, and schools became less ordered. A sense of community and intimacy arose between students and teachers, which can be explored using Turner's (1969) concept of communitas. In the classic sense, subjects in the liminal phase experience a sense of egalitarianism and communion with other initiates but continue to submit to authority figures. One way to make sense of the changing authority relations between teachers and students is that the sense of communitas, typically limited to feelings of solidarity with other students, began to expand to include teachers, who were increasingly seen as being similar to their students. Both teachers and students were, in many ways, the same vis-à-vis National Service—all received the same treatment in military training, all were required to perform the same National Service, and no special accommodations were made for those who had more education. Here I talk about how this flattening of relationships affected the classroom in different ways by looking at two service teachers, Aron and Yesob.

Aron, a biology teacher, was in his second year of teaching. He always looked very uncomfortable in front of the class and struggled to gain the respect of his students, as the following excerpt from my field notes illustrates:

> Aron walked in, unnoticed by the students, and erased the blackboard by himself instead of asking a student to do it, as was customary. Students were talkative, but when Aron told them to stop talking, they became quiet for a few minutes. The students did not stand to greet him as they would have for other teachers, and he did not ask them to. He began to quietly copy from a textbook onto the board. When the students became too loud, he interrupted his writing on the board to silence the students again. Students continued to chat in low voices quietly while they took out their books and began to copy what he had written. After a few minutes, many of them started to shuffle papers noisily and move around the room. A group of boys in the back of the room were laughing and talking loudly in Amharic. About nine students in the back few rows were not writing notes at all. The ones who were writing were talking to each other while they wrote. There seemed to be a shortage of pens in the back of the classroom, and the students were quarrelling over a few pens that they attempted to share between them, grabbing them from each other and laughing. Aron ignored this behavior.
>
> After giving the students some time to copy these notes, he called their attention to the board and read over the notes he had written. In contrast to their rather disruptive behavior while Aron was writing up the notes on the board, the students were quiet while he was talking. One boy was sleeping on the desk, but not disturbing anyone.
>
> Aron left the room to clean his eraser and then returned. He erased the board and wrote up a second set of notes. As with the first time he wrote the notes and had the students copy [them], students were increasingly noisy while he was writing, but when he finished writing the notes and turned to face them, they were immediately quiet. Aron then read over the notes and checked to make sure that

students understood all the words. He then left the class ten minutes early. However, he noticed that students were beginning to leave the room and returned but did not attempt to teach again.[10] He spent the remainder of the period pacing up and down the aisles, assuming, or perhaps hoping, that the teacher's presence would keep the students from leaving the room and disturbing other students. The students were increasingly noisy and disruptive and, except for staying in the room, did not seem to behave as if there was a teacher in the room at all. When the students got too noisy, he left with five minutes still remaining in the period.

In Eritrean schools, certain classroom rituals were supposed to delineate hierarchies and single out the teacher as the authority figure in the classroom. I often stayed in classrooms for an entire morning and observed the radical and immediate shift when a teacher walked in (and conversely, when certain teachers walked in, the complete failure of students to make this transition).[11] When there was no teacher in the room, students would walk around, talk, and yell in loud voices, often chasing each other around the room or throwing things. As soon as a teacher walked in, students were supposed to sit quietly and attentively, ready to begin. When the teacher turned to face them, they would stand together and chorus, "Good morning, Teacher." Then one of them would take the eraser from the teacher and erase the board. Indeed, students often did stop their raucous behavior when a teacher walked in if it were a more senior teacher, and in previous years they had done so even for more junior teachers.

From the beginning, Aron failed to make use of these rituals. He did nothing to indicate that the students should change their behavior, yet they did begin to settle down on their own and start to perform like students, somewhat. In many ways, Aron assumed that students would know how to act, but he did not assert his authority. I knew from conversations with Aron that students did not see him as an authority figure. He complained that students were overly familiar with him and tried to talk to him outside class and befriend him, a line he did not want to cross. But while he did not like students treating him like a friend, he did not assert himself as an authority figure either. In response, the students were not completely out of control in Aron's class, but they did not quite act as they should either. Aron's classroom both was and was not proper "school." Students and teacher went through the motions of schooling, but the balance of power was compromised.

I often asked students why they behaved properly for some teachers but not others, and they invariably described the teachers they showed no respect for as "playing with us," meaning that these teachers were not taking their education seriously, so the teachers, in turn, did not deserve to be taken seriously. After one of Aron's classes, I asked his students why they did not behave properly for him and whether he was playing with them. A debate ensued, with some of them saying that he was playing with them and others saying that he was a "very nice teacher," the opposite of a "playful" one. Aron was in a liminal role—he was almost as young as his students, but he was in a position of authority. Students complied but did not treat him as an authority figure. A tacit agreement, a sense of communitas, existed in his classroom. As a result, his power was tenuous and contingent on whether the students would agree to let him teach them.

While Aron resented the communitas with his students foisted on him by their failure to respect his authority, another young teacher, Yesob, actually embraced the sense of communitas he had with his students. Yesob had a few more years' experience than Aron but still very much looked like a service teacher. Like many of the service teachers, he showed up to teach in baggy blue jeans, a worn-out T-shirt, and flip-flops (professional teachers tended to wear button-down shirts, "dressy" jeans or khaki pants, and lace-up dress shoes or good-quality leather sandals). I recall observing him teach one morning. He walked into a very talkative and rowdy class, smiling, slouching, and shuffling a little. A few students in the front row cheered a little when they saw him. A handful of them stood up and nodded, and he told them to sit down. He grinned at them, walked to the middle of the blackboard, waved his arm dramatically, threw a piece of chalk at the back of the room, and yelled, "Hey!" grinning the whole time. Much to my surprise, the students were immediately quiet. He handed the eraser to a student to clean the board and immediately began teaching.

On another occasion, I recall Yesob sitting on the bench outside the staff room with two girls from his class. They had exercise books and he was ostensibly helping them, but they giggled and laughed as they leaned over him and he smiled up at them. They called him by his nickname, and they clearly were flirting with each other, something that was typically thought to be wildly inappropriate for teachers and students. While Aron was uncomfortable with students' efforts to be familiar with him, Yesob seemed to actually like it. He cultivated these kinds of relationships with students and used them to solidify his authority in the classroom. Judging by the attentiveness of his students, Yesob's approach seemed to be working. I asked some of Yesob's students why they behaved in different ways when different teachers were in the classroom. They told me some teachers were "playing with" them. I specifically asked whether Yesob was playing with them, remembering his teaching style, which seemed playful to me. "No," they told me emphatically. "Teacher Yesob is very brilliant!"

While some classes, like Aron's, arrived at a negotiated in-between and some, like Yesob's, at a playful brilliance, still other classes fell apart entirely due to a lack of teacher authority. In the following section, I discuss one such example of a class that disintegrated into complete disorder and the implications of this. It is also important to recognize that while younger teachers had a harder time controlling their classes, even the more senior teachers were struggling with similar issues, albeit to a lesser degree.

Running for President: Performing Democracy and Disorder

The changing relationship between teachers and students had some interesting side effects. As formal and hierarchical relationships between teachers and students began to flatten, disorder emerged. Students talked loudly and joked around with each other, both in and outside the class, at times even when a teacher was present. They frequently walked out of their classrooms if a teacher was not present or was late. They then heckled students in other classes through open windows. All of this created a climate we can better understand using Mikhail Bakhtin's (1984) concept of the "carnivalesque." This notion shows how conditions in which people are out of control are not just the absence of order but important political spaces that allow for an inversion of hierarchies. Bakhtin's concept allows us to explore how power becomes inverted through disorderly conditions.

Even more significantly, amid this disorder, spaces to rethink and rework how to be national began to open up. The disorderly flag ceremony that I began this chapter with was one such example, but other examples could be found, most significantly, in classroom debates and other interactive activities. Communicative and learner-centered activities in the classroom, such as debates, discussions, and mock elections, were encouraged by the 2003 policy reforms and, thus, became more common in classrooms at this point. These types of activities resulted in disorder and an unusually out-of-control climate in the classroom, during which it was more difficult for teachers to maintain authority, but communicative activities also created an opportunity for students to think through some of the core tenets of Eritrean nationalism. For example, elsewhere I have written about how the animated climate of classroom debates enabled students to think through how to be a good Eritrean citizen by leaving the country (Riggan 2013a). These instances of the disorderly reworking of the nation were both intentional and unintentional, but regardless, they forged the beginnings of a new way of thinking about the nation and citizenship. Teachers and students together opened up spaces in the classroom to critique and debate dominant ways of thinking about Eritrea and being Eritrean. Here I focus specifically on an activity in an English class in which students were asked to pretend that they were running for president and give a speech that explained why the class should vote for them.

Simone, the grade 10 English teacher who introduced this particular activity, struggled with teaching. He was awkward in the classroom, spoke with a slight stutter, and was routinely ridiculed by his students. His difficulties came mainly from inexperience, but, like many of the younger "service" teachers, he also lacked motivation to improve his skills, and when I was not watching, I suspect he was merely trying to fill the time in the classroom. The students often complained that he was a joke, noting that he was "just playing" with them and not really teaching.

I spent several days shadowing Simone exclusively. Unlike many of the more senior teachers, who enjoyed explaining what they were trying to accomplish in the classroom when I spent the day with them, Simone was clearly uncomfortable having me around so much. During this time, he gave a grammar lesson and a test and engaged the students in what he called a "debate." Both the topic of the debate, "if you were president," and the design of the activity were vague. It was unclear to the students and to me whether the students were supposed to be pretending that they were running for president of their class or of the nation. When I asked him for clarification after the class, Simone told me that they were supposed to be running for president of the class, but I thought that all of his prompts were intended to get students to talk about what they would do for the nation, and the students themselves approached the activity this way. Although the students' unruly behavior and Simone's awkwardness prevented them from engaging deeply with the issues that surfaced during the course of the debate, this disorderly attempt to simulate democracy included a complex performance of nationalism. The class I describe below was the second of two sections in which I observed this activity. As with the first section, Simone's inability to manage the class quickly became apparent. The students were immediately playful and irreverent. What became clear in both sections, however, was that amid the carnivalesque environment created by students pretending to run for president, specific political commentary circulated.

It was close to mid-day when this class met. The school day was almost over, and the classroom extremely hot. Ceiling fans clattered noisily and did little to cool off the room. The students were restless. Simone wrote the topic "Running for President" on the board and told the students that he would select five of them to debate.

"About what?" one student called out.

"About the topic," Simone said. "About who will be the president of this year. If you don't do it, I will choose myself." No one volunteered, forcing Simone to choose one student to stand up. The student stood and then sat down again without saying anything.

Another student stood and started to say, "I . . . think. . . ."

Simone interrupted and prompted him, saying, "I would like to be a president." The student mimicked the teacher in a falsetto voice and talked about creating peace within boundaries and economic success. One student clapped slowly and loudly when he finished.

Simone made another student stand, but he promptly sat down again, like the first student. One boy left the room abruptly without permission. Simone then called on a girl. The boys in the back of the room were talking loudly among themselves, and the one who left the room came back in.

The girl Simone called on began in a loud, bold voice: "I don't want to be president of Eritrea. Because this president makes a good one." She then looked nervous and covered her mouth with shaking hands and continued, "I support this president because . . . eh . . . eh."

As soon as her words begin to falter, the other students immediately mimicked her, saying, "Eh . . . eh . . . eh . . . eh." Embarrassed, she still managed to continue. She talked about the WYDC, which engaged students in the process of building villages, and noted that these were good things. She then talked about the president's wanting democracy and peace. She hesitated often in her speech but managed to get out, "The president wants this, this peace agreement."

Other students mimicked her, saying, "This, this." At this point, she sat down giggling and could not go on. It clearly took a great deal of courage for her to stand up and make this statement, and she worked very hard to present it with as much decorum as she could muster. But in the end, despite her show of confidence, her bold attempt to get past her nervousness, and her obvious sense of conviction, which was markedly lacking in the contributions of other students, she was reduced to nervous giggles and compelled to sit down. Effectively, the raucous environment in the classroom silenced this student and her bold endorsement of the president.

After the heckling of the girl who supported the president, Simone walked around the classroom, looking stern and being ignored by the students. Another student stood and then called Simone over to him. They talked quietly for a few seconds, and then the student went to the front of the room. Simone gave him a cue to go on, saying, "I would like to be. . . ."

A boy in back mimicked Simone in a loud high-pitched voice, "I would like to be a president."

A girl in front similarly mimicked, "I would like to be Eritrean government."

The student at the front, seemingly earnest, began, "Okay. Students," he said in a loud, clear, booming voice. "My name is Abdu, and I would like to talk my life." All students laughed raucously and mimicked him, and he sat down instantly.

Another student then stood up and talked quietly. This time, the students did not mimic him. No one interrupted or heckled him, but it was quite possible that this was because no one could hear him. In contrast to the previous student, he spoke so quietly and the rest of the class was making so much noise that it was impossible to hear what he was saying.

Another boy stood up and made his contribution. Although there was noise in the class and it was hard to hear him, he was able to finish. He said that a president should focus on peace and development; however, he made his own stance on the current president clear by differentiating himself with his concluding words: "I wouldn't like to be president, but I would like to say to this president that he [should] build schools and clinics in this country and to use properly natural resources and to import or export things." This student's rather direct critique seemed to change the tone of the class. His words seemed to encourage some students to resist participating even more, but they also led a few others to abandon the façade of "running for president" and instead to simply critique the current president.

The remainder of the class oscillated between student reticence, loud talking, and mockery and outright critique of Eritrea's president. Students continued participating when compelled to. Simone continued trying desperately to get them to contribute to the class. Some were sleeping on their desks. He was having a very difficult time getting anyone to say anything. One student directly refused to participate, saying, "The question is who will be the president of this year? I don't think I will be the president of this year."

Finally, after much effort on Simone's part, one boy stood and read from a paper, "I don't want to be president, but I would like to say to [the] president that the country needs more knowledge and there are no schools in many villages."

Another student followed him, and, after much imploring from Simone, said, "When we see the days and years of [President] Isaias [Afewerki], it is thirteen years, but when we think of this, these are very important days.

These thirteen years, there are more different problems—lack of medicine and hospitals and foods. We see so many travel from our country to our boundaries because of lack of food and water. So, I say to the coming president to see what is very bad and to make it better." As with the previous few students, this student seemed to level a critique at President Isaias rather than advocate for himself as president.

Simone seemed to realize the turn that the class was taking and tried to get the activity back on track, saying, "Try to talk about yourself. About what you will do as a president. Talk about the economy."

In response, a student answered, "Yes, we talk about the economy over the last years." Some students laughed, but many ignored him. The bell rang, and the class ended rather abruptly. Students barely gave Simone and me a chance to leave the room before crowding out behind us, some of them jumping out of the open windows.

It is impossible to fully ascertain the motivations of the students through the course of this debate, and clearly many things were going on simultaneously. Students were critiquing the president and the economic and political conditions in the country. At the same time, their ridicule of the activity itself likely reflected their amusement at the fact that they were being asked to "run for president" in a country that was decidedly not a democracy. Many students were also simply taking advantage of a teacher with poor classroom-management skills to have some fun at the end of the day. This was a mockery of the class, the teacher, the activity, and the president himself.

Whether the heckling students intended to mock President Isaias or to make fun of their English class or teacher, what is significant and clear here is that what should have been sacred—the order of the class, a mock election for president, and especially a commentary on the president himself—was no longer sacred. What Teacher Simone accomplished here, albeit unwittingly and by virtue of his novice performance as a teacher, was to create a classroom climate in which the person of the president and the performance of political debate could be transformed by students into a subject of mockery and ridicule. Indeed, the disorderly climate of the classroom and the fact that the teacher had no authority enabled a mockery of the president, whether it was intentional or not. These disorderly conditions made it possible for students to undermine the teacher's authority and the sanctity of the classroom as a space of orderly hierarchies. They inverted power and, in the process, challenged the president's authority.

While it was a somewhat extreme example of disorder, Teacher Simone's class was certainly not unique. As I noted above, a carnivalesque climate had taken hold across the school. In this particular "carnival," typical norms of classroom behavior altered to produce a chaotic environment, but these radically changing norms also emboldened students to say things that may not have been "safe" to say in other contexts. Bakhtin's (1984) notion of the carnivalesque illuminates the social and political work enabled by disorder. Bakhtin (1984) and others have noted that the carnival locates its participants in a space where norms, rules, and authority are overturned (Mbembe 2001; Woldemikael 2009). As I noted above, a celebratory atmosphere tended to accompany communicative activities. Students became very enthusiastic and engaged, and, as the activity progressed, behaviors tended to get more and more raucous until the teacher or moderator typically gave up any attempt at control. Debates created a space in which the norms for student behavior were more flexible, but they also created a space where broader power relations could be commented on. As the classroom atmosphere became more out of control, students' comments became bolder and more outrageous, as if the suspension of classroom-based rules and hierarchies enabled students to suspend other forms of social censure. Drawing on Bakhtin, Achille Mbembe (2001) shows that quite often under conditions of authoritarianism in Africa, ruler and ruled render each other impotent as the ruled engage in practices of vulgarity, ribaldry, and ridicule oriented toward mocking the ruler, but doing so in a manner that will be largely imperceptible. Similarly, the activity described above turned the president from a sacred figure into an object of laughter. In this process, official power is transformed into something ridiculous but not stripped of its power. At the same time, while stripping power-holders of their sacredness and legitimacy, those engaged in this mockery are not particularly empowering themselves. A condition of mutual impotence in which neither the power-holders nor the disempowered have legitimacy or moral authority ensues.

At the same time, serious opinions were conveyed in the midst of this carnivalesque climate. Whether or not students intended to do so, this activity revealed the reworking of Eritrean nationalism in several ways. First, the activity provided students with a forum in which they could critique or praise the direction the country was going in. Students were given a rare public chance to be engaged civic actors. But at the same time, students knew that the idea of running for president in a nondemocratic country was a game. The activity itself highlighted this. Students mocked the performance of being democratic because the possibility of real democracy was ridiculous in the context of a country where unquestioning obedience was clearly the operable expectation for how one should enact sacrificial citizenship.

Students also reworked the meaning of being Eritrean by critiquing the president himself. In many respects, nationalism was articulated through their attitudes toward President Isaias. In many dictatorships, a cult of personality emerges such that the nation's ruler symbolically represents the nation itself (Wedeen 1999). The leader not only leads the country but also embodies it. In Eritrea, as I have noted earlier, there does not exist the same extreme cult of personality that is found in many other dictatorships. One does not see pictures of Isaias Afewerki in every home or monuments depicting the president's figure. As I noted in Chapter 1, the president has always depicted himself and been depicted as a sort of everyman, but being seen as one of the people does not preclude his being sacred. Even in the absence of a cult of personality that would exalt the image and the body of the president, the stance that one takes toward Isaias Afewerki defines one's stance toward the country, and, more specifically, the ruling party. To this day, many Eritreans (particularly in the diaspora) continue to admire him and trust him to take care of the country. Others may be disillusioned with the president and ruling party but still have a "grudging admiration" for his skill at consolidating the state and maintaining a certain kind of stability (Reid 2009; see also Müller 2012a, 2012b). But still others are tremendously angry with him and express a sense that he has betrayed the nation. Expressions of anger or even outright hatred toward the president were not unheard of during the course of my fieldwork. Even in the absence of a reverent worshipful stance toward the figure of the president, to most Eritreans, Isaias Afewerki is the face of The Struggle, the party, and the nation. He is the essence of the *tegadalai*. Thus, to critique President Isaias is not only to critique the party and its version of nationalism but also to dislodge the centrality of The Struggle itself. To critique him under the auspices of a mock election is to critique his self-proclaimed right to rule the country without being duly elected and to critique a version of nationalism that asserts the legitimacy and necessity of his doing so. Interactive and communicative activities, such as the one described in this chapter, thus enabled students to question meanings of Eritrean nationalism by questioning the authority of the president, who stood in for the nation itself. However, disorder, which both enabled the critique and left the meaning of the critique ambivalent, was also a significant factor. The debate raised questions and challenged the tacit notion that being Eritrean could be equated with tacit support for the president, the party, and fighters.

"Civics Is a Very Nice Subject"

Another way in which national narratives were reworked was through teacher commentary on the teaching, or rather nonteaching, of civics. Like the instances of the classroom debate above, conditions of disorder are integral to the critique of civics. If we see schooling as part of the process of ritually producing national citizens, then we might see the civics curriculum as the sacred teachings of the nation. As I noted in the last chapter, when I asked administrators in leadership posts in the Ministry of Education, who were often former fighters, how education instilled national identities in students, they often immediately referenced the civics curriculum. However, the actual teaching of civics was befuddled by disorderly conditions, and teacher attitudes toward civics were less than reverent.

When I asked the social science teachers about the civics class, they would invariably say, "Civics is a very nice subject" and then break out into laughter. The answer did not vary much, nor did the laughter. Civics, it appeared, had become a collective joke among teachers. During the two years of my fieldwork, I tried many times to observe a civics class. Civics, after all, was the subject that contained the most explicit messages about nationalism and citizenship, but, somewhat ironically, it was one of the least consistently taught subjects. The civics curriculum defines the attributes of Eritrean national "character," describes the structure of government that should be in place, and clearly details a role for students in building the nation. Given this, it was striking that civics was a joke among teachers and seldom taught.

Textbooks play an extraordinarily powerful role in defining national narratives and creating a blueprint for national identity; however, to truly understand the production of nationalism, national duty, and national subjects in schools, it is also necessary to go beyond the written text and explore what is done, or not done, with these texts. In Assab, I found not only that it was impossible to observe a civics lesson because the subject was so seldom taught but also that the only available copy of the civics curriculum was a dog-eared photocopy that a teacher agreed to lend to me for a few hours for research purposes. Text can be a powerful tool to shape collective historical memory and a common sense of national belonging and character, but it is important to explore not only *what* texts say about the nation but also *how* they are taught or, in this case, why they may not be taught.

In Chapter 1, I discussed parts of the grade 6 civics curriculum in more detail. It outlines the Eritrean national character and orients it around qualities of "fortitude" and willingness to sacrifice and be an obedient and disciplined child, student, and worker. The grade 7 civics curriculum reprises many of the characteristics of being a good, patriotic Eritrean but deemphasizes elements of character somewhat and, instead, focuses on educating students about government and governance. Among other things, it includes a unit that outlines various civil rights that are "commonly put into constitutions," such as freedom of assembly, the right to vote and run for election, the right to leave the country, the right to live and work anywhere in the country, the right to due process, and the right to equality (Ministry of Education, CRDI 1995).

The irony of these rights being listed in the Eritrean civics curriculum is not lost on teachers and students, who are, of course, well aware that most of these rights are not guaranteed in Eritrea. Given the content of the civics curriculum and the political realities of Eritrea, it seems obvious why teachers would laugh knowingly and say, with irony, "Civics is a nice subject" every time I asked about the curriculum. But the humor they derived from the question about civics teaching and the statement "Civics is a nice subject" had a number of additional meanings.

The following excerpts from my field notes convey the general sentiments that teachers had about the civics curriculum:

> In the staff room, when I ask about the civics curriculum, Beraki says, "Civics is a very nice subject" in a tone that I can't quite read. Haile passes through and hears what we are talking about and says, "Oh, civics is a nice subject" and exchanges a glance with Beraki. So finally I ask what makes it nice. They laugh and exchange knowing glances again. Beraki says there are some stories that the students like. He tells me that the things they learn are things they already know, like respecting your elders. Then he says that there are also some political things, "a lot of things about 'The Struggle,' but you can just ignore those and teach the other things." (Field notes, April 2005)

On another occasion, Paolo articulated the political nature of his feelings about teaching civics even more clearly:

> When I ask Paolo about teaching civics, he laughs and says, "It's very nice, but not realistic." I ask why it is that every time I bring up the civics curriculum, everyone says, genuinely, "Oh, civics is very nice," and then they start laughing. Paolo tells me that the subjects—democracy, elections, the constitution—are very nice in theory, but everyone knows that it is not realistic now, which is why they laugh. "The theory is nice and it is nice to teach the theory, but it isn't done in practice, so they laugh." Then Paolo says that he doesn't even know what the election and parliament system in this country is supposed to be. (Field notes, April 2005)

The statement "Civics is a nice subject" had several meanings. At one level, teachers actually thought that civics was nice for the students. The idea of teaching about patriotism and how to be a good student and citizen appealed to them. They noted that "students enjoyed" the subject, and that, unlike the other subjects, it was easy, familiar, and fun for the students. It resonated with their identity and felt good. But the statement "Civics is a nice subject" was also deeply ironic. On the one hand, the civics curriculum articulated the official stance that the root of Eritrean national character emerged from The Struggle and its preoccupation with sacrificing for the nation. The fact that reverence for The Struggle was waning and that people were tiring of hearing about sacrifice was reflected in Beraki's comment. Some parts of the curriculum *were* "nice"—the ones about values and discipline and student character—but some should be skipped, such as the ones about The Struggle. Meanwhile, the civics curriculum was also a living testament to where the nation should have been on its trajectory toward political development. It outlined an ideal of democracy and civil liberties that everyone had hoped for but saw little evidence of. The curriculum still existed, even though the trajectory toward elections and implementation of the constitution had been abandoned. Teaching these topics only served as a reminder of this abandoned trajectory.

The statement "Civics is a nice subject" also reflected the irony that little priority was given to the actual teaching of civics, despite the fact that its messages were so integral to the party's understandings of how students would learn to be national. Civics was seldom taught, and, in fact, teachers often refused to teach the subject. In the Senior Secondary School, civics seemed largely forgotten and did not even appear on the course schedule. In the Junior Secondary School, students in grades 6 and 7 were scheduled to take civics, but teachers refused to teach it because it was not their subject and their workloads were already too heavy. Most teachers at one point or another had been compelled to teach civics but later refused. For example, in the Junior Secondary School in 2003, math and history teachers for grades 6 and 7 taught civics for several weeks, but they promptly decided to stop teaching it in protest when a new teacher was assigned to the school and had a lighter course load but was not assigned to teach civics. Thus, when teachers laughed about civics, they were laughing, somewhat defiantly, at the circumstances that surrounded the teaching of civics itself and complaining that no teacher was designated to teach it. No one was willing to take responsibility for teaching civics. Indeed, teachers all believed that it was not their duty to teach the subject, given that many were overloaded with teaching classes in their regular subjects. Laughter was a form of defiant distancing from the responsibility to teach a subject that, while important in theory, was thought to be rather worthless in practice.

Given that the civics curriculum was intended to define the national character, culture, and moral bearing; spell out citizenship rights and duties; and articulate the values—sacred teachings—of The Struggle, we might expect more reverence for civics either from teachers themselves or from administrators responsible for ensuring civics was taught. The civics curriculum instead was a place where the disorder of things was clearly revealed. Everyone seemed to have abandoned it. Civics was at once an embodiment of the Struggle-centric nationalism of the party and an ironic joke. It presented "nice stories" about the nation, but these stories were selectively taught within a disorderly context in which there was no textbook, no teacher allocated permanently to the subject, and seldom a teacher who could be convinced to teach. This combination of disorder and irreverence for the narratives of The Struggle became reflective of the overall condition of disorder in Eritrean schools and, indeed, a sense of impotence in the nation overall.

Communitas and the Negotiated Production of the Educated Citizen

Throughout this chapter, I have given several examples of the ways in which schools produced the nation but not reverence for it. Schools were supposed to produce a sense of reverence, worship, awe, and love for the nation, and yet students refused to comply with the rituals. At the same time, teachers—the state actors assigned to enforce compliance with these rituals and ritualized structures—were often complicit with students in their refusal to comply. In this process, disorder created openings through which to rethink the nation in schools.

If National Service/schooling was supposed to be a liminal space in which young people were transformed into ideal Eritrean educated persons/citizens/soldiers, this process failed when it was no longer clear that National Service was something that was passed *through* and, instead, became an endless stage of subservience to the government. At the time of my fieldwork, limitless liminality had captured the lives of teachers and would soon subsume the lives of their students, who would not pass through National Service but rather get stuck in it. In such a situation, it is hardly surprising that the microrituals of schooling also fell apart, making the very process of becoming national a mockery of itself. As schools were coopted into the machinery of conscription, they also became spaces of limitless liminality, something shown most clearly through the difficulty they had actually starting each year. Liminality played out in more subtle ways in the everyday life of schools as well and was manifest in student lateness, truancy, and chronic misbehavior. A sense of communitas between students and teachers (sometimes cultivated, as in the case of Yesob, and sometimes imposed on teachers by students, as in the cases of Aron and Simone) partially replaced the hierarchical authority that should have enabled teachers to maintain discipline and order. This sense of communitas between teachers and students was encapsulated through student comments that teachers were "playing with" them. In turn, students "played" with their teachers, a behavior that altered the classroom climate from disciplinary and ordered to disordered. Disorder and the carnivalesque environment it produced enabled students to take what was sacred—lessons, learning, teacher authority—and profane it by mocking it. In the classroom, power was inverted, but when power was inverted in these contexts, other sacred objects, such as the president of the country himself, were also subject to mockery, giving rise to an open political critique. Another inversion was present in teachers' refusal to teach civics and their jokes about civics being a "nice subject." Just as a political commentary that made the president less than sacred emerged from students' comments about running for president in their English class, a commentary on the values of The Struggle and the party version of Eritrean nationalism emerged from teachers' comments on the teaching of civics.

The condition of limitless liminality was itself a by-product of National Service and the government's nation-making project. But instead of producing national subjects willing to sacrifice and suffer obediently for the state, the effects of this nation-making program were inverted. Just as Eritreans tried to escape the coercive reach of *gifa*, when schools became a mechanism to conscript, teachers and students began evading schooling. This does not mean that schools failed to produce national subjects, but rather that they produced national subjects differently than the official nation-making project required. Just as imaginaries of the punishing state erased nationalist discourses of honorable sacrifice and service, thereby undermining the government's nation-building project, resistance to school-based rituals and routines recast the official version of the nation as something other than what was intended.

This negotiation, subversion, and mocking of rituals transformed being an educated, national subject into something fundamentally different. At the same time, mocking sacred national ideals ultimately left the state project intact, if illegitimate. Lacking legitimacy, the project became coercive, revealing, once again, the vicious cycle of coercion, evasion, and impotence.

It is particularly significant that this vicious cycle of coercion and evasion played out in schools, which are the state institution best situated to produce national subjects and socialize citizens. The increasingly carnivalesque nature of the classroom and school reflected not an outright rejection of the ideal of becoming an educated citizen but a confused renegotiation of the meaning of doing so. Through this renegotiation, the meaning of being national turned from a statement—Eritreans are like this—into a question: What are we like? The assumption that students should serve and sacrifice for their country embedded in official narratives of being Eritrean were turned into a sometimes-comical conversation about the appropriateness of service, the validity of the stories of The Struggle, and a critique of the president's job. Meanwhile, teachers did have a vision for what educated people should be like; even while teachers themselves were undermining authority in schools, they were also seeking to reinforce this vision through a series of coercive and even violent processes that are the subject of the next chapter.

5

The Teacher State

Morality and Everyday Sovereignty over Schools

A Tale of Two Walls

The Junior Secondary School compound was surrounded on three sides by a wall topped with broken glass and by the Red Sea on the other. This was a relatively small compound, and most of the school and students were within eyesight of a teacher, guard, or administrator at all times. Yet the wall had not been doing a particularly good job of keeping students in place. Large numbers of students had been drifting in late or fleeing from the school compound during the day. Students in the Junior Secondary School were supposed to not only remain in the school during school hours but also have their time and behavior regulated. In early November 2004, teachers could no longer stand the lack of control they had over students. For a week, they warned students that they would lock the school gate promptly at 7:20 and that any latecomers would not be allowed in. On the appointed day and time, the school gate was locked, preventing approximately forty students from entering. The students who were locked out were in an uproar. They began yelling and banging on the gate. Some threw rocks at the school. Determined not to let them in but knowing he could not allow this disturbance to continue, the school director called the police. When the police arrived, the students dispersed, but a handful were arrested and spent up to two nights in jail.

While the director and teachers of the Junior Secondary School were barring its gates against latecomers and calling on the police to help defend the school walls, down the road, the Senior Secondary School was having its own struggles over walls. This school's compound was not enclosed, a situation that had become a source of great frustration for teachers. It was a large compound containing two football fields, a basketball court, and several unused buildings. The school could not afford to enclose the compound with the type of concrete wall that surrounded most Eritrean schools, so students and others could move freely in and out. Teachers constantly complained that because of the lack of enclosure, they could not enforce rules about arriving on time or attending classes. Students often cut class or disrupted other classes. The school director came up with a possible solution: Used shipping containers were donated to the Senior Secondary School and set up to enclose the compound. However, teachers quickly realized that they did not solve the problem. The makeshift walls were easy to climb, students could slip through gaps between the containers, and the compound's large size made it impossible to police. The walls were porous.

Both scenarios reflect teachers' preoccupation with containment and enclosure and with having the power to determine who belonged inside and outside. In the former case, teachers' preoccupation with containment was so powerful that it led teachers, who were themselves subject to state coercion and the arbitrary use of force by the state, to subject their students to a similar type of arbitrary force. This action, while clearly relying on the force of law (the police), was extra-legal and, therefore, a good example of Giorgio Agamben's (2005) notion of the state of exception. In the latter case, teachers' preoccupation with containment led them to extreme, but ultimately futile, ingenuity. Both cases were responses to teachers' decisions that it was time to retake control of their schools.

This preoccupation with enclosing school compounds was reflective of the logics of encampment. The camp, according to Agamben (1998), is a political space that is contained for the purposes of disciplining individuals and managing populations (see also Gupta 2012). The entire country of Eritrea functions according to these camplike logics, contained—its borders sealed—to biopolitically produce a mass of soldier citizens.[1] Camps are a particular manifestation of sovereign control over population and territory that is demarcated by a space of exception, in which the full force of the law exists under conditions in which there is no law (Agamben 2005). Indeed, Eritrean citizens enclosed within the country had few rights guaranteed by law at the time of my fieldwork.[2]

Within the larger national camp were a series of smaller camps—for example, the military camps that dappled the entire country. Furthermore, the prohibitions on moving freely throughout the country meant that each town often felt very camplike. Like military camps and the nationwide camp, school spaces were enclosed for the purpose of discipline, but discipline to a very different end—to produce educated citizens. One of the logics of many types of camps, including schools, is that force can be used against those within the camp with impunity. Building on Carl Schmitt ([1922] 2005), Agamben (1998: 173) notes, "The camp is the space of this absolute impossibility of deciding between fact and law, rule and application, exception and rule, which nevertheless incessantly decides between them," and yet someone has to make these impossible, incessant decisions—the one who "decides on the exception" is the sovereign. Within the space of Eritrean schools, teachers decided on these exceptions and were sovereign over school space and student bodies.

Many scholars have begun to reexamine sovereignty from an actor-centered perspective, arguing that the conventional definitions of sovereignty need to be expanded to look at the work of particular agents in producing sovereignty in a variety of specific locales (Chalfin 2010; Gupta 2012; Herzfeld 1997). Conventionally, sovereignty references the state's right to exert control over its territory and population. It demarcates a nation-state as a distinct entity and sets the terms for its interactions with other nation-states. Sovereignty allocates the right to delineate borders and to control what happens to populations residing within those borders. But, as with other functions of the state, sovereignty is performed in everyday encounters between subjects and citizens. One omission in Agamben's analysis of devolved sovereignty is that it does not allow for an examination of the agency of actors to whom sovereignty devolves.[3] His work falls short of explaining how and why everyday sovereigns enact sovereignty the way they do. As Caroline Humphrey (2007: 433) notes, Schmitt and Agamben's notion of sovereignty "fails to take account of what the ordinary participants bring to the equation. Their everyday life 'throws in' its own exigencies and excitements. These burst beyond the confines of the notion of sovereignty and qualify it by responding to a different logic."

Exploring teachers as sovereign over school space and student bodies complicates Agamben's framework of devolved sovereignty, because teachers bring their own morality, beliefs, and experiences to bear on their decisions about how schools should run. In seeking to contain and discipline students, teachers tried to transform students into their ideal of educated citizens.[4] Their decisions to use coercion, violence, and force, while not quite the same as those of other state actors, may illuminate and help us understand the confluence of prejudices, stereotypes, ideologies, and beliefs that frames decisions to use violence and force among other types of state actors, such as police, military personnel, and bureaucrats. My exploration of teacher sovereignty shows that debates over what it meant to make moral subjects and how to produce such subjects were central to their processes of deciding on the exception—or, in other words, deciding on the appropriate use of force. Building a makeshift wall, locking students out, and calling the police on students were extreme actions that teachers viewed as necessary because they believed that schools were facing a moral crisis that they had little support from the Ministry of Education and parents in resolving. The preoccupation with walls reflected anxieties about their loss of sovereignty at a time of moral crisis. At times, it appeared that teachers believed that their efforts were all that prevented society from falling apart.

In their efforts to claim sovereignty over school spaces and student bodies, teachers were the state, but their *being* the state was shaped by the intersection of how they *saw* or imagined the state (often as inept and at other times as punishing), *saw like* the state (or imagined order, civilization, progress, and their role in bringing it about), and *were seen as* the state (or, in other words, were imagined to be the state by students and parents). The fact that teachers acted *as* the state but not *for* the state raises questions about the locus of the state, even, or perhaps especially, in a place like Eritrea, where the state is thought of as centralized and all-powerful but often operates on the basis of personal decisions by state actors themselves. When acting as the state, teachers responded not only to their own sense of morality—a morality deeply wrapped up with their sense of duty to build a better nation and the ideals of discipline, obedience, and authority—but also to their sense of being abandoned by the state. Additionally, their being the state was in constant tension with parent and student imaginaries of what the state should be.

Much of this book has focused on how teachers were coerced by other state actors, policies, and processes. As a result, teachers behaved evasively along with students and thus were complicit in producing the disorder that they found so problematic. Teachers also attempted to reorder the school in the face of disorder and felt a moral imperative to do so. This chapter specifically sheds light on how and why teachers chose to use coercion, force, and violence when acting as the state. One of my key emphases here is that teacher debates over what constituted this moral imperative were built on clashing notions about obedience and authority over young people. The first half of this chapter shows how the preoccupation with containing school space reflected that moral imperative. Walls not only served to protect and defend sovereign space—in this case, sovereign school space—but also enabled processes of categorization and sorting. Walls also demarcated spaces in which teachers had authority and could set the rules, define appropriate behavior, manage their students and classes as they saw fit, and, if need be, punish. But despite the fact that within this enclosed space of the school teachers acted with impunity, they still responded to moral logics—logics that often varied among teachers and required debating and negotiating what it meant to produce educated citizens. With this in mind, the latter half of the chapter turns to a discussion of corporal punishment, where these debates became particularly pointed, to show how competing notions of punishment, obedience, and authority were contested among teachers. As teachers debated what was "good" for students, they attempted to act on an ethos of care, but some students and parents experienced what teachers took to be forms of caring as arbitrary acts of violence. The intermingling of—and ambiguity between—caring and violence is not only reflective of a state of exception where no clear laws or policies govern the use of force but also manifests the maddening state in which the benevolent state is inextricable from the malevolent one.

The Work of Walls: Controlled Spaces

There were several interrelated components of the work of walls. Walls enabled *control* by creating spaces that could be contained and enforced. Walls created clear divisions between and around spaces, which was essential because space indexed and defined morality, discerning good from bad spaces and people. Walls were also tightly linked to notions of sorting. Below, I talk about each of these components of the work of walls: control, morality, and sorting.

In the quotation below, Teacher Woldemikael reminisces about his own schooling and the value placed on a well-contained, well-controlled school:

> [My high school] in Addis [Ababa] was very nice compared to this one. . . . [T]here was a lot of staff. There is the director, unit leaders, typists, secretaries, storekeepers, guards, many people. The school was *well fenced* with good classrooms. Many classrooms. It was *guarded. A guard by himself has great authority. He has the power to let you in and out. He can even punish you.* He had that power even. If you are beaten by a guard, you will not say anything. *Unit leaders are highly respected. You will not stay in front of them.* He controls the students . . . the whole students. We have two campuses in our school, and he could control the whole campus. *We had three [unit*

> leaders]. They were all very respected. If you see him in the street, you will run away. Run away! If they see classes not occupied by teachers, they will do something. (Interview, Woldemikael; emphasis added)

A "nice" school, according to Woldemikael, was a school that had resources devoted to keeping students in and making sure that they behaved respectfully while inside. There was not only a fence but also a whole range of school personnel situated as authority figures. Even the guard, typically a powerful but uneducated and, therefore, lower-status school employee, had the power to make determinations of who could get in and who could not, thereby regulating and determining who was and was not worthy of being inside school space. Students knew that it was their role to obediently accept and respect this wide array of authority figures. As we can see from Woldemikael's description of his own "nice" school, the notion of a contained (fenced and guarded) school is closely linked with notions of control, respect/fear, and punishment, which are, at one level, prevalent in all forms of modern schooling but are also culturally specific principles in Eritrea.

The management of space was thought to be central to maintaining control. Properly managed spaces, such as those described above, were thought to enable control and thus were key to socializing students properly. Teachers idealized the concept of "control," which referred to specific practices of managing and regulating students. "Control" referred to a process of making expectations about behaviors and norms clear and finding persuasive ways to hold people accountable to those expectations. One teacher defined control as denoted by the pairing of "expectations" and "inspections"—or, in other words, clear rules and policies and a means to monitor and hold students accountable for these expectations. In Tigrinya, the concept of "control" links two interrelated words, both of which translate into "control" in English—*m'kutsitsar* and *m'elay*. *M'elay* means "to manage" or "to guide" and has the more positive connotation of guiding a flock of sheep. Thus *m'elay* tends to refer to the positive, "guiding" work, such as the gentle regulation and management of school space, students, and classrooms. It would be considered ideal practice under "normal" conditions. *M'kutsitsar*, on the other hand, literally means to check up on, thus addressing a more assertive form of control, as one research subject told me. The meaning embedded in *m'kutsitsar* assumes that something is going wrong, or will go wrong, that needs to be corrected through "controlling" activities. *M'kutsitsar* as a more active form of control refers to actions that must be taken when there is a problem to correct or to prevent a problem from arising. Taken together, the two forms of control refer to practices of good management. Teachers suggested that, just as students needed to be controlled to behave appropriately and therefore learn, teachers themselves also needed to be controlled by the administration. Through talking about the ways in which schools and teachers ought to be controlled, teachers constructed a set of ideals of how schools should function through clear and consistent hierarchies and systems of accountability. Walls were key to making this happen.

In contrast to Woldemikael's idealization of the resources devoted to containment in his own childhood, below Iyasu describes the problems caused by the lack of a wall in the Senior Secondary School. The lack of a wall indicated that the school was not attractive or controlled. He complains about the lack of a wall in the quotation below and explains what it indicates about the school:

> Still, the school doesn't have any wall around the compound, and the number of students coming from rural areas . . . is increasing. So we cannot treat those students with the experience we have or with that infrastructure of the school. Our canteen, if you observe, should be good, and there should be some kind of gates that can keep the students in the compound, and actually we are lucky in that aspect. We have a lot of space, but we should rearrange these things and motivate the students to use this compound. Making the school compound more attractive would motivate the students to not go outside. My belief is that this will help the good environment. Then I believe that no one would be motivated to go outside. (Interview, Iyasu)

Iyasu linked motivating students with having an attractive space as well as having a "gate," better "infrastructure," and a contained compound. Interestingly, he also suggested that these provisions were particularly necessary in light of the increased number of students "from the rural areas," which was a reference to the Afar students in the schools. As I discuss in more detail below, Afar/rural students were thought of as less socialized in the ways of schooling and particularly in need of controlled space. As Iyasu suggested, many teachers believed that, due to the large number of students "from the rural areas," containment and a positive school space were essential to control them because teachers did not have the experience to "treat" or teach them. Similarly, at the time of my fieldwork, in light of the lack of "bright future" for the students, teachers generally thought that self-discipline was on the decline and that external discipline was necessary. Walls, thus, were thought to be essential not just to keep students in the school but to regulate external influences. One component of the work of walls thus was to create not only a controlled and controllable space but also a nice, motivating space, a civilizing space of sorts. Teachers' attitudes about space and order here were reminiscent of James Scott's (1998) discussions of the production of orderly spaces as one component of what he calls high modernist ideology and "seeing like a state." Similar to the state-planned cities and villages that Scott (1998) discusses, teachers derived their understandings of space, order, and control from ideological assumptions of what constituted modernity. Space for teachers was also a means to index and define morality; "good" people were in "good" spaces, or in spaces where they belonged. To do their work, schools needed to both be "good" spaces and keep students in, protecting them from bad influences, so that they would become "good" people.

Good and Bad Places: Moralizing Space and Spatializing Morality

Space was deeply moral and moralizing, as I describe below. Morality, as it is understood in Eritrea, is not so much about moral lessons, language, or content but is embodied in practice (Mahmood 2005; Zigon 2008). Resonating with Pierre Bourdieu and Jean Claude Passeron's (1990) notion of habitus and Michel De Certeau's (1984) conceptualization of the "practice of everyday life," Jarrett Zigon (2008) depicts morality as "embodied dispositions" (see also Bourdieu 1977). One's morality is apparent through the way one behaves rather than through one's beliefs. One is moral because one acts in the right way. Teachers envisioned moral students as embodying discipline, diligence, and hard work, but moral students also knew how to maintain a particular set of relations with authority and understood how to engage in everyday performances that indicated respect. These performances required knowing where to be and not to be and how to act in particular places and, thus, were highly spatial.

Teachers' moral coding of space and the morally transformative power they ascribed to certain spaces resonated with Mary Douglas's ([1966] 1984) notions of purity and impurity. Anxieties about purity often emerge at times of categorical indistinctness—for example, during the liminal phase, which, as I illustrated in the previous chapter, had become an endless condition in Eritrea. Morality is also incarnated through notions of cleanliness that are equated with order and care versus uncleanliness that is equated with disorder and chaos. The profound moral distinctions between states of purity/cleanliness and impurity/disorder index a much broader array of concepts (Douglas [1966] 1984). For example, as Douglas notes, that which is clean or pure often comes to represent hope, development, civilization, and progress. According to Eritrean teachers, "good" spaces for students were ordered spaces that were well cared for and controlled, as I noted above. In contrast, "bad" spaces were spaces where disorder reigned and where no one was "controlling" students. The space of the school was supposed to be not only ordered and clean but also emblematic of progress. In contrast, in other spaces, students were not monitored and "good things" were not taught to them.

Teachers' imagined geography of the town of Assab illuminates these categories of moral and immoral spaces and makes clear which categories of people were allowed to be in certain spaces. Through this imagined geography, teachers effectively articulated a sense that there were clear, student-free zones. Morality was articulated through the ascription of value to particular spaces, but this was only one valence of the imagined morality of space. Space was also thought to have the capacity to *make* people moral or immoral largely because certain spaces were more controlled. Teachers' memories of their own schooling or their earlier years of teaching more often than not provided an outline of their moral imaginary of school space. These accounts, in most cases, tended to create a somewhat idealized portrait of a time when schools were better controlled and students were acting like students.[5]

Teacher B'ruk, who grew up in Assab, depicts this imagined geography of moral and immoral spaces and explains the implications of students finding themselves in the "wrong" space in response to my asking during an interview about the school he attended:

> When I was grade 9, we were very disciplined. Up to grade 11 and 12, I would not enter into any tea room that had a teacher in it. Especially in Campo Sudan or Assab Kebir. No student would go to that area. Because of the bars and tea rooms, that area was a bad area. No lady was wandering around that area. So you would never see a student either. The teacher didn't do anything if he saw a student, but the student would feel bad. At that time, not only my mother controlled me, but the place, the society controlled me. But now it's different. Then, I didn't observe students going to [tea shops] in Seghir or anything. Then, no one would sell students tea, because they knew. But now, they sell them tea. (Interview, B'ruk)

B'ruk equated discipline with avoiding certain spaces, thus drawing a clear line between a moral imaginary of a disciplined student and a division of public space. The disciplined students would not find themselves in a public space with their teacher. Furthermore, B'ruk articulated an imagined geography of the town of Assab, distinguishing its "bad" areas. These bad areas, Campo Sudan and Assab Kebir, are neighborhoods in Assab noted for having many bars and tea rooms. Although many students lived in these areas, they had a bad reputation because sailors and truck drivers frequented them when Assab still functioned as Ethiopia's main port; they had a reputation as places where people drank too much, got into fights, and could find prostitutes. Magnus Treiber's (2010) comparison of good and bad bars in the capital city, Asmara, and the different social groups attracted to these bars reflects a similarly imagined spatial geography. According to Treiber (2010: 11), so-called clean bars are typically recently renovated, more expensive, and places where people go to socialize rather than to drink heavily. Clean, therefore, is often equated with civilized, tempered behavior and modernity. In contrast, "bad" bars are not renovated and, like Assab's bars in Campo Sudan and Assab Kebir, are reputed to be dangerous, dark, and in a state of disrepair.

B'ruk also noted in his response to me how this separation of spaces was maintained. It was not teachers who upheld this moral ordering of space. Indeed, he went out of his way to note that a teacher "wouldn't do anything" if he saw a student. Rather, a student behaving improperly would have an internalized sense of shame for entering the same space as a respected adult. Similarly, other teachers commented that if students saw an authority figure, like a teacher, while outside in a public space, they would be "afraid" and would "run away." In Tigrinya, the notion of fear is often linked with shyness or embarrassment and is a characteristic that is often valued, particularly for those that are supposed to be subservient, such as students. Students should be appropriately fearful, or shy, when they encounter teachers in public spaces. Fear not only indicates respect and deference for authorities when a student encounters them in unexpected spaces but is also produced through notions of authority based on maintaining hierarchies and distinctions between student and nonstudent spaces. Another key point that B'ruk made was that a properly functioning society would help keep students "in their place" by not selling things to them when they were out of place (i.e., not in school). B'ruk lamented that shop owners sold students tea, which he saw as a violation of the separation of spaces and an indication that society was not helping students understand where and what their place was.

This same moralization of space applied to teachers as well. Some teachers described their own moral transformation when they became teachers. This transformation involved not only changing behaviors but also, more importantly, choosing to occupy only certain spaces that were regarded as morally appropriate for a teacher. Woldemikael noted that when he became a teacher, he could no longer "go everywhere." Because he had to be respected as a teacher, he had to limit the kinds of places that he frequented. Instead of going to smaller bars in some of the seedier areas of town, he went to the "big hotels," which were thought to be more respectable and were places where he was not likely to run into his students. Woldemikael also noted that as a teacher, he had to start spending more time at home as well. Home, of course, is the most moral space of all. Students are supposed to spend most of their time in the home engaged in the moral activities of reading and working. Woldemikael had become "like a student," mostly staying home and engaging in these activities.

Schools not only were coded as good, moral spaces where "good" students could be found but were also thought to have a moralizing influence. As Iyasu notes:

> The longer you stay there [in the school], the longer you learn something from the school. You meet with your fellow students and with your teacher. You might ask him something and you look at the walls and you might see the [educational] pictures on the walls. . . . If you stay in the school, you learn something. If you stay out of the school, you learn something different, especially staying in the bars. What do you do when you see a student sitting in a bar with a bottle of beer? You don't feel good. So if you make the school attractive, you can keep students in the school longer, and they can learn more academic things. They learn a lot from the society. But if the students stay in the school, they learn more academic things. (Interview, Iyasu)

The school compound was filled with positive educational and social influences, so it would motivate the students to become the type of moral person that teachers sought to create.

Despite the fact that teachers idealized certain spaces as appropriate for students and other spaces as inappropriate, the behaviors of those who inhabited them were inevitably blurred and, in reality, always had been. For example, while teachers may have categorized certain kinds of recreational spaces as "good" and "bad," there was no shortage of teachers recreating in "bad" bars, particularly given that a teacher's salary seldom allowed them to frequent the more expensive, modern "hotels." Additionally, the perceived clear-cut distinction between good and bad spaces shifted over time as economic realities changed. Campo Sudan, once thought to be the roughest neighborhood in Assab, especially at night, was far less raucous once the war began and the port and truck route to Ethiopia closed. At the same time, the clean, "good" bars and more upscale hotels fell into some disrepair as the economy, and their businesses, floundered.

Similarly, teachers often encountered students in spaces where they "should not be." Ideally, if this were to happen, students would show some sort of "fear," manifested through the type of shame or embarrassment that Woldemikael mentioned above or by running away and avoiding meeting their teacher in a public space, as many teachers noted was the correct reaction. In blurred spaces, according to teachers, students should respond with proper deference, respect, and fear to maintain the appropriate moral stance between teacher and student. Teachers noted that when students did not "fear" teachers, they could not know right from wrong, and they lamented that students did not seem to have fear anymore. As Woldemikael notes:

> I mean, there is no one to be afraid of. I mean, afraid of, I mean it in a positive sense meaning respecting . . . a deep respect. The fear that comes out of deep respect, not to be shocked of someone, to be frightened of someone. That deep respect is not there. (Interview, Woldemikael; emphasis added)

The lack of fear was a by-product of the blurring of the boundaries between spaces where students should and should not be. Many teachers made comments suggesting that students feared less because they were less controlled.

Spoiled Students and Polluting Influences

Teachers' worries about the moral and moralizing properties of "good" and "bad" spaces were reflected in their anxieties about a variety of polluting influences that they believed to be making students "less moral." Teachers often talked about the students and the "teaching-learning process" becoming "spoiled." When I asked what was causing this "spoiling," teachers described a variety of what we might think of as "polluting" influences. Interestingly, the elements that were thought of as "spoiling" the students were typically regarded as foreign, outside influences because they were unfamiliar to the teachers. Although these attributes of "foreignness" varied depending on which teacher was characterizing it, definitions of what is foreign, in general, differentiate between what or who belongs on the inside and what or who is an outsider. As such, these distinctions can be seen as a means to code who, or what kind of person, belongs to the nation and the community of educated nationals.

For younger teachers who had spent little or no time outside the Eritrean highlands, the entire city of Assab was foreign due to its proximity with Ethiopia and the fact that historically it had had a large number of Ethiopians residing in the town. These younger teachers, who were relative newcomers to Assab, often suggested that Assab's students had picked up bad habits or a sort of bad "culture" from the Ethiopians that made them "not like the highlands," as one teacher told me when I asked for his explanation of the behavioral difficulties in schools.[6] Teachers who had lived in Assab for a longer period of time did not talk about Assab as being corrupted by Ethiopian influences but rather seemed to celebrate its hybridity and cultural diversity (Riggan 2011).

Other teachers blamed what they perceived to be a condition of moral decline on the number of Afar students, many of whom came from rural desert areas. Afar students, most of whom came from remote parts of the South Red Sea region, historically had little access to schooling, something that the Eritrean government had been trying to rectify since independence. Larger numbers of Afar students began attending schools in Assab in the late 1990s and early 2000s, when the government expanded access to elementary and Junior Secondary Schools in the South Red Sea region. Despite the fact that Afar students were by no means the only ones who were misbehaving, many teachers attributed the shift in student behavior to Afar students attending in larger numbers. Teachers, the vast majority of whom were from the majority Tigrinya ethnic group and most of whom were raised or lived for many years in cities, tended to have a civilizational prejudice toward the Afar and regarded them as somewhat "backward," largely because they were more rural. Additionally, some teachers, who, with some very notable exceptions, tended to have a fairly cursory knowledge of Afar culture, often took cultural differences as evidence that the Afar did not care about education.[7] They often talked about the amount of money the government was spending on education in the rural areas and spoke of the Afar students as if they were ungrateful for what the government was doing for them. Furthermore, as I discuss in more detail below, teachers suggested that the Afar notions of respect and authority were quite different from those of the Tigrinya people. Tigrinya notions of respect tended to be hierarchical, and strict codes of behavior proscribed how children should behave in the presence of adults. Indeed, both the overall norms for classroom behavior (that students should be silent, obedient, and respectful) and the beliefs about how students should behave in spaces where adults were present derived from patterns of child-rearing and beliefs about childhood prevalent in Tigrinya culture. Tigrinya teachers who had worked in Afar areas often commented warily that Afar families were "very democratic" with regard to child-rearing and that "even the smallest child could speak" in a gathering of adults. Additionally, teachers noted that Afar families did not practice corporal punishment, implying that this made it difficult to ensure that children would respect adults. B'ruk's reference above to students going to "tea shops in Assab Seghir," an Afar area, was an indirect complaint about what teachers interpreted as permissiveness in Afar culture, in which students could go where they wanted and act like adults. Teachers believed that the proximity of this very different culture was affecting their ability to control students. Their response was to contain students in the school so that teachers could free them from other influences.

Students having money was also referenced as a corrupting influence. Money and the desire/necessity to earn money took students into the world outside the school, with its plethora of potentially bad influences. Many teachers attributed blurred social spaces to conditions of economic decline, which, for example, led tea shop owners to sell tea to students rather than send them back to school where they belonged. At one level, working students were seen in pragmatic terms. The fact that students needed to work meant that they did not have enough time to focus on their studies. However, students' work was also seen as locating them in nonstudent spaces and exposing them to influences that were inappropriate. Working students, some of whom were employed as taxi drivers or in bars, had access to money, which gave them the capacity to engage in such practices as smoking and drinking. Teachers thought of students who worked as blurring the boundaries between student and adult spaces and behaviors. These students could engage with adults who might not know that they were students and therefore in need of protection from negative influences. Having access to adult spaces and participating in adult activities, such as smoking and drinking, would make these students see themselves as adults and would make it more difficult for teachers to command their respect and obedience in the classroom. Although teachers acknowledged that students had to work to support their families, there was a perception that once a student began to earn money, he or she would no longer see the value of being a student. Finally, another less common explanation for students' out-of-control behavior was their increased level of exposure to Western media. Several teachers suggested to me that the problem with students was that they listened to too much Western music and watched too many Western movies, which depicted students in America as being disrespectful toward their teachers.

Although teachers had a variety of perceptions of what was "spoiling" students and education, all spoke to fears of what was foreign, different, or potentially uncontrollable. Significantly, all of these polluting influences also blurred teachers' normative sense of the distinction between the categories of child/student and adult/teacher. Cultural patterns that were thought to derive from "Ethiopian" or from "Afar" culture were depicted by teachers as problematic because they pushed students to behave in a more egalitarian way with their teachers, challenging hierarchical notions of authority. Students' needing to work also put them in the world of adults, further blurring these lines. Additionally, each of these foreign influences in some way made it difficult for teachers to distinguish a student from a nonstudent and, in turn, made it difficult to know how to treat students. It is also important to recall that the merging of military training and education put into place by the 2003 policies, which I discussed in previous chapters, fundamentally blurred the distinctions between the roles of teacher and student. This profound blurring of categories provided the backdrop against which teachers' concerns about and interpretations of other forms of category blurring were conceptualized. Concerns about blurred roles led to deep moral anxieties about their ultimate inability to categorize in the face of these broader political and policy changes.

Sorting Small from Large

Sorting and categorizing are key functions of the camp. Camplike enclosures enable and require sorting. Walls themselves sorted by differentiating between students and nonstudents, keeping one group out and another group in. At the same time, within the enclosure, student life was ordered in very specific ways. I now turn to a fuller discussion of teachers' efforts to sort and contain as a manifestation of teacher sovereignty that responded to these particular concerns about moral blurriness and the capacity of schools to contain and maintain categories.

When teachers in the Junior Secondary School locked out students, they were effectively giving them a choice to respect the rules of school space and time or to face consequences—to act like a student by coming to school on time or to fail to act like a student and be locked out. The walls effectively categorized those who were "acting like students" and "not acting like students."

Ultimately, the "nonstudents" were locked out. They were regarded as a polluting influence and abandoned by teachers. Beyond the school wall, these nonstudents were relegated to the much more violent forms of sovereignty enacted by the police or military commanders. Young people who were not students in Eritrea would eventually be rounded up and forced to join the ranks of those in National Service or, if they chose not to, would have to find a way to evade service by escaping the country or living as a fugitive within the country. Any of these outcomes—service, escape, or the fugitive life—effectively relegated these nonstudents to a condition that Agamben (2005) calls "bare life," or life that is abandoned by and inconsequential to the state, rather than life that is cultivated, nurtured, and protected. Within the school walls, teachers made their best effort to help students who were "acting like students" to do well to avoid the fate that would befall those who were outside the wall. Teachers cultivated those who acted like students. However, in light of the 2003 policy changes, it became increasingly difficult to distinguish between who was and was not a "real" student, in part because students and nonstudents alike all wound up the same place—Sawa—and in part because many young people who were seeking to evade service were using school as a means to do so. This made it difficult for teachers to do this work of cultivation and caring. Locking the school gate was one attempt to clarify these distinctions. The intensive process of sorting students within the school that occurred a few days earlier was another.

Within a few days of the "lockout" of late students, grade 8 teachers gathered the entire grade, approximately two hundred students, in the large field in front of the flagpole in the center of the school compound. They lined the students up and walked among them, sorting them by size and "character." Children who were either physically small or known by the teachers to be age-appropriate for their grade were placed in one group and asked to stand on one side of the field. Students who were known to the teachers or by reputation to be "repeaters and disturbers" or who simply appeared to be physically big or old were put in another group. Two groups were created for students who were somewhere in the middle. The sorting was very public, and teachers openly negotiated with each other about which group students were to be put in. At first they had too many students in the "repeaters and disturbers" group and had to place some of them in one of the in-between groups.

Teachers were sorting students into new sections based on age and reputation for behavior. This sorting, along with the lockout, was a strategy to regain control over the school. Teachers had decided that the overly large number of older, disruptive students made it impossible for them to control their classes and that sorting students into different sections by age, number of years repeated, and level of "disturbance" they caused would improve the situation. Students in one section, 8A, were seen as the innocents who could do no wrong; if they misbehaved in class, the act was usually just seen as youthful exuberance rather than deviance. One section was created for students who were known to have repeated grades multiple times and had reputations for causing trouble. Indeed their section, 8D, became known as the "disturber section." The other sections were somewhat ambivalent and created for students in the middle. The teachers' approach to sorting was, effectively, to isolate the big from the small, the innocent from the poorly behaved, those who should be in school from those who should not.

Some context of what was going on at the time of these incidents illuminates why teachers in the Junior Secondary School felt the need to sort and categorize students at this moment. Education was, in theory, open to everyone through the end of the Junior Secondary School level—grade 8.[8] At the end of grade 8, all students took the highly competitive National Examination, which determined whether they would go on to the Senior Secondary School. Although a school rule stipulated that students were supposed to repeat grades only once, there was no consistent national policy about this. Because of this, students could keep repeating grades for as long as they wanted to, and increasing numbers of students seemed to be doing so. The Junior Secondary School teachers were frustrated because the regional Ministry of Education officials in Assab had not developed or enforced a consistent rule regarding how many times students were allowed to repeat a grade. Students quickly figured out that they could fail grades in Junior Secondary School and thereby indefinitely delay their terms of National Service. Ministry of Education officials, not wanting to upset parents by removing their children from school, tended to support this de facto policy that allowed students to stay in school. Teachers in the Junior Secondary School believed that students were using schools as a strategy to evade military service rather than taking schooling seriously, something that challenged their ability to distinguish between students and nonstudents. They believed that larger numbers of nonstudents were filling their classrooms simply because these people were using school as a means to avoid service. Teachers worried that older students would negatively influence younger students and that this negative influence would prevent teachers from having a positive influence on the younger students. They commented that classes were increasingly hard to control due to these older students. In addition, the number of disciplinary incidents had increased, including fights between teachers and students, something attributed to the higher number of older students.

Teachers in the Junior Secondary School were responding to exceptional times, times when rules regarding student promotion were unclear. Teachers both did and did not have control in their school. They did not have the ability to promote students into the Senior Secondary level, because students were promoted only when they passed a national exam, and many Junior Secondary students had been intentionally failing this exam for several years. Nor did teachers have the ability to remove a student from the school permanently, because only the Ministry of Education could do that. But they could and did decide how to organize, discipline, and manage students within the enclosed space of the school.

The sorting process was reflective of the state of exception in several ways. The state of exception is marked by a lack of clarity between law (rules) and the enactment of the exception to these rules by an array of state actors who become sovereign over citizen bodies (Agamben 2005). In the absence of clear rules regarding promotion policy, Junior Secondary School teachers created a mechanism for sorting that was an exception to Ministry of Education rules and policies (or lack thereof). By sorting students, teachers were acting of their own accord and not according to a "higher" authority. Tracking, ability grouping, and other forms of sorting that are widespread elsewhere are almost unheard of in Eritrea. When they occur, they are almost inevitably a school-based practice rather than a national policy. This made the teachers' decision to sort students even more remarkable. In fact, the regional Ministry of Education administration threatened to force teachers to change the grade 8 groupings, saying that this was unprecedented in Eritrea, which left the director caught between his teachers and the administration (he ultimately sided with the teachers). Additionally, as the actors who were sovereign over this sorting mechanism, they made decisions about the exceptions based on highly subjective, arbitrary, intimate, and interpersonal criteria for was good and bad. The decisions that teachers made about each student were based on observing students and understanding their reputations. Ultimately, teachers were pleased with the results of their efforts and believed that these categories would make it easier to manage students. In fact, the sorting was perceived to have worked so well that the grade 7 teachers also considered sorting their students, although they never got around to doing so.

Although these large numbers of older, repeating students presented a pragmatic problem for teachers, teachers' worries about older students reflected deeper moral concerns related to the purity of the student identity. Teachers worried that the blurring of adult and child categories would result in "matter out of place" (Turner 1969). Similarly, teachers described older students in their classes as being out of place. They often made such comments as "How can you teach a class when you have a big man sitting next to a small boy?" Indeed, the age range in classes was striking. In an average class of sixty students, as many as half of the students might be well into their teens, while the other half was a grade-appropriate age. Thus, the problem with older students was not just a pragmatic problem of management but a moral hazard of category blurring. Teacher sovereignty emerged in response to this sense of moral breakdown. When the capacity of the state to provide appropriate stability to schools was found unsatisfactory, teachers took things into their own hands.[9]

Similar but less extreme forms of sorting happened every day in the Senior Secondary School. For example, at different points in time, teachers would position themselves at the school gate after school had started to catch late students and punish them. At some points, teachers would decide to crack down on students not in uniform and would stand at the school gate to send home or punish students who failed to show up dressed appropriately. However, these efforts in the high school were short-lived. The key reason for their failure was the lack of a wall around the school compound. If students were turned away at the gate, they could circle around and find another way into the school compound. Thus, in the Senior Secondary School, the preoccupation with control related to figuring out how to build a wall, something that was seen as essential for the functioning of the school.

Some of the Senior Secondary School teachers also talked about problems of blurred categories, but they did so in different ways. One day I came upon two teachers discussing a particular student. Teacher Mateos was noting that this student was married, had children, and despite this was trying to continue with his schooling. Teacher Iyasu began to laugh with embarrassment and then shook his head and put his head in his hands. He then told us that the student had come to school late the day before and that Iyasu had beaten him. Teacher Iyasu said he wished he had known this particular student's circumstances, because if he had, he would not have beaten the student. Discipline was not universally applied but was applied differently based on understandings of different students' circumstances. This "adult" student who was in school was matter out of place, and, because he was out of place, this teacher made what he considered the rather embarrassing error of beating him (that is, he should not have beaten an adult, an equal).

In contrast, many Senior Secondary School teachers described being furious when students came to school smelling like cigarettes and beating them for having smoked outside school. Although few teachers want their students to smoke, in Eritrea smoking has a particular moral value as well.

It is considered immoral for women to smoke, and most adults would not smoke in front of their parents. Students' smoking was seen as a behavior that was morally out of place and inappropriate for their age. Teachers had similar reactions if they found love letters in students' notebooks. Similar to smoking, love and romantic relationships were seen as immoral acts that were antithetical to being a student. Indeed, if a love letter was found in a student's possession, it was often seen as such a moral aberration that several of the teachers would come together to discuss it and strategize about what action to take. Romantic relationships, like smoking, were intended for adults and thus had no place in the school.[10] When students engaged in these practices, they threatened teachers' sense of moral categories, because they were engaged in behaviors restricted to adults.

Being Seen as the State: Part I

There was a great deal of controversy over teachers' decision to sort students. Effectively, state actors (teachers) believed they were working against their own state institution (the Ministry of Education). Teachers faced opposition from students, Ministry of Education officials, and parents. Indeed, many teachers expected that the Ministry of Education would eventually force them to detrack the grade 8 students and braced themselves to fight back against the ministry. Teachers were criticized for these measures, but they defended their right to divide students and the necessity of doing so. Ultimately, they were not forced to detrack the students, but this sorting (and their defense of it) revealed that teachers were willing to place themselves in an antagonistic relationship with the community and their superiors to take back control of the school.

This controversy illuminates the ways that teachers not only saw (imagined) the state (which I've discussed in previous chapters) and "saw like" the state (by embracing their understanding of how to order schools and educated students); they also were "seen" as the state. In their study of governance and governmentality in India, Stuart Corbridge et al. (2005) capture the notion that the state is brought into being through techniques of governance, technologies of power inherent in governmentality, *and* the way citizens themselves understand, interpret, and "see" the state. My phrase "being seen as the state" references this idea of people "seeing" teachers as the state. Although my main focus here is on the morality and beliefs that framed teachers' utilization of technologies of power and techniques of governing schools (ordering, organizing, containing, sorting, categorizing, and punishing), it is also essential to remember that in utilizing these technologies of power, teachers were "seen" by students and parents as the state even though they would not see themselves that way. These tensions between how teachers saw themselves, saw the state as an entity "out there," and were seen as the state accounted for a number of tensions and struggles over legitimacy. Teacher sovereignty, as with many forms of devolved sovereignty in the state of exception, was always riddled with struggles and tensions over legitimacy and questions about the limits of the use of force. Teachers struggled against each other; against other state actors, such as their own supervisors and administrators; and against students and parents to define the appropriate limits to their use of force. They were seen as the state, but not always in a positive light. As an entry point into this examination of how teachers were seen as the state, it is useful to look at the reactions of students who were placed in the infamous section 8D, the section allocated for "overage students" and "disturbers."

One of the reasons why teachers' sorting of students was controversial among students and parents was because the division of grade 8 students coincided with other, more coercive encounters with the state—both within the school and in the nation as a whole. In Chapter 2 and elsewhere, I suggest that despite the fact that different state institutions and actors may behave completely autonomously, imaginaries of the state create linkages between discrete actions of different state actors and institutions. These linkages characterize and delegitimize the state while they simultaneously imagine it as coherent and translocal. In Eritrea, an imaginary of the coercive, punishing state plays this role (Riggan 2013b). The fact that the sorting of students and the lockout occurred within days of each other and that many of the locked-out students had been assigned to 8D made this particular class believe they were targets of coercion and state punishment. More broadly, around this same time period, in an attempt to reduce the number of students who were enrolling in school simply to receive an ID and thereby avoid military conscription, the Ministry of Education announced that grade 8 students would not be given student ID cards.[11] Many saw this policy as another government effort to militarize schools and target students. While this was happening in Assab, a massive *gifa* took place in Asmara, during which the infamous Adi Abeto incident occurred. Although the events that occurred in the school, the incident of *gifa* in Asmara, and the changed Ministry of Education policy on student ID cards were not directly connected in any way, teachers' actions—locking students out of the school, calling the police, sorting students—need to be examined as imaginatively and discursively linked to the larger notion of the punishing state.

A few days after the students were locked out of the school, I spent several mornings in the 8D classroom, which gave me a chance to hear about how these students felt about the teacher's actions. When I first walked into the class, I was struck by how cramped the room seemed when full of adult-sized bodies. Indeed, if the categorization of 8D were simply based on student size, it would seem that they were distinct from other classes of students. Otherwise, student behavior during their classes struck me as rather ordinary. A few more students than usual appeared to have their heads down on their desks, sleeping. One difference I did note was that when the teacher left the room at the end of each period, the majority of students also left the room, a behavior that teachers generally regarded as problematic.

The few students who remained chatted with me. I asked them what they thought of this new arrangement. A few said it was good to have all the older students together, but many had complaints. One girl told me that she thought the teachers did this so the students in 8D would not copy from other students. Her thoughts reflected teachers' assertions that 8D students performed poorly academically and needed to rely on copying from "clever students" to pass. A couple of other students mumbled something about Sawa that I could not completely make out. Then, interestingly, students almost immediately brought up the arrests that occurred outside the school wall and coincided with the separation of the classes. I did not ask them directly about these arrests, yet the fact that students brought them up on their own shows that they linked the arrests with the sorting process.

For students, being separated into age-based categories, being locked out of school, and having the police called on them were linked as punitive actions and thus reflected the broader sense that the state was punishing in Eritrea. They told me that the police arrested approximately twenty students, and they narrated the events of that morning as if it were a police raid on the school. In contrast, teachers depicted this event as necessary to keep the peace and as only affecting a small number of students. Students described the police infiltrating the school and seeking out particular students for detention. Students in 8D believed the police were particularly targeting them. Later I asked teachers about this discrepancy between teacher and student narratives, and they said that only one student was taken out of the school, while the others were taken from in front of the school, where they were causing a disturbance. In contrast, the students linked sorting the students with locking the gate and calling the police. They imagined the series of events as examples of arbitrary, unpredictable, and inappropriate force used by teachers against students.

The story that one particular student who was taken out of his classroom by the police told me illuminates the way students experienced being the victims of state force. This student made a point of coming over during the break between classes to sit down next to me and tell his story. He told me that he was only fifteen years old (slightly old for grade 8, but not unheard of) and "very small" (in size), so he did not know why he was assigned to 8D. He then told me that he was, in fact, not late the day that the police arrived and was already in the school when they came to arrest students. According to the student, one teacher brought the police into the classroom where he was studying and had him arrested. The teacher hit him and then handed him over to the police. The student told me that he spent two nights in jail.

The student's story was somewhat vague. When I spoke to the teacher involved, he told me that he thought the student had been one of the disturbers outside the school wall but that the student had managed to slip inside while the police were arresting the other students. To rectify the situation, the teacher brought the police to the student and had him arrested. Later, when the student was released from jail, the teacher realized his mistake. The student told me that when he got out, the teacher apologized and bought him a sandwich. "Now we are OK," the student said.

Several dynamics were revealed in this incident. While teachers saw locking the school and calling the police as a necessary means to rectify the situation of moral decline in schools, students experienced it as an arbitrary and violent use of state force against them. This also shows that while teachers thought they were being fair, the sorting mechanisms through which students were labeled disturber and nondisturber resulted in the arbitrary and exceptional use of force against students. Under a state of exception, where there are no clear laws or rights, exceptional force can be used simply because an authority figure wills it. Arguably, this is what happened to students in this school. Furthermore, students believed they had been categorized unjustly and singled out for punishment for a reason that they could not entirely fathom, thereby linking teacher actions with the broader coercive state.

In this particular student's case, the teacher admitted to having been wrong. But it was also curious that the teacher could make it right so easily by buying the student a sandwich. This speaks not to the use of extreme force against students but rather to the rationalization of the use of force, which is far more ordinary and mundane. The use of punishment, including corporal punishment, is highly intimate. It binds teachers and students in a particular relationship of authority that is intimate and familial in many ways. We see state power that is sometimes violent, sometimes nurturing, but always engaged in a process that brings students and teachers into a close and familiar relationship with each other. Students were sorted not on the basis of arbitrary categories thought up in a remote office in Asmara. These categories were developed in the school itself, based on a sense of moral order, a threat to that order, and an intimate knowledge of the students themselves.

Teacher Sovereignty and Student Bodies

Teachers' sense that they were supposed to act in a fair and even legal manner often clashed with their sense that they had to do whatever it took to make students moral. This mandate to make students moral was so important to teachers that they were willing to use their power to subject students to coercion and even violence, effectively punishing students much as other state actors punished teachers. Although technically illegal, corporal punishment was ubiquitous throughout Eritrea at the time of my fieldwork. The law was typically ignored. The vast majority of teachers carried sticks or pieces of hose with them to class, and it was common for them to have students kneel and/or extend their palms to be slapped with the stick or hose if they arrived late, talked in class, failed to do their homework, or behaved in any other disruptive way. Teachers were positioned to decide on the exception, in Agamben's sense. Sometimes this literally involved deciding when to make exceptions to the law prohibiting the use of physical violence against students, and sometimes this involved deciding which type of force or coercion to use when the law was ignored, as it often was. But teachers' decisions on the exception also drew on their sense of moral crisis. Two imaginaries of the state were reflected in this conflict between legality and morality—on the one hand, that the state should be fair, predictable, and orderly, and on the other hand, that the self-imposed mandate that teachers shape students into moral beings might transcend fairness and regulatory predictability. These different imaginaries often came to a head around several contested instances of corporal punishment, which I discuss below.

Much emphasis has been placed on the sovereign's capacity to kill or do physical harm. In Agamben's depiction, this capacity is absolute. What I emphasize here is how debates over the efficacy, appropriateness, and morality of using force frame and temper this capacity. The everyday sovereign may act with impunity vis-à-vis the law under the state of exception, but there are always forces and factors that shape and constrain the use of force. What made debates over corporal punishment complicated was the variety of perspectives on what the conditions, limits, and purpose of violence should be, which were infused not only by the broader political context and the sense that teachers were on their own but also by a sense of fairness and wanting to enact "law" fairly. Several anecdotes illustrate the range of approaches to corporal punishment and their contested nature.

"Corporal Punishment Is the Only Way"

One morning, in between classes at the Junior Secondary School, Teacher Paolo struck up a conversation with me. "I've decided to give up corporal punishment," he announced somewhat proudly. He explained to me that it was not fair to use corporal punishment with the Afar students, because they were not accustomed to it. Sometimes they would even hit the teacher back when beaten, and he wanted to teach and avoid fights. Paolo was a thoughtful teacher who seemed to grasp some of the subtleties of cultural differences. I told him I admired his sensitivity and eagerness to experiment with different approaches and that I looked forward to hearing whether he was successful. Although other teachers talked about limiting their use of corporal punishment, this was the first time I had ever heard anyone plan to give it up entirely.

There was a widespread sentiment among teachers that students would not respect them if the teachers did not hit them. Teacher Haile explained to me that in teacher training, they were taught that corporal punishment was bad for children, but once they began teaching, they found that they could not control their classes without it and that there was no support for not using it:

> We had learned that corporal punishment was not allowed and not good for students, but the students wouldn't take us seriously. You want to look like a good teacher, but you can't do that as long as you avoid this corporal punishment. Students push you. Senior teachers tell you corporal punishment is the only way. (Interview, Haile)

Paolo eventually came to a similar conclusion. When I interviewed him several months after his bold declaration that he was not going to use corporal punishment and asked how it was going, he explained why his plan did not work: "I was not successful. I went back to physical punishment. But I am trying to do other things. Before I was punishing them all of the time, but now only when the students become crazy."

Like many teachers before him, Paolo came around to see corporal punishment as a pedagogical necessity, but one that could and should be used sparingly. He learned that while a teacher could limit his or her use of corporal punishment, it was difficult to teach without it. In fact, in my own experience teaching in Eritrea, I admit that I inadvertently came to a similar realization. Although I never resorted to hitting students, I did make them kneel down at times and, once, when faced with a thoroughly unmanageable class, I called the school director, who, much to my shock and dismay, hit the students.

Several points are illuminated by Paolo's bold experiment. First, it reflected the strength of the belief that students would not respect their teacher if he or she did not resort to corporal punishment. This attitude was so widespread that most teachers never considered *not* resorting to corporal punishment. It was a daily part of schooling in Eritrea, as it is elsewhere. But Paolo's experiment also reflected a sense that there were limits and alternatives to the use of force. Paolo's attitude, like that of many teachers, was that corporal punishment was part of a teacher's pedagogical tool kit, necessary to create an orderly climate for teaching, but to be used sparingly and strategically. There were other understandings of the pedagogy of punishment, however. Some teachers believed not only that corporal punishment was necessary to create orderly conditions in which students could learn well but also that violence itself would make students more moral.

"He Is a Very Stupid Boy"

Four teachers and the school director sat in a semicircle around a student who was kneeling on the ground in front of them. They questioned him sternly for several minutes, and then the director stood up and asked him to stretch out his arm. He hit the student several times on his palm with a stick. The boy, who was obviously in pain, at one point pulled his hand back and was roughly ordered to put it back for more blows. He cried out in pain, and a smile flickered across one teacher's face. After the boy had been dismissed, I asked what he had done. One teacher answered, "He is a very stupid boy."

Another added, "He is very bad."

Finally, the director explained to me that the boy had disappeared from his home and from school for three days. His mother and sister had been looking frantically for him, and his mother had asked for the assistance of the school staff in disciplining her child. Corporal punishment was used here as a means to teach the student a lesson—that running away was bad. The assertion that the boy was "stupid" combined with the blows suggested that they hoped he would learn something from his punishment.

"His parents are divorced," another teacher added, as if this explained things. In this instance, teachers were rather directly being asked to stand in for the student's father and were being placed in a disciplinary role by the student's mother. State actors—teachers— were acting in the place of the parent. This suggested that the teachers' sense of their moral role as disciplinarians extended beyond education and into the realm of the family. Indeed, the teachers' sense of their moral mandate linked the realms of the home, school, and state.

This case illustrates the pedagogical role of the use of force, something that is prevalent in schools and other state institutions, such as the military. Corporal punishment was used to teach students to be better people. Inflicting pain showed the punished subjects that they had done something wrong and trained them not to do it. Teachers and parents thought pain would teach young people the difference between right and wrong. The pedagogical role of state violence illuminates Begoña Aretxaga's (2003) concept of the "maddening state." In the instance recounted above, a state employee beat a student at the request of a mother. The state here was simultaneously caretaking and violent, or, more precisely, violent in its caretaking. Much of teachers' work as sovereigns over school space and student bodies reflected a similarly maddening condition. One way to think about this is that many teachers assumed that beating students showed that they cared about their development—students needed to be punished sometimes so that they would learn properly. On the other hand, beatings could incline toward the brutal and sadistic. The maddening nature of state violence is reflected in the use of corporal punishment in other state institutions as well. Arguably, when corporal punishment is used in the military, it has a similarly pedagogical role. Military trainees are often beaten (or worse) for not correctly learning skills—for example, failing to shoot a target or committing minor infractions of rules. The logics of this use of corporal punishment suggest an attitude among military trainers that is similar to that of teachers—violence has a pedagogical role. However, at times, in schools and elsewhere, force was used to assert dominance without any specific lesson being taught other than the lesson that the punished subject should obey the authority figure. The anecdote below illustrates this.

"He Will Learn Respect"

Every day, teachers would drag chairs out of the sweltering cement tea shop and sit in the shade overlooking the Red Sea. Often they would call to students to bring them cups of tea, sandwiches, sodas, or cigarettes. Students gave teachers a lot of space unless they were summoned. One day, a student whom I recognized from one of the grade 6 classes I had recently observed was standing and talking, jokingly, with three teachers—Lemlem, Beraki, and Yakob. He was a student who was large for grade 6 but did not seem to act his age. He seemed very eager to participate in his classes and was animated, playful, and enthusiastic. Teachers often seemed annoyed with him even though he was engaged in his studies. The other students often laughed mockingly at his enthusiastic attempts to participate in class.

Lemlem, Beraki, and Yakob were trying to get the student to dance. "He is going to show us how Michael Jackson dances," Lemlem said to me. Lemlem and Yakob explained to me that the student had been "dancing like Michael Jackson" in the staff room the previous day, to the amusement of the other teachers. I looked at the student and became aware of the fact that the student did not want to dance and was looking apprehensive. The teachers were becoming more and more insistent that he dance, and he was becoming more and more visibly nervous about doing so, saying that the other students would laugh at him. Beraki, in particular, was getting increasingly angry because of the student's refusal to dance.

At this point, Weldeyesus, another teacher who was known for his liberal use of corporal punishment, had arrived and became involved in the situation. He began talking to the student in a fairly calm voice. I became distracted and looked away for a minute, and the next thing I knew, Weldeyesus had clubbed the student on the side of the head.

"Is this because he won't dance?" I asked, incredulous. They said yes. By this point, two other teachers, Ezekiel and Haile, had arrived and watched the situation unfolding. It became clear that they were also unhappy about Weldeyesus's hitting the student. The student, who was crying by this point, was made to kneel down. Ezekiel, Haile, and I were furious and said, "If he doesn't want to dance, why make him dance?" The other teachers ignored us. Beraki, Yakob, and Weldeyesus seemed intent on punishing the student. At that point, break time was ending, and Lemlem, Ezekiel, and Haile had to leave.

A few minutes later, Weldeyesus made the student run around the field. The student returned and sat on the wall near us, and Yacob, his homeroom teacher, spoke to him for a while. After some time, the student was excused.

I was deeply shaken by this experience, not so much because of the physical violence done to the child, which was not uncommon, but because of the reason for his punishment, which felt like an exception to the pedagogical role of corporal punishment as I understood it. The student was not doing anything wrong. He was not breaking a rule. He just did not want to dance for his teachers.

Finally, I asked Beraki and Yakob, the only teachers who remained seated around the table at that point, "How can you expect a student to learn right from wrong when you give him the same punishment for not dancing as you do for doing something else? What will he learn from this?" My question reflected my understanding, at that time, that corporal punishment was typically used pedagogically—to teach students to behave appropriately and to follow rules.

Yakob's answer revealed a very different manifestation of the pedagogy of punishment. He glared at me and answered without hesitating, "He will learn respect."

A few minutes later, I saw the student walking quickly across the school compound with his books in hand. He was trying to leave the school grounds. Weldeyesus happened to be crossing his path and saw him, stopped him, hit him a few times with his fists, and kicked him before sending him back to class.

The incident described above, like other instances of corporal punishment, was an enactment of sovereign power. The teacher/sovereign commanded the student body. This sovereign could make student/citizen bodies dance, hop, kneel, sit, or stand at whim. At various times, teachers did all of these. Teacher power here was very much the coercive power of the state, with its capacity to command the bodies of its subjects. If the student body failed to comply, the teacher/sovereign could punish it, thereby inscribing sovereign power on that body. However, unlike the incidents that I described previously in which corporal punishment was used pedagogically to teach specific lessons (do not run away from home; sit quietly and do not talk in the classroom), here it was used to teach absolute obedience to authority. The only lesson being taught was that students must obey teachers no matter what, even when the teacher was making an innocuous request like asking the student to dance. This was an empty but essential lesson for life in a coercive state—obey your superiors, because otherwise they will beat you.

There are thus two notions of corporal punishment: (1) that it should be used sparingly, strategically, pedagogically, and as a technique to create order; and (2) that it should be used to assert dominance and authority and produce obedience and subservience. The distinctions between the two are sometimes subtle but significant. In these distinctions between the pedagogical role of force and the authoritarian/coercive one, we can see two different state effects prevalent in Eritrea at play and in tension with one another. On the one hand, the state orders and disciplines; state actors might use force to produce order, but always with constraint and purpose.

On the other hand, the state punishes arbitrarily and with impunity, producing the coercive state effect. These distinctions played out in debates among teachers, and later parents, over several controversial instances of corporal punishment, which I discuss below. However, the overall political climate, the moral crisis of disorder, and a sense of threat to teachers' sovereignty over school space also influenced the outcome of these debates over corporal punishment.

Lions versus Laws

The following controversial case of corporal punishment illustrates the distinctions between teachers' understandings of the roles and limits of corporal punishment. I became aware of this case when some members of the discipline committee brought it to my attention and explained it to me as it developed. It involved a fight between a teacher and an older grade 7 student who was probably in his late teens. The teacher slapped the student in the face in the classroom for not completing his homework assignment. The student raised his hand to defend himself and backed away, arguing that he was being punished unfairly. The teacher dragged him out of the class and continued fighting with him in the staff room. This particular teacher was known to treat students strictly and harshly. The atmosphere in his class was absolutely silent, and he did not tolerate the most minor disturbance. Several of his students commented to me that he was generally disliked and feared by the students, in part because of his strictness and in part because he often failed many students.

The discipline committee consisted of three teachers and the director. One of the teachers, Ezekiel, almost never hit students and was frustrated with the increased emphasis in the school on using force discipline. He told me that he had recently walked out of a discipline committee meeting in frustration at the teachers' insistence on emphasizing control rather than learning. Another teacher on the committee, Weldeyesus, used corporal punishment on a regular basis and was frustrated that more of the teachers were not stricter. The third teacher on the committee occupied the middle ground. Teklay often carried a stick with him to his classes and would use it when he felt it was warranted, but he used it pedagogically, not to terrorize or assert authority over students.

Members of the committee debated whether the student or the teacher should be punished. Yosef, the teacher involved in the incident, wanted the student punished for fighting with him. In many cases if a student fought with a teacher, this kind of behavior could warrant suspension or expulsion from school, depending on the severity of the fight. On the other hand, the student and many of the teachers believed that Yosef was the one who needed to be punished for continuing to beat the student even after he had stopped fighting. Punishment for teachers would include a letter from the supervisor that would go in a teacher's permanent file. Teachers feared having such a letter in their files because it could impede future opportunities, such as transfers, training sessions, or any other opportunities that came up. Yosef very much hoped for a transfer to Asmara and a chance to continue his education, and a negative letter in his file would have a detrimental impact on either possibility.

Ezekiel and Teklay initially convinced Weldeyesus that, according to the disciplinary rules of the school, Yosef needed to be punished because he had continued to beat the student long after he needed to defend himself and because he had been too harsh to begin with by hitting the student for not completing his homework. Additionally, according to the law, the student was in the right, since corporal punishment was officially illegal. Although Weldeyesus argued against this view, he could not argue against the logic that Yosef had broken the law. However, in a second meeting, Weldeyesus came across more strongly, having apparently discussed the issue with Yosef. He commented in this meeting that he believed that only three teachers in the school were "like lions." He was clearly disappointed that more teachers were not willing to be "lions" and, furthermore, were not willing to defend the lions. He considered himself and Yosef to be among the few teachers who cared about correcting students' behavior. Ezekiel held his ground, contending that Yosef was fundamentally in the wrong and that the rules of the school were very clear in this case. Teklay agreed with Ezekiel, and Weldeyesus, outnumbered, was forced to comply with their decision.

Predictably, Yosef was furious at this decision. In the meeting when they told him the outcome of their decision, he banged on the director's desk and threatened Ezekiel, accusing him of defending the students. The student was suspended for two weeks (Yosef thought he should be expelled), and Yosef would have a permanent letter placed in his file. Ezekiel continued to argue that he was simply following the "law" of the school and upholding the right principles. According to Ezekiel, a teacher could not complain about a student fighting with him when the "law" clearly said that the teacher did not have the right to hit the student in the first place. This was an interesting instance because, although teachers often noted that corporal punishment was illegal, no one attempted to adhere to these laws.

I would argue that this was not a debate over the legality of corporal punishment itself. Rather it was a debate about the nature of teacher sovereignty, or, in other words, a debate about when and how teachers could make decisions about the exception. A variety of issues were at stake. Did teachers have the "right" to use unchecked force against students? Could they act with total impunity? Or were there limits to their use of force? As is apparent by the ubiquity of corporal punishment as well as the range of instances of corporal punishment discussed in this chapter, the legality of the everyday use of corporal punishment was not questioned, and yet members of the discipline committee evoked the law in this instance to enable other teachers to place limits on Yosef's use of force. Yosef, according to some teachers, had gone too far. He had decided on the exception inappropriately, and other teachers held him accountable for making the wrong decision.

Questions about the limits of the use of force not only challenged teacher sovereignty but also reflected different assumptions about student subjectivity. Teachers who stood by their right to use unchecked force tended to believe that a moral, respectful student was one who would not question authority and would do whatever the teacher ordered. If they did not, they could be punished in as brutal a manner as the teacher chose. This stance was reflected in Weldeyesus's claim that teachers should be "lions" and also in the incident where the student was beaten severely for not dancing like Michael Jackson. In contrast, teachers who believed that force had limits believed that students needed to be taught to be moral and respectful and that force was a key means to do so, but that students also had rights and that teachers had responsibilities to constrain their use of force. The perspective that emphasized law was, thus, less about enacting the law and more about evoking it as a stand-in for limits to teacher sovereignty.

Weldeyesus's and Yosef's assertions that (1) teachers should be "lions" and (2) if they cared about education, they had to be willing to be brutal gained purchase during this particular time period. At a time when all teachers perceived that students were increasingly out of control and in need of greater discipline and control, this argument was powerful. At the same time, teachers such as Yosef were increasingly frustrated with their own work and lives. Their frustration, combined with deep-seated beliefs about the efficacy of corporal punishment, made them far less amenable to alternate perspectives about the use of force in punishing students. Below, I complicate this even more by exploring another controversial instance of corporal punishment that was, in many respects, very similar, except that in this case teachers found themselves in solidarity with each other rather than challenging each other's use of force.

Teacher Rights

As we saw above, some teachers were often extremely defensive about their "right" to use force against student bodies even when other teachers suggested that their use of force had extended the boundaries of what was commonly regarded as appropriate. In many ways, this perceived right to use force against student bodies was the epitome of teacher sovereignty. The following incident illustrates the interplay of these particular tensions.

This highly controversial disciplinary incident involved the school director's hitting a student for failing to obey him. The director warned the student not to leave his classroom and later found him outside the class. He took the student into his office to punish him by hitting him on the palm with a piece of rubber hose, but the student apparently flinched away from the swing, resulting in the director's hitting the student in the stomach with the piece of hose. No one witnessed the incident. The student was later taken to the hospital, where the doctor considered surgery. Although ultimately it was decided that no surgery was necessary, there was much talk about the director's facing charges for physically hurting the student. The director realized that he hit the student inappropriately and visited the family, which was the culturally appropriate action to take under the circumstances; the court decided several months later that he was required to make a monetary reparation of 1,000 nakfa (roughly $50, the equivalent of a bit less than one month's salary) to the family.

Several factors were interesting about the conversations about this incident that occurred among teachers over the course of several months. First, the level of solidarity among teachers and the support they had for the director were striking. Even teachers who never or seldom hit students advocated for the director in this case. In fact, no teacher in the school condemned or criticized the director's actions. Unlike the case discussed earlier in which some teachers claimed that they were "lions" and other teachers stood by the "law," here teachers were in agreement that the director had not behaved inappropriately. Second, many teachers commented that by attempting to run away from punishment, the student had brought a harsher punishment on himself. Running away from a punishment was thought of as a moral aberration. Blaming the student for running away indicated that teachers thought of this incident as a reflection of the general "out-of-control" environment in the school—morally aberrant students were not accepting their punishments, leading to greater extremes of violence and problems for everyone.

Other narratives that circulated around this event illuminated the larger issues at stake in Eritrea and reflected several imaginaries of the state. It was notable that at the time of the incident, teachers frequently complained about the ineffectiveness of the (government-run) hospital. A wide array of Junior Secondary School teachers engaged in this discourse of complaining about the hospital and together recounted many harrowing tales about the same hospital and doctor. When discussing the director's case, one teacher described another teacher's wife's miscarriage, blaming it on the negligence of the hospital staff. Stories circulated that this doctor had a habit of performing unnecessary surgeries. One teacher even said he had heard nurses complaining that this doctor seemed to perform surgery to "practice" on his patients. Another teacher noted that when his sister gave birth, this same doctor wanted to perform an unnecessary cesarean section on her. These tales of an inept hospital and doctor served to discredit the accounts that the school director had seriously injured the student by casting suspicion on another state institution—the hospital. Although many of the teachers did have a good deal of evidence to doubt the doctor and the hospital (which suffered from shortages of well-trained and educated manpower), the timing of these tales of hospital horrors was strategically placed to discredit the doctor and, thus, vindicate the director. At the same time, these stories of hospital incompetence also projected an imaginary of another state institution—and, by extension, the state itself—as incompetent.

Another narrative that emerged in response to this incident related to the lack of Ministry of Education support for teachers' efforts to regain control over schools. When discussing the accusations against the school director, teachers brought up the lack of ministry support for their reorganization of grade 8, for their broader efforts to better control students, and for their specific efforts to have certain older students removed from school. This was notable because the boy who was injured by the director was neither an older student nor a grade 8 student and thus had no direct connection to these complaints. However, teachers narrated the accusations against their director as evidence of the lack of support for their work by the Ministry of Education. The criticism that the director had behaved inappropriately was seen as further evidence of the lack of support by the ministry, thereby making teachers feel somewhat akin to vigilantes in working on their own to reclaim control over their schools.

It is interesting that there was widespread solidarity in support of the school director's case while there was criticism in Yosef's case. One reason for solidarity was that the director was generally seen as a fair person, whereas Yosef often was not. But, even more significantly, teachers saw these accusations against their director as an attack on the school and on their work as teachers. The narratives I discussed above—the narrative of the inept state and the narrative of being abandoned by the ministry—served to galvanize teachers in support of the director, but they also reflected imaginaries of the impotent, incompetent state, one that could not or would not support the work teachers were trying to do.

Being Seen as the State: Part II

Parents provide a different commentary on teachers' use of force, and in these comments we find another way in which teachers are "seen as the state." Two meetings were called for teachers and parents shortly after the start of the spring semester in February 2004. The semester was getting off to a late start, and students were still not showing up for school. At the first meeting, Ministry of Education officials responded to pressure by teachers to get parents to help send their students to school by telling parents that they would face "consequences" if they did not send their children to school. This approach suggested that parents were complicit in the disordered and chaotic conditions of schooling. At the same meeting, the Ministry of Education told teachers to "be serious" about taking attendance and following other procedures, such as cleaning the classrooms, suggesting that a teacher's failure to do his or her job properly also produced conditions of disorder and chaos. While the "consequences" parents would face were not made clear, the threat to parents effectively functioned to remind them that it was their responsibility to send their children to school. This reminder, combined with the pressure on teachers to tighten mechanisms of controlling students, was enough to get the semester off to a start. Almost immediately following this meeting, students started showing up for school, and the semester was able to begin.

Although the school got started a few weeks later in mid-March, parents and teachers continued to be disturbed by the conditions in schools and the behavior of students, so another meeting was called for them—this time by the town's administration, with the meeting itself run by the mayor. Unlike the previous meeting, which was intended to specifically address the issue of students not coming to school, there was no clear objective or outcome to the second meeting. Also, in contrast to the previous meeting, which placed the responsibility for student behavior on parents, this meeting seemed to give parents a chance to vent their feelings and the teachers a chance to reply. In this meeting, a debate ensued as to who was responsible for the failure to control the students. Parents blamed teachers' lack of motivation for the disorderly condition of schools, while teachers blamed parents' failure to make their children come to school. Everyone, however, was generally anxious about students' "immoral" behavior. What was in tension here was a perspective in which teachers were "seeing like a state" and being seen as the state. Teachers were aspiring to impose a system of regulatory, disciplinary order on students such that they could accomplish their goals of transforming them into educated citizens. In doing this, teachers believed it necessary to enforce regulations, to utilize technologies of categorization and containment, and to use force if need be.

Meanwhile, parents were "seeing the state" but seeing it in two ways—as overly coercive, controlling, and punishing on the one hand, but also as inept, disorganized, and irresponsible on the other. Parents' complaints suggested that teachers were too strict and unfair in their punishments at times, thereby depicting teachers *as* the punishing state. Specifically, several parents found it unjust that particular students had been dismissed from school for disciplinary infractions. They also found teachers' reasons for suspending students from their classrooms unfair. Parents complained in particular about relatively new procedures in both the Junior Secondary School and Senior Secondary School whereby late students were locked out. At the same time, parents complained that teachers were not able to "control" the students and often questioned teachers' motivation, or lack thereof, accusing them of not doing their jobs properly and suggesting that this failure was the reason for schools' being out of control. Parents picked up on the tight controls that teachers tried to put in place, which I have described in this chapter, but also on the evasiveness and disorder that I discussed in the last chapter. In effect, their imaginaries of the teacher state reflected the condition of impotence. The teacher state, as imagined by parents, was simultaneously disorderly and coercive.

Conclusion

Teachers experienced these years as a time of moral crisis. Teacher sovereignty, which was enacted through practices of containment, categorization, and corporal punishment, was a response to this condition of moral breakdown. I began this chapter with a discussion of encampment and the work of walls. Walls enabled control and categorization by demarcating good from bad spaces and good from bad people. Encampment enabled teacher sovereignty, because within walled-off spaces teachers could act with impunity on student bodies—they decided on the exception. Students were at the whims of teachers who could decide when force was appropriate and inappropriate, but, significantly, teachers' use of force was also framed and constrained by a number of factors, complicating our sense that just because state actors can use force, they will.

The state is imaginatively produced on the basis of everyday encounters between citizens and state actors, such as those I have described in this chapter. Teachers were imagined as the state, sometimes criticized as inept, and sometimes regarded as overly coercive. Interestingly, these are the same two poles that framed Eritreans' imagination of their state more broadly. Recall in Chapter 2 that Eritreans complained that *gifa* was overly coercive but then also attempted to make sense of *gifa* by commenting that the state had to resort to these measures because it was too inept to catch those who legitimately deserved to be detained; on the one hand, the state is seen as punishing, but on the other hand, it is seen as unfortunately stumbling in its efforts to create order.

In closing, I suggest that we can draw many parallels between teacher sovereignty and the sovereignty of other state actors, including police, military personnel, and bureaucrats. All of these state actors "see like the state" in the sense that they, by virtue of their own education and training and their appropriation of "high modernist" ideologies, have been disciplined and socialized into believing in the ordering of space, the clear organizing of categories, and the imposing of procedures to order and organize (Scott 1998). Other state actors authorized to use force are similar in many respects to Eritrean teachers, although there are clearly differences between teachers, whose state function is to socialize and teach, and the police or military, whose state function is to use force. By its very nature, the state of exception authorizes state actors to use force with a good degree of impunity—to decide on the exception. But deciding on the exception also requires making a decision that often is not constrained by law, regulation, or procedure. What I have shown here is how the confluence of political conditions, frustration with the political and social climate, a sense of being criticized by other state actors and by "society," and, most importantly, culturally specific notions of morality all help determine how decisions to use force are made. What constitutes morality and what constitutes an appropriate way to produce moral subjects is not constant but rather shifting, contested, debated, and negotiated. I suggest that this framework might illuminate the decisions to use force among all kinds of state actors in Eritrea and elsewhere. Having said this, it might be tempting to read the school as a microcosm of the country, teachers as a microcosm of the state, and the use of force against students as an indication that they are being socialized as mindless, obedient automatons primed for authoritarian rule. Indeed, some work on schooling for democracy has made the argument that students are pedagogically primed for authoritarian rule (Harber and Mncube 2012). My argument, however, is that teachers are not merely mirroring the state by using force but constituting the state. The teacher state, in Eritrea and elsewhere, is certainly reflective of the ongoing state of exception, which allows teachers to act with a good deal of impunity and strips students of any legal rights. But teachers are not merely mirroring the broader state, because they enact the state of exception on the basis of their own unique prejudices, assumptions, beliefs, stereotypes, and morality, all of which are contested and debated. The teacher state is, thus, a manifestation of the state of exception, but one that is demarcated by teachers' own attitudes about education, morality, the future of the nation, and their students.

CONCLUSION

Escape, Encampment, and the Alchemy of Nationalism

Escape

September 12, 2005, was the day after New Year's in the Ge'ez (Orthodox) calendar. It had been a tense two months as we tried to get an exit visa for my husband. My fieldwork was finished, my funding was ending, and our nerves were growing frayed by the constant uncertainties of the coercive state—would my husband be sent to the desert, transferred to Asmara, or left indefinitely in Assab? Would we have enough money to live on with my funding ending? Would a war break out again, drawing everyone into the military? Would he be detained in another round of *gifa*? Would we be able to stand the constant stresses as our lives were incessantly controlled by the state? Would things worsen and become more repressive, or was this all temporary? Our long process to receive the exit visa was grueling and full of hopes and fears.[1] Several days before the New Year's holiday, miraculously, we had an exit visa in our hands, and on New Year's Eve, we bought plane tickets. It is hard to describe the emotions of those days. We were eager because it finally looked like he was leaving after years of trying, but we could not feel excited because so many things were likely to go wrong. Few people had the power to let us leave, while many had the power to stop us. I slept little during those days, anticipating, hoping, but trying not to hope too much.

On New Year's Eve, we had tea with a trusted family member who warned us in hushed tones not to tell *anyone* we were leaving. Common wisdom was that a jealous person might tip off someone with the power to bar our departure. We knew this was a real possibility. It had happened to people we knew. For this reason, Eritreans often leave without telling even their closest relatives and friends of their plans, especially if they are leaving illegally and making a dangerous trek across borders, but even if they are leaving legally with an exit visa by plane. Departure is shrouded in secrecy for fear of the plethora of state actors who have the ability to block their escape.

We packed in a daze and ate a meal at my in-laws' house in Asmara. My father-in-law worked for Eritrean Airlines, but when he departed for work that evening, we did not tell him we were leaving that night, fearful that, out of excitement, he would share our plans with someone at the airport who would then prevent us from getting on the plane. But aside from not telling my father-in-law, we did not do a very good job of taking our relative's advice. We took two cars full of friends and relatives to the airport with us, probably making far more of a spectacle of ourselves than we should have. As we crammed our belongings and our friends into two small cars, our dog, which we would be leaving with my brother-in-law, ran in manic circles around us, yapping. She would not come to me. I hugged and kissed friends and relatives, including my mother-in-law, who would not be making the trip to the airport with us. She was a small, strong woman, and her hands engulfed mine as we kissed multiple times on each cheek. Greetings and salutations in Eritrea are always full of restrained emotion and were particularly so that evening. I remember the calm, kind expression on my mother-in-law's face, an expression that could, and often did, quickly break out into broad laughter and always reflected her faith that everything would work out, despite the fact that she had lived through multiple wars and multiple dictators. That night her expression only hinted at the combination of happiness and loss that she must have been feeling. I know she was worried that she would not see us again for a very long time, if ever.

It was a cold summer night in Asmara, foggy and drizzling slightly. We hugged everyone good-bye, thanked them all for coming, and entered the bright fluorescent haze of the airport. Walking up to the check-in counter was surreal. The mixed emotions of the past weeks crystalized. I could not help but become giddy as we inched toward the check-in counter and got closer to getting on the plane. I also could not believe we were really leaving, not only because this was something we had dreamed of and longed for but also because we knew that it still might not happen. Hope, fear, and disbelief were inseparable. I felt like I was walking around in several bodies at the same time, each in its own emotional state.

The airport was chaotic. A throng of passengers negotiated their wildly oversized bags, jostling and pushing each other, loading and unloading bags from the scales at the check-in counter. I felt distant from all of it. My hands shook as I handed our passports and tickets to the airline employee. As we passed through immigration, my husband was pulled into one of the small offices next to the immigration counter. "Go ahead. It's OK," he told me, but as the door shut behind him, I froze. I went on through security and up to the departures lounge, but I do not remember anything until he joined me a few minutes later. Then, as we waited for our flight, a man wearing civilian clothes with a badge dangling around his neck approached him and asked to see his passport. He flicked through the document while we tried not to look nervous. I felt cold and tried not to show that I was shivering. He handed the documents back without making eye contact, and we began boarding the plane shortly after.

As we climbed the staircase to the plane, we turned around and saw through the fog a group of Eritrean Airlines employees clustered together, wearing thick jackets to keep out the cold. I could make out the thin frame of my father-in-law, standing slightly to the side of the group. We know he saw us. We wanted to wave but were afraid of doing so. Staring at each other through the fog, across the tarmac—that was how we said good-bye.

Even once we were sitting on the plane, bound for Rome and then New York, we half expected that a government official would barge onto the plane, tell us they had made a mistake, and whisk my husband away, imprisoning him (metaphorically and perhaps literally) in Eritrea forever. We did not start breathing until we stumbled out of the airport in Rome into the September sunlight, seeing the world differently, somehow changed, free.

This book ends, as it began, with a departure. The evacuation of Assab in 2000 profoundly and permanently changed the town. Many did not return. After that, the town came to feel like a military encampment, a place where people were forced to be. The border war and its failure to completely end set Eritrea on its current, securitized course. Its leaders became preoccupied with the potential for renewed war and oriented the entire country toward being under a state of siege (Tronvoll and Mekonnen 2014). The evacuation of Assab, which led to mass conscription, was a threshold, an entry point into the limitless liminality of National Service. Teachers who returned to Assab after summer 2000 were changed and living in a changed country.

In the years since the conclusion of my fieldwork, departures such as ours, and other far more harrowing escapes, have become all too common in Eritrea. As this book goes to press, the United Nations has noted a vast increase in the already enormous numbers of Eritreans fleeing the country (Al Jazeera 2014; Gedab News 2014c; UN News Centre 2014). When I first went to Eritrea in 1995, leaving the country was unheard of for most. "Why would anyone want to leave the country?" one teacher asked, incredulous. "There is nothing sweeter than living in one's own country." That particular teacher is now in the United States. Of the teachers who taught in the Junior and Senior Secondary Schools in Assab during the years of my fieldwork, I know of only one who remains in Assab and three, when I last checked, who remain in Eritrea. Of the educational administrators, civil servants, and teachers in other schools whom I know and am friends with, countless more have left. They have spread across the world now, living throughout western Europe, the United States, and East Africa. I know Eritreans in Australia, New Zealand, Mozambique, Angola, Yemen, Saudi Arabia, and South Africa. Some left legally, with a much coveted exit visa, by plane. Others were not so fortunate and made the treacherous journey by land or sea to Yemen, Sudan, or Ethiopia. Some managed to make their way to South America and then traveled across the southern border to claim asylum in the United States. Others made their way north by land across Sudan, Egypt, and Libya, risking being kidnapped, tortured, and held for ransom in the Sinai Desert or dying at sea while crossing the Mediterranean. I know that at least one of the teachers who appears in this book has died making this journey.

For Eritreans, a life outside the country is much coveted, but leaving involves intensive sacrifices. For years after my husband and I left, we constantly reminded ourselves how lucky we were. Life in Eritrea and leaving Eritrea was so difficult that freedom felt like a dream for a very long time. Over time our life there came to seem like the dream. Then the longing and the loss began to set in. Most who flee are not able to return. Some find that it is impossible to make enough money in their destination country to afford a trip back home. Some fear political repercussions upon return or worry they will not be given permission to leave again. Some take a principled stance in protest of the government's policies and refuse to comply with government requirements that would make their return safe and sanctioned (which I discuss below). In the ten years we have been gone, we have not believed that returning would be safe. During that time, both of my husband's brothers have gotten married, as have countless cousins and friends. Children have been born, including my husband's niece and nephew. We have had two children who have never met their uncles, aunts, or cousins. My father-in-law and mother-in-law have both passed away without our seeing them again. Our children will never know their grandparents.

When we left Eritrea, we did not realize we were saying good-bye forever. We did not realize we were severing our lives. These losses born from escape have become integral to the experience of being Eritrean. We mourn long-distance by Skype, Facebook, and phone with relatives and friends who are scattered around the world.

Many ethnographies end with an epilogue. The anthropologist revisits the village, chats with interlocutors, notes how the children have grown, and discusses how much has changed or not changed to bring the findings up to date. Instead, I end with departure, loss, and erasure—the literal hollowing out of the nation. The "village" of teachers and students that I studied no longer exists. The vast majority of the teachers who so generously shared with me their lives, their criticisms and insights into their country, town, school, and profession, are gone. Perhaps out of fear, perhaps frustrated with the inability to grow up, perhaps angry at a state that insists on militarizing them, they have left and now reside abroad, where they can recalibrate their lives and their relationship with the nation. They are no longer positioned to do the work of the state or to reproduce the nation by socializing a new generation of young people. What could be more emblematic of the impotence of the state than a generation of teachers—the ones charged with reproducing the nation—who have fled?

In many ways, I neither chose to do fieldwork in Eritrea nor chose when to leave. Going to Eritrea, in my case, and leaving—for thousands of Eritreans and for my husband and me—was framed by the strictures of the coercive state and, more specifically, by the prisonlike nature of Eritrea. My husband was not allowed to leave, and so I went to Eritrea instead; he could not get out, but I could get in. Two years later, the imperative to leave and the timing of our departure were also a by-product of the intense, prison-like nature of the Eritrean enclosure. Being enclosed and imprisoned means that when you have the chance to leave, you must take it. You do not wait and hope for another chance, because that chance might not come. The experience of being imprisoned drives Eritreans to escape into what is often exile, a condition from which they cannot return. Our leaving, like the departures of so many Eritreans, is an effect, a by-product, of the dynamics of encampment.

Encampment in Eritrea and Elsewhere

Throughout this book, I have suggested that Eritrea, with its prohibitions on leaving, its tight controls, and its biopolitical management, can be better understood through the logics of encampment. Enclosures—camps—are a means of creating spaces that can be controlled, regulated, and managed. Governance through camps is the modus operandi of the Eritrean state. Not only is the whole country enclosed and regulated like a camp; a plethora of actual camps, such as military camps and work camps for students, also punctuate the national space and are visible throughout the country. The country is a series of literal camps within a larger figurative camp. Camps, both literal and figurative, are political spaces preoccupied with containing elements regarded as threatening and dangerous by keeping them in or out while also utilizing extremes of coercion and control and devolving sovereignty to state actors. Here I have also argued that schools are camps in their own right.

Processes of encampment, enclosure, and mass imprisonment are far from unique to Eritrea. It has been noted that nation-states in the late twentieth and early twenty-first centuries face "waning sovereignty," arguably giving rise to this preoccupation and near obsession with enclosure (Brown 2010). A large number of nations are building walls, barriers, and security fences along their borders, while other nations are building security barriers to protect communities within nations (for a discussion of both of these phenomena, see Brown 2010). Some of these forms of securitized enclosure—security barriers between national territories, gated communities, security gates around property—are intended to keep those who are unwanted *out* and, thereby, protect those who are *in*. In this sense, the enclosure is like a "gated community" (Brown 2010: 19). What is inside the walls is protected from the dangers outside. When communities or nations build security barriers around themselves, they simultaneously respond to perceived threats and produce a sense of identification with what is inside the enclosure.

Camps are intensely concerned with security and risk management in their myriad forms. Securitization leads to the utilization of the extremes of coercion, sometimes to keep people out, as in the case of walling off national borders with security barriers, and sometimes to keep dangerous elements in to protect society from their influence, such as in the case of prisons and detention centers. Eritrea is perhaps somewhat unique in that it has created a nationwide camp not to keep people out but to seal the nation and keep nationals *in*. Additionally, as I discuss below, this camp regulates the terms under which nationals who are able to get out may return. As with other countries that are anxious about waning sovereignty and concerned about security, enclosing the population within the national territory in Eritrea is a response to a sense of siege and security threats (Tronvoll and Mekonnen 2014). The most pressing threat, of course, is the lingering border conflict, which produces the ongoing state of siege in Eritrea and, for some, justifies the mass militarization of the population. However, the logics of encampment in Eritrea are not just about protecting the nation from security threats but also about making Eritrean subjects who ascribe to the ruling People's Front for Democracy and Justice's (PFDJ's) version of what it means to be Eritrean. The instinct to govern through enclosing, while rooted in the country's military ethos, is about the party's revolutionary project and its desire to produce a nation oriented around these revolutionary notions of progress, unity, and *wholeness* that would fuse together disparate ethnic, religious, and regional identifications. In this regard, Eritrea is, perhaps, similar to Cold War–era, revolutionary dictatorships, which sealed borders and prevented people from leaving to protect "fragile" societies, promulgate the ideologies of socialism, and reinvent "new" societies (Brown 2010: 40; see also Hinton 2005). Total social change was the ultimate goal of these powerfully moral Cold War–era projects, and encampment was the key strategy to bring about this goal. Thus, in seeking to protect its national community from polluting influences, Eritrea is a complex "gated community" seeking to protect itself from external threats and take care of its population.

In contrast to the gated community, other forms of enclosure, such as prisons, concentration camps, and detention centers, are intended to guard sovereignty by keeping those deemed to be dangerous or polluting away from those to be protected. Imprisonment, detention, and mass incarceration are arguably a product of the same concern about weakened sovereignty and the subsequent securitization that emerges from perceptions that the government cannot keep us safe without removing those deemed to be dangerous. While the impetus to secure borders and communities looks to keep those deemed dangerous and unwanted *out*, prisons enclose those deemed a threat within a tightly controlled environment. They keep the dangerous elements *in*. The rationale for concentration camps, detention centers, and prisons is still to ward off security threats, but these camps do so by containing elements deemed to be threatening. They serve to imprison and punish those regarded as not fit to belong to the larger, protected whole. Because Eritrea protects itself by coercing and imprisoning its own nationals, it combines the two forms of encampment—the gated community that protects and purifies those inside and the prison that punishes those inside and deems them dangerous.

One of the core objectives of this book is to explore what happens to national identifications under these extremes of encampment. The large swathe of the population whose relationship with the state is mediated by the biopolitical metrics of imprisonment and punishment fundamentally recalibrates its relationship with the nation. Arjun Appadurai (1996: 39) has noted that the hyphen that binds nation to state in most countries, if not all, is now more an "index of disjuncture" than an "icon of conjuncture." He suggests that nations and states "have become one and another's projects" (1996: 39). Even in a country like Eritrea, which initially appeared to be extremely adept at hyphenating its nation to its state, we can observe how the state has struggled and ultimately cannibalized its nation, its nationals, and its national project (Appadurai 1996: 39). At independence in Eritrea, the liberating and ruling party instituted an intensive, revolutionary nation-making project. As I showed in Chapter 1, the party developed and disseminated an ideology based on the legacy of The Struggle, values of equality, the commonalities of all Eritrean peoples, and, above all, the willingness to sacrifice and die for the country. It also set in place a variety of technologies designed to produce this type of subject. However, because those technologies were coercive, particularly after the failure to demobilize when the border war ended, they unraveled the party's version of nationalism, leaving Eritrean nationalism intact but fragmented. The party's unitary and unified vision for the country coexists with multiple notions of what it means to be Eritrean. This turned the meaning of being Eritrean into a question, a debate, no longer defined by party hegemony based on the tropes of revolution and sacrifice.

The party and the government it had put in place now struggled to reproduce the values of the struggle for independence. In the absence of effervescent buy-in from Eritreans, the government wound up forcing people into National Service, leading Eritreans to imagine the party's nation-making project as emblematic of the punishing state. They thought of themselves as punished subjects, forced to serve rather than valiantly sacrificing for the good of the nation. Attempts by the leadership to stay true to its nation-building agenda, which tried to maintain the hyphen between nation and state, produced a vicious cycle of coercion and evasion. Once committed to forcing citizens to comply with its nation-building agenda (and to National Service in particular), the leadership had no choice but to continue to coerce. Meanwhile, the more coercive the state became, the more Eritreans evaded forms of coercion. This in turn led to more coercion and more evasion, ultimately leading to large numbers of people fleeing the country.

The vicious cycle of coercion and evasion is not simply a battle between a monolithic state with the will and capacity to *force* and a population intent on escape and evasion. Rather, it is also enacted between middle actors, such as teachers and citizens. This vicious cycle plays out not between The State and The People, writ large, but through everyday encounters between people who have multiple commitments as people and as state employees. Thus, this cycle occurs within the state apparatus itself, leading to multiple contradictions, inconsistencies, and inefficiencies that reveal the impotence of the state. In other words, as state employees struggle to *be* the state, they embody the cycle of coercion and evasion.

Under a regime of encampment, state sovereignty devolves into a plethora of individual state actors. If the camp is the embodiment of the state of exception, which normalizes the use of force and abandons the rule of law, then there is little to stop state employees from utilizing coercion or violence with impunity (Agamben 1998, 2005). This is certainly the case in Eritrea and elsewhere; it is evident in the behavior of bureaucrats, who may deny people documentation that will give them the freedom to leave the country, change jobs, pursue higher education, or even take annual leave. Many in Eritrea, including my husband and me, experienced this when trying to acquire exit visas; we became aware of how many people have the power to deny, contain, and constrain. Impunity is also apparent in the many accounts of punishment, torture, and detention within military units as well as among the police, who commonly use force and generally make decisions about the use of violence outside any guidance of law.[2] Impunity is present in schools, where teachers seal off school compounds, have students arrested, sort students, and use violence liberally as a punishment. Under a state of exception, particular places—schools, military units, and even ministry offices—become their own sovereign spaces where power is diffused to those who act with impunity, making decisions about the use of force on behalf of the state, but not according to any coherent state mandate or policy.

State employees, including bureaucrats, military commanders, police, and teachers, may act coercively and even violently. Though they act without the constraint of law, there is usually a complex logic to their use of violence and force, which may constrain violence or unleash it. Morality, beliefs, prejudices, and attitudes frame their decisions about the use of force and coercion, while debates about all of these complicate their decisions. Uncertainty about the future and a sense of moral crisis heighten the stakes of these debates, reframing these decisions about coercion and violence. Additionally, state actors' own imaginaries of the state—in this case, imaginaries of the state as failing to maintain order—amplify their sense of responsibility for the morality of the nation. Thus, state actors may act with impunity under a devolved state of exception, but they do so in response to a complex configuration of factors, including their own contested morality, the insecurity brought on by an uncertain future, and their own imaginaries of what the state is doing to rectify this insecurity.

To further complicate our understanding of the state, these same state actors, who produce coercive state effects within the sovereign space of their own encampment, are also subject to regimes of encampment and coercion within the larger nationwide camp. Middle actors respond to being evaded with coercion and respond to being coerced with evasion, thus embodying the vicious cycle of coercion and evasion. Due to the limitless liminality of National Service, teachers believed they could not help students "grow up." Indeed, they could not grow up themselves. As a result, they gave up, slacked off, and joined the students in a kind of foot-dragging resistance that made the schools ineffective. Teachers showed up late and generally "did not act like teachers." They mocked the national narrative and created opportunities, willingly or unwillingly, in which students could do so as well. Many sought ways to escape the teaching profession and, ultimately left the country, seeing few other options. At the same time, the ensuing disorder that teachers helped create gave rise to their resurging sense of moral crisis and an effort to retake control that was almost vigilante-like in its determination to do better than the government at governing students.

Coercion and evasion inevitably produce each other, particularly within the enclosed conditions of encampment. This was certainly apparent in schools, but also in Eritrea as a whole. Imprisoning the nation produces desires and, indeed, a sense of the necessity to escape, which in turn produces the necessity of more coercive measures to prevent people from escaping. Containing people within enclosed military units, where violence is rampant, produces the need to evade National Service but also creates the state's need to enact more coercive means to conscript. *Gifa* was one such method; utilizing schools as a technology of conscription was another. Student attempts to use schooling to evade National Service led teachers to become more coercive by tightening the school enclosures and shoring up school walls, which, in turn, led students to slack off more in schools and led teachers to believe that they were justified in using even more force. Although the examples I provide are mostly from schools in Eritrea, the mutuality of coercion and evasion certainly has played out more broadly in Eritrea and also plays out elsewhere, particularly in light of the rising preoccupation with walled sovereignty and the logics of governance that accompany an increased preoccupation with encampment worldwide.

Ultimately, the cycle of coercion and evasion reveals the state as impotent. Teachers were impotent, failing to either make schools into controlled spaces or to provide students with an alternative to the broader imprisonment, punishment, and coercion of life as a subject of the Eritrean regime. More broadly, the government was impotent in several ways. It came to rely on coercion and violence to enact its nation-making project—specifically, National Service. Meanwhile, it lacked the capacity to regulate and control the use of force by its own employees. Thus, this use of force did not accomplish any desired ideological or imaginative effects. Instead, it made state subjects feel coerced and evasive. These coerced subjects came to imagine the state negatively, delegitimizing and mistrusting the government's national project but not abandoning the nation or their sense of belonging to it.

Eritrea, with its hearkening back to an earlier era of Cold War authoritarianism, is a notably difficult case to compare. It might, at first glance, look like an artifact of an earlier political era in which it was not unheard of for countries to seal their borders, lock in their citizens, and exert extreme controls over their people. But I suggest that it is also a harbinger of things yet to come, an extreme form of encampment that punishes the punishers, coerces those who coerce, imprisons its citizens, and thereby cannibalizes the nation and renders the state impotent. Eritrea illuminates rising, and often hidden, forms of authoritarianism worldwide. This apparently odd case of Eritrea can shed light on state struggles elsewhere.

Much of the literature on authoritarianism, most of which comes out of political science, has attempted to differentiate authoritarian from democratic regimes. Despite a growing literature on the hybrid regimes in the post–Cold War era, which makes the important point that there is a complex politics within authoritarian regimes, most of the work in this area still distinguishes between distinct regime types (see, for example, Brownlee 2007; Gandhi 2008; Levitsky and Way 2010; Svolik 2012). It also tends to focus on political elites rather than on everyday life, meaning that we know very little about microlevel politics under conditions of authoritarianism. Anthropology would seem to be the field that might illuminate these dynamics; however, there has been little to no work in anthropology explicitly on authoritarianism. Several studies are incisive in this regard, but at present there is no readily identifiable anthropological literature on authoritarianism (see, for example, Mbembe 2001; Skidmore 2004; Wedeen 1999). This is a significant omission in the field given that forms of authoritarian governance are proliferating despite the widespread transition to formal democracy in many countries over the last two decades. Indeed, we might argue that so-called democracy and authoritarianism seem to be moving toward each other, with what are labeled authoritarian regimes holding elections and what are categorized as democracies utilizing increasingly authoritarian tactics to manage their populations.

This is particularly apparent at the level of lived experiences of people who live under all regime types. This makes it all the more necessary for anthropology, and ethnography more generally, to examine the phenomenon of authoritarianism. From the vantage point of lived, everyday authoritarianism, I have focused on the effects of three facets of this experience: coercion, and particularly the use of force; encampment, including imprisonment; and punishment, particularly as it frames a sense of subjectivity around being punished. As I have noted above, these facets of everyday authoritarianism are common in Eritrea and elsewhere. Indeed, a focus on these three elements makes Eritrea look much less like a unique case.

As I have written this book, I cannot help but be aware of how these three facets of authoritarianism play out in other, very different contexts where extremes of imprisonment are present, including neighborhoods fifteen minutes from where I live in Philadelphia. In the urban United States, a hugely disproportionate number of men of color come in contact with the carceral state through the police, the legal system, or prisons. The urban poor in the United States increasingly encounter the state predominantly through the auspices of being a suspect or a criminal—in short, being a punished subject. As this happens, not unlike in Eritrea, whole populations come to see the state as punishing and equate their status as citizens with being punished subjects (Lerman and Weaver 2014; Rios 2011). Ethnographies in these contexts suggest that as a guilty-until-proven-innocent mentality takes hold in these communities, subjects come to understand that there is no reliable rule of law, only a series of policing and legal practices that strip them of their humanity, constrain their everyday lives, and limit the way they think about their future (Goffman 2014; Rios 2011). A series of encounters with the force of law strip punished subjects of their humanity, rendering them "bare life" and repeatedly subjecting them to the state of exception.

Eritreans have responded to the inevitability of being punished by the state with evasiveness. This also resonates with accounts from the urban United States, where young men will go so far as to avoid signing up for government benefits that they are entitled to, avoid going to hospitals when injured or to see the birth of their children, and avoid attending public services and public places out of the knowledge that they may be punished or imprisoned if they do so (Goffman 2014; Rios 2011). This is not so different from Eritreans' learning to avoid public streets, the workplace and, at times, weddings and other events to avoid *gifa*. Ongoing attempts to avoid being punished frame life in the urban American police state similar to the way they do in the prison state of Eritrea. As the vicious cycle of coercion and evasion plays out, Eritreans and members of urban, poor, American communities master intricate strategies to live life "on the run" (Goffman 2014).

While there is an expanding understanding of what it is like to be a punished subject, little work helps us understand the symbolic and actual violence used by middle actors within these contexts. While my work has focused on teachers, I suggest that this complex configuration of coercion and evasion, morality and power, frames decisions to use force and coercion among other state actors in Eritrea and elsewhere. In the United States, public institutions, particularly schools, not only are aligned with the carceral state and thereby positioned to punish citizens but are punished by the state as well. American schools increasingly have metal detectors, random police sweeps, no-tolerance policies, and other measures that make schools ever more like the larger carceral system (Kupchik 2010; Lyons and Drew 2006). At the same time, American public schools are mandated to educate students but must do so amid intensive regulatory scrutiny and face increasing sanctions (punishments) if they do not perform well (Kupchik 2010; Lyons and Drew 2006). Similarly stringent accountability measures regulate teachers' work. Although there is no study that looks at American teachers as state actors in light of the overall climate of punishment, an examination of teachers—middle actors who are both punishers and punished—in this context would be fruitful. We know little about how teachers respond to the mandate to punish when they themselves are punished; however, lessons from teachers in Eritrea might shed light on this paradox. It would seem logical that the same vicious cycle of coercion and evasion, tinged with morality, prejudices, and imaginaries of the state, would apply under conditions in the United States and elsewhere that teachers face the strictures of encampment. Understanding teachers, whose job it is to socialize citizens, under these types of conditions is important, because it allows us to understand nationalism at a historical juncture when identifications with nations are increasingly fragmented.

Imprisoned, punished subjects do not identify with national values or notions of citizenship in conventional or official ways. A growing literature on the punished and punishing culture of the carceral state in the United States (Goffman 2014; Kupchik 2010; Lerman and Weaver 2014; Lyons and Drew 2006; Rios 2011) and elsewhere in the democratic world (Waquant 2009) shows that citizens in these communities have a fundamentally different relationship with the state. Again, there are important resonances between the way this plays out in Eritrea and in other punishing contexts.

As in Eritrea, populations susceptible to mass incarceration and state punishment in the United States recalibrate their understanding of citizenship and reimagine the nation. These populations in the United States, whom I would consider to be punished subjects, feel alienated from any sense of democratic citizenship or civic duty, arguably the cornerstones of American nationalism (Lerman and Weaver 2014). There are parallels between America's punished subjects abandoning notions of democratic citizenship and Eritreans abandoning the ideals of party-sponsored nationalism in the face of mass punishment and coercion. In both cases, a large proportion of the population effectively opts out of any attempt to be good nationals, as per official definitions, and instead embraces and legitimates various forms of evasiveness and political subjectivity that are counter to those subject positions carved out by official state discourse.

Alchemical Nationalism

Escape and encampment demarcate the experience of being Eritrean and ascribe meaning to it; they are the two modalities through which citizens understand their relationship with the regime and vice versa. Eritreans can remain imprisoned and coerced subjects of the state, or they can flee from state repression. However, a third modality enables the state to recalibrate its relationship with citizens and citizens to reimagine the meaning of the nation and therefore recalibrate their relationship with the state. I call this third modality "alchemical nationalism." If alchemy is the magic of taking something base, bare, and without value and turning it into something valuable and precious, then efforts of both the regime and opposition groups to transform unfortunate circumstances into something meaningful and sacred can be thought of as alchemical. Through bureaucratic procedures, the regime turns those who flee the country, and are therefore regarded as traitors and de facto criminals, into good citizens. Meanwhile, opposition groups discursively transform Eritreans' experiences of suffering and bare life into meaningful narratives of opposition to the regime.

Over the past ten years, the number fleeing the Eritrean regime has exploded, leading diasporic citizenship to take two significantly different forms. Tricia Redeker Hepner (2009a) introduces this dynamic through her discussion of "generation asylum" and "generation nationalism." Generation nationalism references the earlier generation of patriotic, government-supporting diasporic citizens, while generation asylum references the more recent explosion of Eritreans fleeing the current regime.

The government, however, has more recently begun to recalibrate its relationship with generation asylum, seeking out ways to alchemically transform generation asylum into citizens who perform as loyal citizens. Shortly after we left Eritrea, we learned that a teacher whom we knew well had managed to leave the country around the same time we did. (In keeping with the secrecy that surrounds departures in Eritrea, to this day, I have no idea how that family managed to secure exit visas.) We have visited them periodically over the years and were quite surprised to learn that they planned a visit to Eritrea. Around the same time, after years of witnessing Eritreans' struggles to flee the country and their anguish at being unable to return because the government regarded leaving as a crime, I suddenly became aware of many Eritreans, including those who had fled their National Service or left without permission, returning to the country to visit. I also started to hear more stories about those who fled, particularly those who arrived in Sudan, making the embassy one of their first stops so that they could receive documentation and identity papers. At some point in the last few years, the government began allowing Eritreans who left illegally to acquire consular services, including an ID card that would, in theory, allow them to travel back to Eritrea, provided they would sign a *te'asa*, a formal letter of apology that stated: "I regret having committed an offence by failing to fulfill my national obligation and I am willing to accept the appropriate measures when decided" (Hepner 2009a: 200). Signing the *te'asa* along with paying a mandatory 2 percent income tax and other additional fees effectively altered the relationship between Eritreans and the government (Hepner 2009a; Hepner and Tecle 2013). The *te'asa* is emblematic of the process of alchemical transformation of citizenship status and the reframing of the relationship between citizens, the state, and the nation. With a signature on a letter that the government has formulated (and the payment of fees and taxes), these Eritreans are instantly altered from criminals—who if caught while trying to flee Eritrea would have been imprisoned, quite likely tortured, and possibly killed—to legal, diasporic citizens with the right to return home and leave again freely. Through the use of the *te'asa*, the government coercively recalibrates notions of citizenship on a case-by-case basis, yet it still imprisons the broader population of Eritreans within the country.

As the diaspora is populated with larger and larger numbers of people who have fled the regime, opposition groups in the diaspora are involved in a national alchemy of their own. This becomes most clear in their appropriation and inversion of the language and symbolism of The Struggle to cast those who flee as the "sacrificial citizens" who are valiantly opposing the government (Bernal 2014). In October 2013, a boat that was carrying several hundred Eritreans capsized near the island of Lampedusa, off the coast of Italy. These events pulled at the heartstrings of those around the world who are concerned for humanitarian issues, highlighting the plight of refugees and asylum seekers and Italy's lack of preparedness to cope with the routine influx of immigrants. However, the way these events played out in Eritrean politics was quite different. While the world expressed concern about this grave humanitarian problem, the Eritrean government tried to distance itself from these events, initially pretending that these were not Eritreans who had died (Awate Team 2013). After some criticism for failing to mention the crash, on October 4, three days after these events, an announcement was made on Eritrean TV, referring to "illegal African immigrants" from "horn of Africa nationality" who had died, without specifying where they were from (Awate Team 2013). The dead, officially for the Eritrean government, were alchemically transformed to country-less African immigrants. Later, the Eritrean government acknowledged that the losses were mainly Eritrean, offered condolences to the families of those who died, and offered to repatriate the bodies of the deceased (Clottey 2013).

Meanwhile, Eritrean diaspora opposition groups were nationalizing these subjects and depicting them with the most sacred language of the nation. For those opposed to the government, these were martyrs, equated with those who had fought and died for the country. Opposition websites posted pictures of long rows of coffins, some of them child-sized. The websites juxtaposed these images with pictures of mourning Eritreans, critiques of government policies that drive people out of Eritrea, and declarations of anger at how the government was dealing with the boat crash. For these opposition groups, those who died in Lampedusa were martyrs who died fleeing, and therefore opposing, the policies of an oppressive regime. Furthermore, for Eritreans in Eritrea and, particularly, in the diaspora, the tragedy in Lampedusa was deeply personal—many people knew or imagined they could have known people on that boat. Opposition groups yoked this affective climate of loss to a critique of the government. This was certainly not the first time that diaspora opposition groups appropriated the language of martyrdom. As Victoria Bernal (2014: 120) describes, in 2005, the opposition website Awate posted the "Martyrs Album," a "virtual war memorial" to commemorate the lives of those who had died in the border war. This Martyrs Album, according to Bernal, was subversive not only because it enabled an opposition website to usurp the role of the state by publishing the names of the war dead but also because Awate claimed the power to "sacrilize" the dead, categorizing those who died in the border war as sacred "martyrs" along with those who died in the war for independence (2014: 121). Opposition groups that have martyred those who died making the dangerous escape from Eritrea take this one step further by labeling flight from the regime as the ultimate sacrifice.

Both the state and the people recalibrate nationalisms. Spaces of encampment produce and protect notions of national purity and pure belonging; they differentiate good citizens from bad and sort those who "really belong" from those who do not. The state may imprison or dispose of those who are deemed to be bad citizens. Indeed, the state in Eritrea has done so to a large number of people. But nationalism under conditions of encampment and exile also becomes alchemical. A symbol, image, person, or process that does not have value in one context can be transformed into someone or something that does. The state turns criminalized escapees into valued diasporic citizens. Opposition groups weave horrific tales of escape and suffering into valorous, brave acts of martyrdom for the nation. The government is intent on alchemically transforming citizenship status to bind these newly escaped diasporic citizens to the state. Meanwhile, opposition groups are intent on appropriating the sacred symbols of the nation and wresting the nation away from the ruling regime. While the country is enclosed and encamped—a space of coercion, evasion, and impotence—the places to which Eritreans are exiled become the spaces in which we can observe a multiplicity of actors and organizations, including the government, struggling over the meaning of the nation and the capacity to act as the state. In contrast to the enclosed space of the territorial nation, where the state cannibalizes its nation, weakening the hyphen between nation and state, outside the national territory the nation and the state "become each other's project" (Appadurai 1996: 39), remaking the relationship between nation and state in new ways. Governing institutions redefine citizenship. People wrest the nation away from the state. And nationalism is constantly reimagined and remade by state, nonstate, and middle actors.

Notes

INTRODUCTION

1. This is a point that has been made by a number of scholars, including Arjun Appadurai (1996), Akhil Gupta (2012), Michael Herzfeld (1997), and Lisa Wedeen (2008).

2. This definition of the state is common in much of the anthropology of the state, but I am specifically influenced by Herzfeld's (1997) and Gupta's (2012) work in this regard. See also Jean-François Bayart's work in the conclusion of *The Politics of the Belly: The State in Africa* (2009).

3. The concept of collective effervescence comes from Emile Durkheim (1965) and is borrowed by Tricia Redeker Hepner (2009b) to describe the passionate sentiments of support and joy for independence around which Eritrean nationalism coalesced during these years.

4. David O'Kane (2012) also uses the theme of struggle to illuminate the challenges of the regime to acquire legitimacy among its people. He identifies three struggles: a military struggle (the border war), a developmental struggle, and a struggle to instill national identities. I emphasize the regime's struggle to produce national identities, but I do so in a way that neither reifies nation or state nor equates the state with the regime, but rather illuminates the struggles of people to constitute nation and state and to fuse the two.

5. Achille Mbembe's (2001) and Wedeen's (1999) work draws on these frameworks but also attends to state violence specifically. Work on sovereignty that draws on Giorgio Agamben's notion of devolved sovereignty also addresses the productive and unstructured nature of state violence (see, for example, Das and Poole 2004; Hansen and Stepputat 2005). Finally, work on vigilantism has also used these frameworks to show how extra-state violence functions as the state (Buur 2003; Goldstein 2003; Lyons 2008; Smith 2004).

6. Imaginaries that emerged from state coercion reflect the maddening nature of the state. On the one hand, a sense that the country is under a state of siege and that therefore the government is legitimately taking exceptional measures to protect people may legitimate state coercion. Indeed, Eritrea galvanized its people, both during the war and after it ended, with this sense of being under siege and has often been described as "a siege state," or a

"garrison state" (International Crisis Group 2010; Müller 2012a, 2012b; Tronvoll and Mekonnen 2014). On the other hand, when the state of emergency extends beyond the point at which people legitimately sense that there is a threat, people interpret the emergency powers of coercion ascribed to state actors as the state turning against its people. However, in people's imagination of the state, there is no clear delineation between when the state legitimately derives powers from being truly "under siege" and when it has illegitimately turned against its people. This uncertainty and the unevenness of imaginaries of the state that this uncertainty produces constitute the maddening condition.

7. Wedeen makes a similar point: that these types of perspectives that focus on discipline are important to look at even in authoritarian, coercive regimes. In her work on Syria, overall she is interested in looking at how the state enacts symbolic power as well as disciplinary power and how the two become fused, leading subjects into a situation where they have to behave "as if" they support the regime. I think the symbolic power in Eritrea was somewhat different. Because liberation was so recent and there still was a powerfully lingering sense of effervescent revolutionary nationalism, Eritrean nationalism was more conflicted than performative. This is why I think Begoña Aretxaga's framing of the "maddening state" works better to understand Eritrea than Wedeen's notion of performing "as if" one is compliant with authoritarianism.

8. For example, "the state" that is held accountable for human rights violations in instances of arbitrary detention, imprisonment, or torture is assumed to have malicious intent; it is imagined as an all-powerful state that decides to behave maliciously. However, what are often thought of as state violations of rights and liberties are the result of actions by individuals who may or may not have been incentivized or forced to engage in those actions by other state actors.

9. In addition to Eritrean teachers, there were nine Indian teachers over the course of the two years I was in Assab, although only four stayed for the full two years. A complete examination of the role of these teachers and their role as "foreign" state actors is far beyond the scope of this book. Indian teachers were remarkably similar to Eritrean teachers in terms of pedagogy as well as in their understanding of their role as nation-builders. Thus, I have included the Indian teachers when their outlook and understanding of their role as teachers and "nation-builders" mirrored that of Eritrean teachers.

10. Historically, in eighteenth-century Europe, arguably the era in which the modern nation-state dawned, schools and the military worked together to create national identities, a sense of territoriality, and the mandate to protect that territory (Weber 1976). But while historical work tends to assert, quite rightly, that schools and the military have worked together to forge national attachments, the vast majority of more contemporary studies treat them separately, which does not allow for an exploration of the complex convergence and divergence of the two. There are some notable exceptions to the separation of studies of education and studies of militarization. Work on the relationship between militarization and schooling in Turkey (Altinay 2005; Kaplan 2006) makes similar observations. Additionally, there is historical work on this topic, most notably Eugene Weber's *Peasants into Frenchmen* (1976), which treats schools and the military as key. But there is still a need for this relationship to be explored more fully.

11. This is similar to the bureaucratic pilgrimages that Benedict Anderson (1991) describes as being essential to forging national identifications in eighteenth-century America; the life trajectories of educated citizens and soldiers serve as a sort of pilgrimage that nationalizes their everyday experience in local settings, such as schools or military training.

12. Militarism references not only a government's orientation toward defense and war

readiness but also the infusion of military symbols and practices into citizens' daily lives combined with a variety of symbolic and ritualized practices that valorize the nation's military past and present (Bickford 2011; O'Kane and Hepner 2009; see also Enloe 1988 and Lutz 2002). I understand militarization to be, as Andrew Bickford (2011: 24) notes, "an intentional process; something the state must set out to accomplish." Militarism becomes a way of life promoted by the state, in service to the state, and, indeed, enabling citizens to imagine the state. Militarism becomes a way of understanding the past, present, and future of the nation. Additionally, in militarized societies, experiences and encounters with military personnel and institutions mediate social experiences.

13. Exceptions to this include ethnographic studies conducted in Eritrea, which focus on various facets of everyday life in post-liberation Eritrea (see, for example, Bozzini 2011, 2013; Mahrt 2009; O'Kane 2012; Poole 2009, 2013; Treiber 2009, 2010; Tronvoll 1999; Woldemikael 2009, 2013); however, with the exception of Tronvoll 1999, no other full-length ethnographic monograph has been published until this book.

14. Eritrea has also provided fertile ground for scholars of transnationalism (Al-Ali, Black, and Koser 2001; Bernal 2004, 2005, 2014; Hepner 2009b). The ruling party's extensive organizational structure, which incorporates its diaspora into the national polity, has enabled Eritrean nationalism to remain strong among its citizens around the world (Hepner 2009b). The government is one of few to effectively levy a mandatory tax (2 percent) on members of the diaspora, which is an important source of revenue for the government. Scholars historically have used Eritrea as a case in point to show that the nation-state was not, in fact, weakening or disappearing as a result of globalization, as many predicted it would, but that nations like Eritrea could learn to operate transnationally and actually strengthen the nation-state (Bernal 2004).

CHAPTER 1

1. There is increasing and very interesting scholarship on the forms of nationalist consciousness that emerged from the colonial era in Eritrea. Because my focus here is on Eritrean government–sponsored nationalism and the genesis of the ruling party itself, there is no space to delve into this very interesting form of Eritrean nationalism, but for more information, see Makki 2011a, 2011b and Taddia 1994.

2. Earlier thinking on identity in Africa suggested that these were diverse and varied populations that were not easily turned into national populations. Kwame Anthony Appiah (1992) asserts that these were states seeking nations. Similarly, this is a central piece of Basil Davidson's (1993) argument that the nation has been a "curse" and a "burden" for Africa. Complicating these earlier arguments, more recent work suggests that in an effort to lay legitimate claim to the state, the nation is co-opted by particular groups who seek to define national belonging more narrowly. Whereas earlier literature suggests that this is a process of rejecting the idea of the nation, more recent literature argues that because of the processes of democratization and the changing political field in Africa, nationalism is now an exclusionary process. This point is made in work on autochthony (Geschiere 2009; Geschiere and Ceuppens 2005; Geschiere and Jackson 2006; Jackson 2006, 2007). The principle of nationalism has taken hold, but it has become an exclusionary principle that allows groups to lay particular claims to the state rather than a unifying one that allows the government to spread its influence over "the people" (Young 2007).

3. Family members may have feared that a loved one they had not heard from had died in the war, but absent an official announcement, they could still hold out hope. Because

many soldiers were given little or no leave to visit family, many wrote home infrequently, and letters were easily lost, there was room for hope that family members with whom they had not had contact were still alive and serving in the military.

CHAPTER 2

1. At the same time that the G-15 was arrested, several Eritrean U.S. Embassy employees were also arrested.

2. Officially, Eritreans are considered of military age until they reach forty-five, but there are accounts of people being conscripted up to age fifty.

3. It is important to remind the reader that my definition of "the state" assumes that we understand that "the state" is not a material thing or a totality. Throughout this chapter, it is necessary for me to use language that may appear to be reifying the state, but all references of the state are to how the state is imagined and conceptualized.

4. Michel Foucault shows that the modern military was a disciplinary institution extraordinarily adept at producing the modern, disciplined state subject. Indeed, Foucault (1995: 136) singles out the soldier in his discussion of seventeenth-century technologies of power that "discovered the body as an object and target of power" that could be "manipulated, shaped, trained." Soldier bodies are intensely disciplined. The experience of being in the military requires extensive temporal, spatial, and bodily control. Military training thus produces "isolation effects," which lead individuals to think of themselves as disciplined subjects (Mitchell 1991, 2006).

5. Foucault's (1995: 1) depiction of the seventeenth-century soldier emphasizes the "recognizability" of external attributes of the corps of soldiers. Their posture, coordinated movements, uniforms, and uniformity produce a collective, singular, uniform entity—the military. Extending Foucault's argument, Timothy Mitchell (2006) argues that military discipline creates not only a disciplined state subject/soldier but also the very concept of "the military" as a whole.

6. Although initially there was widespread support for these various forms of service and Eritreans reflected a sense of pride in seeing televised images of National Service cadres, even in those early years, prior to the border war, there were complaints about the overly coercive and punitive nature of National Service, which belied docility while producing obedience. But despite these early complaints about National Service, it was largely an acceptable practice as long as the government honored its part of the agreement. Until 2001, few questioned National Service and the moral authority of the government to conscript. Indeed, when the war broke out, many, including those who had been critical of the institution, were thankful that the country had a ready fighting force to defend the country.

7. Katherine Verdery (1996) notes that the etatization of time could occur both when people have to engage in daily activities, such as waiting in food lines, and more coercively, when people are compelled to participate in lengthy parades and state performances.

8. Lisa Wedeen (1999) makes a very similar point. As I noted in the introduction, she refers to subjects of authoritarian leaders performing "as if" they supported the regime but transgressing in subtle ways.

9. The United Nations High Commission on Refugees (UNHCR) estimates that there were currently 252,000 Eritrean refugees and asylum seekers as of 2011, a number that steadily increased from 124,121 in 2003 (UNHCR 2000, 2002, 2005, 2011). The number continues to rise. As of December 2014, UNHCR estimates that there are 363,077 Eritrean refugees and 53,662 asylum seekers (UNHCR 2015). In the first ten months of

2014, 36,678 Eritreans requested asylum in Europe, compared to 12,960 in the previous year (UNHCR 2014).

10. In January 2013, a group of soldiers briefly occupied the Ministry of Information and read a statement on Eritrean television, demanding the implementation of the constitution and the release of political prisoners. There has been no further open opposition or protest since this event, which has come to be known as "Forto 2013," although many opposition groups in the diaspora protested at Eritrean embassies around the world. Forto 2013 was the first open protest since students protested the arrest of their student union leader in 2001.

CHAPTER 3

1. Standards-based curricula have become prominent in the United States and are usually about integrating state curriculum with state standards and state tests. The Texas curriculum was notable for its early efforts to match statewide standards to statewide examinations, thereby holding schools and students to these standards.

2. This is a commonly understood assertion in a variety of literatures in the field of education. That schools reproduce class structures, particularly in the industrialized world, has been well asserted statistically and ethnographically (Althusser 1971; Anyon 1981; Bowles and Gintis 1976). Pierre Bourdieu and Jean Claude Passeron (1990) have taken up this argument and thoroughly theorized it, showing the ways in which schooling cultivates particular tastes, habitus, and therefore cultural capital. This assertion about the reproductive qualities of education is also at the core of work on social reproduction (Levinson and Holland 1996). Building on this, one of the core tenets of theories of cultural production is that schools reproduce broader social locations and positions, but in contrast to social reproduction theories, cultural production theories allow more agency and more understanding of the shifting, mutable nature of these structures. The vast majority of these studies explore the industrialized north, and, in general, much more work needs to be done in places where schools, and class structures themselves, function somewhat differently.

3. A robust literature on cultural production and social reproduction has illustrated the ways in which the subjectivity of an educated person is produced. This particular subjectivity maps onto racial, ethnic, or class privilege, thereby reinforcing broader societal inequalities, but it can also alter social structures and identities in meaningful ways. For an overview of this literature, see Levinson, Foley, and Holland 1996. For a discussion about how this literature applies to national identities, see, for example, Benei 2008, Hall 2002, and Levinson 2001.

4. The old system included clear written guidelines for what constituted failing a grade. In contrast, the new system never made clear to teachers what constituted "failure" for the year. Previously, under the old system, what constituted "failure" for the year was quite complex but was written in policy. For example, under the old system, in the Senior Secondary School, students "failed" their grade if they failed several different combinations of classes: (1) if they failed English or math and one other subject or (2) if they failed any other combination of three subjects out of the remaining five to seven subjects offered in Senior Secondary Schools (biology, chemistry, physics, history, geography, and sports were always offered, and sometimes Arabic and civics). The new system had no such clear policy regarding what constituted failure. One of the problems when the "new curriculum" was implemented was that the standard, academic courses were weighted differently; for example, students no longer took all three natural sciences every semester, as they had previ-

ously. Other "enrichment" courses were added, including "Family and Consumer Science," "IT," and "Health Science." No policy ever clearly stated which courses would be included when calculating whether students would fail for the year.

5. These comments, made the same year that the new policies were implemented, might suggest that Eritrea's choice of reforms were informed by (or resulted from) direct pressure from foreign donors. However, while it has been noted in many other countries that developing nations may have to succumb to pressures from international donors to fund their education systems (Berman 1992), Eritrea has long shown itself to be highly resistant to any type of coercive relationship with international donors and has been willing to reject aid to reject that which does not allow the government significant autonomy over its own policies. The director general of General Education described relationships with donors in the following way: "We share with our partners as long as they believe that we have the ownership and we have the program. They focus on what we are interested in and what we want to focus on." Another interviewed curriculum writer went into more detail about what he thought the process of international influence might be, concluding that it was ultimately a national process: "I am quite sure there must be some kind of influence [from donors]. They have some ideas. But the good thing about our educational transformation is it has been initiated exclusively internally."

CHAPTER 4

1. Ethnographies that show how schooling produces identities, including national identities, have focused a great deal on the use of school-based rituals to instill a sense of the meaning of being an educated person (Levinson, Foley, and Holland 1996; McLaren 1986; Quantz 2011).

2. Victor Turner (1969) discusses millenarian movements and hippies as examples of groups in a stage of extended liminality. Liisa Malkki's (1995) work suggests that certain groups of people, such as refugees, are liminally located between categories produced by the nation-state system or "national order of things."

3. In addition to the two roughly defined categories of Eritrean teachers, there were also Indian teachers, but for reasons outlined in the Introduction (because they were cultural outsiders), they do not figure into my discussion in this particular chapter.

4. Teachers who had already fully completed military training and National Service were called to the front lines during the third offensive and then were allowed to return to their teaching posts when the fighting stopped. University students and teachers who had not yet received training were called to training and after that began their National Service.

5. Indeed, historically the Eritrean People's Liberation Front's (EPLF's) egalitarian ideology attempted to break down "traditional" hierarchies and empower youth. The People's Front for Democracy and Justice (PFDJ), and its predecessor during the war for liberation, the EPLF, specifically targeted youth as a vulnerable and disenfranchised category of the population and has had a long history of organizing youth and breaking down earlier alignments of power (Hepner 2009b; Pool 2001).

6. According to Peter McLaren (1986: 82), the macrorituals refer to the "overall passage of students through the school system," while the microrituals are the smaller, everyday rituals.

7. Control, as teachers described it, referred to managing the students and holding them accountable for their behavior by taking attendance, administering tests, and imposing consequences for lateness.

8. In Eritrean schools, students remain in their classroom throughout the school day, while teachers rotate from room to room; thus, the room belongs to the students.

9. Teacher lateness was not only a product of wanting to extend summer vacations and avoid returning to work. Some teachers worked during the summer, and their summer work encroached on the school year. Others experienced problems with finding transportation to Assab. New National Service teachers fresh from the university, who, depending on the year, composed a good percentage of school staff, had always been assigned to their posts belatedly and generally arrived once the semester was well underway.

10. It was common for teachers to leave the class a few minutes early if they had completed their lessons or to stay a few minutes late if their lessons ran over. However, it is possible that Aron felt self-conscious about leaving the class early because I was present. This was a problem, particularly in some of my observations of younger teachers. Despite my efforts to assure them that I wanted to see what they did normally in their classes, I often had the sense that, in contrast to the older teachers, they believed they had to perform in a particular way for me.

11. Perhaps surprisingly, students did not seem to make much of my presence in the room. In some classes when I first observed, when the teacher left the room, some students would glance at me and tell the others to be quiet, gesturing at me. But as soon as I indicated to them that I was not a teacher and they should carry on, they did so with little hesitation. In other classes, the students figured out on their own that I was not in a teacher role and paid no attention to me. This speaks to the fact that how the teacher behaved, in a particular ritualized manner, cued to the students how they were supposed to act. I was doing nothing that indicated to students that I was an authority figure. I sat in the back or the middle of the room, quietly taking notes as they were. I typically did not leave when the teacher left. I did nothing to command or require their obedience and docility. In some classes, the students tried to draw me into their conversations, sometimes even when the teacher was teaching. But mostly, they ignored me.

CHAPTER 5

1. Notions of sovereignty discussed by Giorgio Agamben (1998) and introduced by Carl Schmitt ([1922] 2005) are deeply entwined with notions of containment or "enclosure" (Brown 2010), which for Agamben is epitomized by the concentration camp. Law blurs with what is outside the law but enforced by state actors. State actors who are charged with upholding or following laws and policies find themselves positioned, and often expected, to behave in ways that are technically illegal but are considered necessary in times of crisis or emergency. In the state of exception, the force of law acts with violence on citizens, especially those categorized as dangerous or impure, stripping them of the rights that would be guaranteed to them by law. Those who encounter the full force of the law without the rights guaranteed by that law exist in a condition that Agamben refers to as "bare life," not necessarily denied rights by the law but existing outside the law itself and effectively invisible to the law.

2. The lack of rights applies to a greater extent to those evading military service, who may be arrested at any moment, detained indefinitely, gravely mistreated, and perhaps killed with impunity. It applies to a lesser extent to civil servants, who also have minimal rights, but a few more than conscripts and many more than those evading service. In Chapter 2, I noted the absolute level of bodily control that conscripts experience. Additionally, no one has the right to own property or leave the country until National Service has been

completed. Furthermore, no written policies allocate when, how often, or under which conditions soldiers in National Service are awarded leave or under which conditions they may return home. Reports from those who have fled National Service suggest that considerations such as when a soldier may visit his or her family are made on a highly personal basis by commanding officers and that they may be denied for equally personal reasons.

3. Caroline Humphrey (2007) notes that Agamben's notion of sovereignty is tremendously useful for anthropologists to work with, as it allows for an exploration of very specific forms of state regulation and control of populations outside the traditional centralized notion of the state. However, she cautions that while we need to consider seriously the ways in which sovereignty devolves from the state, we need not treat Agamben as too prescriptive.

4. My thinking about morality and violence is illuminated by recent work on the anthropology of vigilantism, which shows that much vigilante violence is an attempt to rectify perceived or real weaknesses of the state. Like vigilantes, teachers behaved in ways that they saw as holding the state accountable to its moral obligations (Goldstein 2003). This work on vigilantism draws on a reinterpretation of Agamben's (1998) notion (which in itself is adopted from Schmitt [1922] 2005) to show the ways in which sovereignty becomes devolved and decentralized (see also Das and Poole 2004; Hansen and Stepputat 2005).

5. Not surprisingly, teachers described these memories of well-ordered schools when I asked them directly what they thought was wrong with schools at the time of my fieldwork. But during life history interviews, when asked to recount their own education, they also spontaneously drew comparisons between well-ordered schools and respectful students of the past and the disorder of the present. Only a couple of teachers who grew up in Eritrea during the war noted that their schools were not as disciplined. One of these two teachers attributed this to their being taught by Ethiopian teachers who did not care about Eritreans. Another noted that there were many fights between Eritrean and Ethiopian students in the school. In both cases, the ongoing conditions and Ethiopian rule were implicated in the lack of order in schools. But, in general, most teachers noted that until the border war, schools in Assab were more disciplined.

6. When I spoke with teachers and directors in the highlands, they were experiencing similar or more serious behavior problems with their students, so the perception that students in Assab behaved worse than students in the highlands was more an expression of teacher frustration than a reality related to Assab.

7. It should be noted that because my research focused on teachers, my own knowledge of Afar culture is also very cursory and superficial. For this reason, I do not comment on these cultural differences in depth. The point here is that what were likely differences in cultural habits and practices were often coded by teachers as evidence of Afar students' being more "backward" and less "modern."

8. In practice, because of the dearth of Junior Secondary Schools throughout the country, relatively few students actually attended school up to grade 8, though according to educational policy, anyone could attend. Furthermore, the government was rapidly expanding access to grade 8 education by building more schools.

9. Parallels with the measures teachers took and the work of vigilantes can be seen here. If vigilantism is an attempt to retain order, justice, and morality when the state is not capable of doing so (Buur 2003; Goldstein 2003; Lyons 2008; Smith 2004), vigilante violence comes from a crisis of state legitimacy, such as existed in Eritrea, and challenges the state's capacity to maintain control and enforce justice but simultaneously reinforces these same ideals of justice and an ordered society (Buur 2003; Goldstein 2003). Its purpose is not to "overturn the state" but to "recall it to its legal obligations, its social contract with its citizens" (Goldstein 2003: 25). In times of moral anxiety, vigilante justice can be seen as an

attempt to restore a sense of morality: "It is through the constant enactment and embodiment of violence that the moral community is performed" (Buur 2003: 25).

10. Even adult married couples typically did not tend to overtly express romance, emotion, or affection for each other in public. There were very certain bars where more liberal men and women could go on a date; usually they were dimly lit with secluded areas where one would not be seen. In more public areas, women typically sat with their backs to the room to avoid being seen.

11. Generally students were not given ID cards. An exception was made for grade 8 and Senior Secondary School students, many of whom looked old enough to be of military age and were therefore at risk of being detained and forced into military training by the authorities.

CONCLUSION

1. I have detailed this process in Riggan 2014.

2. Although a systematic examination of the police was well beyond the scope of my research, anecdotally, I know of enough examples of police deciding how long to detain people and using violence liberally as an interrogation technique or punishment to make the claim that police officers in Eritrea, even more so than teachers, were generally at liberty to decide on the exception.

References

Abrams, Phillip. 1988. "Notes on the Difficulty of Studying the State." *Journal of Historical Sociology* 1:58–89.
Adams, Laura. 2010. *The Spectacular State: Culture and National Identity in Uzbekistan.* Durham, NC: Duke University Press.
Agamben, Giorgio. 1998. *Homo Sacer: Sovereign Power and Bare Life.* Stanford, CA: Stanford University Press.
———. 2005. *State of Exception.* Chicago: University of Chicago Press.
Al-Ali, Nadje, Richard Black, and Khalid Koser. 2001. "The Limits to 'Transnationalism': Bosnian and Eritrean Refugees in Europe as Emerging Transnational Communities." *Ethnic and Racial Studies* 24 (4): 578–600.
Al Jazeera. 2014. "Spike in Eritreans Fleeing into Ethiopia." Al Jazeera.com, October 29. Available at www.aljazeera.com/news/africa/2014/10/spike-eritreans-fleeing-into-ethiopia-20141029101248192297.html.
Althusser, Louis. 1971. "Ideology and Ideological State Apparatuses." *Lenin and Philosophy and Other Essays,* 127–186. New York: Monthly Review Press.
Altinay, Ayse Gul. 2005. *The Myth of the Military Nation: Military, Gender and Education in Turkey.* New York: Palgrave.
Anderson, Benedict. 1991. *Imagined Communities.* London: Verso.
Anyon, Jean. 1981. "Social Class and School Knowledge." *Curriculum Inquiry* 11 (1): 3–42.
Appadurai, Arjun. 1996. *Modernity at Large: Cultural Dimensions of Globalization.* Minneapolis: University of Minnesota Press.
Appiah, Kwame Anthony. 1992. *In My Father's House: Africa in the Philosophy of Culture.* New York: Oxford University Press.
Arbi Harnet. 2014a. "Eritrea: Asmara Residents Will Retaliate against Roundups by Ethiopian Mercenaries Deployed by the Regime." Asmarino.com, October 24. Available at http://asmarino.com/news/4021-eritrea-asmara-residents-will-retaliate-against-roundups-by-ethiopian-mercenaries-deployed-by-the-regime.

———. 2014b. "Eritrea: Asmara Tense but Hopeful Following Mass Resistance to Forced Militarization." Asmarino.com, October 22. Available at http://asmarino.com/news/155-breaking-news/4017-eritrea-asmara-tense-but-hopeful-following-mass-resistance-to-forced-militarization.

———. 2014c. "Eritrea: Residents of the Capital Quietly Resist the Government's Militarisation Campaign." Asmarino.com, October 10. Available at http://asmarino.com/news/3991-eritrea-residents-of-the-capital-quietly-resist-the-government-rsquo-s-militarisation-campaign.

Aretxaga, Begoña. 2003. "Maddening States." *Annual Review of Anthropology* 32:393–410.

Argenti, Nicholas. 2007. *Intestines of the State: Youth, Violence and Belated Histories in the Cameroon Grassfields*. Chicago: University of Chicago Press.

Awate Team. 2013. "Isaias Regime and Lampedusa: A Week Late, a Weak Explanation." Awate.com, October 10. Available at http://awate.com/isaias-regime-and-lampedusa-a-week-late-a-weak-explanation.

Bakhtin, Mikhail. 1984. *Rabelais and His World*. Bloomington: Indiana University Press.

Bayart, Jean-Francois. 2009. *The State in Africa: The Politics of the Belly*. Cambridge: Polity Press.

Bayat, Asef. 2010. *Life as Politics: How Ordinary People Change the Middle East*. Stanford, CA: Stanford University Press.

Benei, Veronique. 2008. *Schooling Passions: Nation, History and Language in Contemporary Western India*. Stanford, CA: Stanford University Press.

Benjamin, Walter. 1978. *Reflections: Essays, Aphorisms, Autobiographical Writings*. New York: Schocken Books.

Bereketeab, Redie. 2010. "The Politics of Language in Eritrea: Equality of Languages vs. Bilingual Official Language Policy." *African and Asian Studies* 9 (1): 149–190.

Berman, Edward. 1992. "Donor Agencies and Third World Educational Development, 1945–1985." In *Emergent Issues in Education: Comparative Perspectives*, edited by Robert F. Arnove, Philip G. Altbach, and Gail P. Kelly, 57–74. New York: State University of New York Press.

Bernal, Victoria. 2004. "Eritrea Goes Global: Reflections on Nationalism in a Transnational Era." *Cultural Anthropology* 19:3–25.

———. 2005. "Eritrea On-line: Diaspora, Cyberspace, and the Public Sphere." *American Ethnologist* 32 (4): 660–675.

———. 2014. *Nation as Network: Diaspora, Cyberspace and Citizenship*. Chicago: University of Chicago Press.

Bickford, Andrew. 2011. *Fallen Elites: The Military Other in Post-unification Germany*. Stanford, CA: Stanford University Press.

Billig, Michael. 1995. *Banal Nationalism*. London: Sage.

Bolten, Catherine. 2015. "A Great Scholar Is an Overeducated Person: Education and Practices of Uncertainty in Sierra Leone." *Journal of Anthropological Research* 71 (1): 23–47.

Bourdieu, Pierre. 1977. *Outline of a Theory of Practice*. Cambridge: Cambridge University Press.

Bourdieu, Pierre, and Jean Claude Passeron. 1990. *Reproduction in Education, Society and Culture*. London: Sage.

Bowles, Samuel, and Herbert Gintis. 1976. *Schooling in Capitalist America: Educational Reform and the Contradictions of Economic Life*. New York: Basic Books.

Bozzini, David. 2011. "Low-Tech Surveillance and the Despotic State in Eritrea." *Surveillance and Society* 9 (1/2): 93–113.

———. 2013. "The Catch-22 of Resistance: Jokes and the Political Imagination of Eritrean Conscripts." *Africa Today* 60 (2): 39–66.
Brown, Wendy. 2010. *Walled States, Waning Sovereignty*. New York: Zone Books.
Brownlee, Jason. 2007. *Authoritarianism in an Age of Democracy*. Cambridge: Cambridge University Press.
Buur, Lars. 2003. "Crime and Punishment on the Margins of the Postapartheid State." *American Anthropological Association* 28 (1): 23–42.
Chabal, Patrick, and Jean-Pascal Daloz. 1999. *Africa Works: Disorder as Political Instrument*. Oxford, UK: James Curry.
Chalfin, Brenda, 2010. *Neoliberal Frontiers: An Ethnography of Sovereignty in West Africa*. Chicago: University of Chicago Press.
Clottey, Peter. 2013. "Lampedusa Boat Tragedy a Crime against Eritrea, Says Official." Voice of America, October 15. Available at www.voanews.com/content/lampedusa-boat-tragedy-a-crime-against-eritrea-says-official/1770413.html.
Coe, Cati. 2005. *Dilemmas of Culture in African Schools: Youth, Nationalism, and the Transformation of Knowledge*. Chicago: University of Chicago Press.
Connell, Dan. (1993) 1997. *Against All Odds: A Chronicle of the Eritrean Revolution*. Trenton, NJ: Red Sea Press.
———. 2001. "Inside the EPLF: The Origins of the 'People's Party' and Its Role in the Liberation of Eritrea." *Review of African Political Economy* 89:345–364.
———. 2005. *Conversations with Eritrean Political Prisoners*. Trenton, NJ: Red Sea Press.
———. 2011. "From Resistance to Governance: Eritrea's Trouble with Transition." *Review of African Political Economy* 38 (129): 419–433.
Corbridge, Stuart, Glyn Williams, Manoj Srivastava, and Rene Veron. 2005. *Seeing the State: Governance and Governmentality in India*. Cambridge: Cambridge University Press.
Corrigan, Phillip, and Derek Sayer. 1985. *The Great Arch: English State Formation as Cultural Revolution*. Oxford, UK: Basil Blackwell.
Das, Veena, and Poole Deborah, eds. 2004. *Anthropology in the Margins of the State*. Santa Fe, NM: School of American Research Press.
Davidson, Basil. 1993. *The Black Man's Burden: Africa and the Curse of the Nation-State*. New York: Three Rivers Press.
De Certeau, Michel. 1984. *The Practice of Everyday Life*. Los Angeles: University of California Press.
Dorman, Sarah. 2005. "Narratives of Nationalism in Eritrea: Research and Revisionism." *Nations and Nationalism* 11 (2): 203–222.
———. 2006. "Post-liberation Politics in Africa: Examining the Political Legacy of Struggle." *Third World Quarterly* 27 (6): 1085–1101.
Dorman, Sarah, Daniel Hammett, and Paul Nugent, eds. 2007. *Making Nations, Creating Strangers: States and Citizenship in Africa*. Leiden, Netherlands: Brill.
Douglas, Mary. (1966) 1984. *Purity and Danger: An Analysis of the Concepts of Pollution and Taboo*. Boston: Ark.
Downey, Charles Aiden. 2007. "'You Can't Save Them All': The Moral Economy of Teacher Work in a 'Failing' Inner City High School." Ph.D. diss., University of Pennsylvania.
Durkheim, Emile. 1965. *The Elementary Forms of the Religious Life*. New York: Free Press.
Enloe, Cynthia. 1988. *Does Khaki Become You? Militarization of Women's Lives*. London: Pandora.
EPLF. 1977. *National Democratic Program of the Eritrean People's Liberation Front*. Adopted at the 1st Congress. January 31.

———. 1994. *A National Charter for Eritrea: For a Democratic, Just and Prosperous Future.* Nakfa, Eritrea, February.

Feldman, Allen. 1991. *Formations of Violence: The Narrative of the Body and Political Terror in Northern Ireland.* Chicago: University of Chicago Press.

Ferguson, James, and Akhil Gupta. 2002. "Spatializing States: Towards an Ethnography of Neoliberal Governmentality." *American Ethnologist* 29 (4): 981–1002.

Foucault, Michel. 1990. *The History of Sexuality: An Introduction.* New York: Random House.

———. 1995. *Discipline and Punish.* New York: Vintage.

———. 1997. *Society Must Be Defended: Lectures at the College de France 1975–1976.* New York: Picador.

———. 2004. *Security, Territory, Population: Lectures at the College de France 1977–1978.* New York: Picador.

Frederik, Laurie. 2012. *Trumpets in the Mountains: Theatre and the Politics of National Culture in Cuba.* Durham, NC: Duke University Press.

Gandhi, Jennifer. 2008. *Political Institutions under Dictatorship.* Cambridge: Cambridge University Press.

Gebremedhin, Jordan. 1989. *Peasants and Nationalism in Eritrea.* Trenton, NJ: Red Sea Press.

Gedab News. 2014a. "Crisis in the Eritrean Army." Awate.com, April 3. Available at http://awate.com/crisis-in-the-eritrean-army.

———. 2014b. "Intense Anxiety Engulfing Eritrea." Awate.com, October 23. Available at http://awate.com/intense-anxiety-engulfing-eritrea.

———. 2014c. "A New Wave of Escapees Leaving Eritrea." Awate.com, October 21. Available at http://awate.com/a-new-wave-of-escapees-leaving-eritrea.

———. 2014d. "The Plight of 'Zuria 26' Enrages Eritrean Youth." Awate.com, October 27. Available at http://awate.com/the-plight-of-zuria-26-enrages-eritrean-youth.

Gennepp, Arnold Van. 1960. *The Rites of Passage.* London: Routledge.

Geschiere, Peter. 2009. *The Perils of Belonging: Autochthony, Citizenship and Exclusion in Africa and Europe.* Chicago: University of Chicago Press.

Geschiere, Peter, and Bambi Cueppens. 2005. "Autochthony: Local or Global? New Modes in the Struggle over Citizenship and Belonging in Africa and Europe." *Annual Review of Anthropology* 34:385–407.

Geschiere, Peter, and Stephen Jackson, eds. 2006. "Autochthony and the Crisis of Citizenship." Special Issue, *African Studies Review* 49 (2): 1–7.

Glaeser, Andreas. 2011. *Political Epistemics: The Secret Police, the Opposition and the End of East German Socialism.* Chicago: University of Chicago Press.

Goffman, Alice. 2014. *On the Run: Fugitive Life in an American City.* Chicago: University of Chicago Press.

Goldstein, D. M. 2003. "'In Our Own Hands': Lynching, Justice, and the Law in Bolivia." *American Ethnologist* 30 (1): 22–43.

Gorham, Eric. 1992. *National Service, Citizenship, and Political Education.* Albany: State University of New York Press.

Gottesman, L. 1998. *To Fight and Learn: The Praxis and Promise of Literacy in Eritrea's Independence War.* Trenton, NJ: Red Sea Press.

Government of Eritrea (GoE). 1995. Proclamation of National Service. Proclamation No. 82/1995. *Eritrean Gazette*, no. 11, October 23, 1995. Available at www.refworld.org/docid/3dd8d3af4.html.

Green, Linda. 1995. "Living in a State of Fear." In *Fieldwork under Fire: Contemporary Studies of Violence and Survival*, edited by Carolyn Nordstrom and Antonius C.G.M. Robben, 105–127. Berkeley: University of California Press.

Gupta, Akhil. 2012. *Red Tape: Bureaucracy, Structural Violence, and Poverty in India*. Durham, NC: Duke University Press.

Hailemariam, Chefena, Sjaak Kroon, and Joel Walters. 1999. "Multilingualism and Nation Building: Language and Education in Eritrea." *Journal of Multilingual and Multicultural Development* 20 (6): 475–493.

Haile Selassie. (1961) 1965. "An Address by the Emperor of Ethiopia at the Inauguration of Haile Selassie I University." Reported in the *Voice of Ethiopia*, December 18. Reprinted in *Education and Nation-Building in Africa*, edited by L. Gray Cowan, James O'Connell, and David Scanlon, 303–308. New York: Frederick Praeger.

Hall, Kathleen. 2002. *Lives in Translation: Sikh Youth as British Citizens*. Philadelphia: University of Pennsylvania Press.

Hansen, Thomas Blum, and Finn Stepputat, eds. 2005. *Sovereign Bodies: Citizens, Migrants and States in the Postcolonial World*. Princeton, NJ: Princeton University Press.

Harber, Clive, and Vusi Mncube. 2012. *Education, Democracy and Development: Does Education Contribute to Democratization in Developing Countries?* Oxford, UK: Symposium Books.

Hellweg, Joseph. 2011. *Hunting the Ethical State: The Benkadi Movement of Cote d'Ivoire*. Chicago: University of Chicago Press.

Hepner, Tricia. 2009a. "Generation Nationalism and Generation Asylum: Eritrean Migrants, the Global Diaspora, and the Transnational Nation-State." *Diaspora* 18 (1/2): 184–207.

———. 2009b. *Soldiers, Martyrs, Traitors, and Exiles: Political Conflict in Eritrea and the Diaspora*. Philadelphia: University of Pennsylvania Press.

Hepner, Tricia, and Samia Tecle. 2013. "New Refugees, Development-Forced Displacement, and Transnational Governance in Eritrea and Exile." *Urban Anthropology* 42 (3/4): 377–410.

Herbst, Jeffrey. 2000. *States and Power in Africa: Comparative Lessons in Authority and Control*. Princeton, NJ: Princeton University Press.

Herzfeld, Michael. 1992. *The Social Production of Indifference: Exploring the Symbolic Roots of Western Bureaucracy*. Chicago: University of Chicago Press.

———. 1997. *Cultural Intimacy: Social Poetics in the Nation-State*. New York: Routledge.

Hinton, Alexander. 2004. *Why Did They Kill? Cambodia in the Shadow of Genocide*. Berkeley: University of California Press.

Hirt, Nicole, and Abdulkader Saleh Mohammad. 2013. "'Dreams Don't Come True in Eritrea': Anomie and Family Disintegration Due to the Structural Militarisation of Society." *Journal of Modern African Studies* 51 (1): 139–168.

Hoyle, Peggy. 1999. *Eritrean National Identity: North Carolina Journal of International Law and Commercial Regulation* 24:381–416.

Human Rights Watch. 2009. "Service for Life: State Repression and Indefinite Conscription in Eritrea." New York: Human Rights Watch. Available at www.hrw.org.

———. 2011. "Ten Long Years: A Briefing on Eritrea's Missing Political Prisoners." Available at www.hrw.org. Accessed November 17, 2014.

Humphrey, Caroline. 2007. "Sovereignty." In *A Companion to the Anthropology of Politics*, edited by David Nugent and Joan Vincent, 418–436. New York: Blackwell.

Hyden, Goran. 2006. *African Politics in Comparative Perspective*. Cambridge: Cambridge University Press.

International Crisis Group. 2010. "Eritrea: The Siege State." September 21.
———. 2014. "Eritrea: Ending the Exodus?" August 8.
Iyob, Ruth. 1995. *The Eritrean Struggle for Independence: Domination, Resistance, Nationalism 1941–1993*. Cambridge: Cambridge University Press.
Jackson, Stephen. 2006. "Sons of Which Soil? The Language and Politics of Autochthony in Eastern D.R. Congo." *African Studies Review* 49 (2): 95–123.
———. 2007. "Of 'Doubtful Nationality': Political Manipulation of Citizenship in the D.R. Congo." *Citizenship Studies* 11 (5): 481–500.
Kanaaneh, Rhoda Ann. 2009. *Surrounded: Palestinian Soldiers in the Israeli Military*. Stanford, CA: Stanford University Press.
Kaplan, Sam. 2006. *The Pedagogical State: Education and the Politics of National Culture in Post-1980 Turkey*. Stanford, CA: Stanford University Press.
Kibreab, Gaim. 2009a. *Eritrea: A Dream Deferred*. London: James Curry.
———. 2009b. "Forced Labor in Eritrea." *Journal of Modern African Studies* 47 (1): 41–72.
Kupchik, Aaron. 2010. *Homeroom Security: School Discipline in an Age of Fear*. New York: New York University Press.
Lerman, Amy, and Vesla Weaver. 2014. *Arresting Citizenship: The Democratic Consequences of American Crime Control*. Chicago: University of Chicago Press.
Levinson, Bradley. 2001. *We Are All Equal: Student Culture and Identity at a Mexican Secondary School*. Durham, NC: Duke University Press.
Levinson, Bradley, Douglas Foley, and Dorothy Holland. 1996. *The Cultural Production of the Educated Person: Critical Ethnographies of Schooling and Local Practice*. Albany: State University of New York Press.
Levinson, Bradley, and Dorothy Holland. 1996. "The Cultural Production of the Educated Person: An Introduction." In *The Cultural Production of the Educated Person: Critical Ethnographies of Schooling and Local Practice*, edited by Bradley Levinson, Douglas Foley, and Dorothy Holland, 1–56. Albany: State University of New York Press.
Levitsky, Steven, and Lucan Way. 2010. *Competitive Authoritarianism: Hybrid Regimes after the Cold War*. Cambridge: Cambridge University Press.
Lipsky, Michael. (1980) 2010. *Street-Level Bureaucracy: Dilemmas of the Individual in Public Services*. New York: Russell Sage.
Lutz, Catherine. 2002. *Homefront: A Military City and the American Twentieth Century*. Boston: Beacon Press.
Luykx, Aurolyn. 1999. *The Citizen Factory: Schooling and Cultural Production in Bolivia*. Albany: State University of New York Press.
Lyons, B. J. 2008. "Discipline and the Arts of Domination: Rituals of Respect in Chimborazo Ecuador." *Cultural Anthropology* 20 (1): 97–127.
Lyons, William, and Julie Drew. 2006. *Punishing Schools: Fear and Citizenship in American Public Education*. Ann Arbor: University of Michigan Press.
Macleish, Kenneth. 2013. *Making War at Fort Hood: Life and Uncertainty in a Military Community*. Princeton, NJ: Princeton University Press.
Mahmood, Saba. 2005. *Politics of Piety: The Islamic Revival and the Feminist Subject*. Princeton, NJ: Princeton University Press.
Mahrt, Michael. 2009. "War, Spatiotemporal Perception, and the Nation Fighters and Farmers in the Eritrean Highlands." In *Biopolitics, Militarism, and Development: Eritrea in the Twenty-First Century*, edited by David O'Kane and Tricia Redeker Hepner, 17–33. New York: Berghahn Books.
Mains, Daniel. 2012. *Hope Is Cut: Youth, Unemployment, and the Future in Urban Ethiopia*. Philadelphia: Temple University Press.

Makki, Fouad. 2011a. "Culture and Agency in a Colonial Public Sphere: Religion and the Anti-colonial Imagination in 1940s Eritrea." *Social History* 36 (4): 419–442.

———. 2011b. "Subaltern Agency and Nationalist Commitment: The Dialectic of Social and National Emancipation in Colonial Eritrea." *Africa Today* 58 (1): 28–52.

Malkki, Lissa. 1995. *Purity and Exile: Violence, Memory, and National Cosmology among Hutu Refugees in Tanzania*. Chicago: University of Chicago Press.

Mamdani, Mahmood. 1996. *Citizen and Subject*. Princeton, NJ: Princeton University Press.

Markakis, John. 1987. *National and Class Conflict in the Horn of Africa*. Cambridge: Cambridge University Press.

Mbembe, Achille. 2001. *On the Postcolony*. Berkeley: University of California Press.

McLaren, Peter. 1986. *Schooling as Ritual Performance: Towards a Political Economy of Educational Symbols and Gestures*. New York: Routledge.

Ministry of Education. 2002a. "Concept Paper for a Rapid Transformation of the Eritrean Education System." Ministry of Education of Eritrea, July.

———. 2002b. "Proposal for the Development Plan for RaTEES: The Rapid Transformation of the Eritrean Education System." Ministry of Education of Eritrea, December.

Ministry of Education, Curriculum Research and Development Institute (CRDI), English Panel. 1993. *English for Eritrean Schools, Grade 10 Reading Book*. Asmara, Eritrea: Curriculum Development Institute.

———. 1994. *English for Eritrea Grade Six Textbook*. Asmara, Eritrea: Garnet Publishing and Adulis Printing Press.

———. 1995. *English for Eritrea Grade Seven Textbook*. Asmara, Eritrea: Garnet Publishing and Adulis Printing Press.

Mitchell, Timothy. 1991. "The Limits of the State: Beyond Statist Approaches and Their Critics." *American Political Science Review* 85 (1): 77–96.

———. 2006. "Society, Economy, and the State Effect." In *The Anthropology of the State: A Reader*, edited by Aradhana Sharma and Akhil Gupta, 196–186. New York: Blackwell.

Müller, Tanja 2005. *The Making of Elite Women: Revolution and Nation Building in Eritrea*. Leiden, Netherlands: Brill.

———. 2008. "Bare Life and the Developmental State: Implications of the Militarisation of Higher Education in Eritrea." *Journal of Modern African Studies* 46 (1): 111–131.

———. 2012a. "Beyond the Siege State—Tracing Hybridity during a Recent Visit to Eritrea." *Review of African Political Economy* 39 (133): 451–464.

———. 2012b. "From Rebel Governance to State Consolidation—Dynamics of Loyalty and the Securitization of the State in Eritrea." *Geoforum* 43:793–803.

Nader, Laura. 1972. "Up the Anthropologist: Perspectives Gained from Studying Up." In *Reinventing Anthropology*, edited by Dell Hymes, 284–311. New York: Pantheon.

NOKUT (Norwegian Agency for Quality Assurance in Education). 2013. "Report on Recognition of Higher Education in Eritrea and Ethiopia: A Study Trip to Eritrea and Ethiopia in October 2012 and January 2013." Available at www.nokut.no/Documents/NOKUT/Artikkelbibliotek/Kunnskapsbasen/Rapporter/UA%202013/Gullik sen_Anne-Kari_Audensen_Erik_Report_on_recognition_of_higher_education_in_ Eritrea_and_Ethiopia_2013-1.pdf. Accessed August 19, 2013.

O'Kane, David. 2012. "Limits to State-Led Nation-Building? An Eritrean Village Responds Selectively to the Plans of the Eritrean Government." *Studies in Ethnicity and Nationalism* 12 (2): 309–325.

O'Kane, David, and Tricia Redeker Hepner, eds. 2009. *Biopolitics, Militarism, and Development: Eritrea in the Twenty-First Century*. New York: Berghahn Books.

Ong, Aihwa. 2007. *Neoliberalism as Exception: Mutations in Citizenship and Sovereignty.* Durham, NC: Duke University Press.

Peteet, Julie. 1994. "Male Gender and Rituals of Resistance in the Palestinian Intifada: A Cultural Politics of Violence." *American Anthropological Association* 21 (1): 31–49.

Plaut, Martin. 2014. "Eritrean Resistance Steps Up Pressure on President Isaias Afewerki." *Guardian*, October 28. Available at www.theguardian.com/global-development/poverty-matters/2014/oct/28/eritrean-resistance-pressure-isais-afewerki.

Pool, David. 2001. *From Guerillas to Government: The Eritrean People's Liberation Front.* Oxford, UK: James Curry.

Poole, Amanda. 2009. "The Youth Has Gone from Our Soil: Place and Politics in Refugee Resettlement and Agrarian Development." In *Biopolitics, Militarism, and Development: Eritrea in the Twenty-First Century,* edited by David O'Kane and Tricia Redeker Hepner, 34–52. New York: Berghahn Books.

———. 2013. "Ransoms, Remittances, and Refugees: The Gatekeeper State in Eritrea." *Africa Today* 60 (2): 67–84.

Quantz, Richard. 2011. *Rituals and Student Identity in Education: Ritual Critique for a New Pedagogy.* New York: Palgrave Macmillan.

Reid, Richard. 2005. "Caught in the Headlights of History: Eritrea, the EPLF and the Postwar Nation-State." *Journal of Modern African History* 43 (3): 467–488.

———. 2009. "The Politics of Silence: Interpreting Stasis in Contemporary Eritrea." *Review of African Political Economy* 120:209–211.

Richard, Analiese, and Rudnyckyj, Daromir. 2009. "Economies of Affect." *Journal of the Royal Institute of Anthropology* 15:57–77.

Riggan, Jennifer. 2009. "Avoiding Wastage by Making Soldiers." In *Biopolitics, Militarism, and Development: Eritrea in the Twenty-First Century,* edited by David O'Kane and Tricia Redeker Hepner, 72–91. New York: Berghahn Books.

———. 2011. "In Between Nations: Ethiopian-Born Eritreans, Liminality and War." *Political and Legal Anthropology Review* 34 (1): 131–154.

———. 2013a. "Imagining Emigration: Debating National Duty in Eritrean Classrooms." *Africa Today* 60 (2): 85–106.

———. 2013b. "'It Seemed like a Punishment': Teacher Transfers, Hollow Nationalism, and the Intimate State in Eritrea." *American Ethnologist* 40 (4): 749–763.

———. 2014. "Biopolitical Departures: A Love Story." *Journal of Narrative Politics* 1 (1): 44–60. Available at http://journalofnarrativepolitics.com/wp-content/uploads/2014/09/JNP-Vol-1-Riggan.pdf.

Rios, Victor. 2011. *Punished: Policing the Lives of Black and Latino Boys.* New York: New York University Press.

Rippberger, Susan J., and Kathleen A. Staudt. 2003. *Pledging Allegiance: Learning Nationalism at the El Paso–Juarez Border.* New York: Routledge Falmer.

Rodney, Walter. 1974. *How Europe Underdeveloped Africa.* Washington, DC: Howard University Press.

Schmitt, Carl. (1922) 2005. *Political Theology: Four Chapters on the Concept of Sovereignty.* Chicago: University of Chicago Press.

———. 2003. *Nomos of the Earth.* New York: Telos Press.

Scott, James C. 1985. *Weapons of the Weak: Everyday Forms of Peasant Resistance.* New Haven, CT: Yale University Press.

———. 1998. *Seeing Like a State: How Certain Schemes to Improve the Human Condition Have Failed.* New Haven, CT: Yale University Press.

Silver, Patricia. 2007. "'Then I Do What I Want': Teachers, State, and Empire in 2000." *American Ethnologist* 34 (2): 268–284.

———. 2010. "'I Am a Worker-Professional': Teachers and Their Classes in Puerto Rico." *Identities: Global Studies in Culture and Power* 17:86–107.

Skidmore, Monique. 2004. *Karaoke Fascism: Burma and the Politics of Fear*. Philadelphia: University of Pennsylvania Press.

Sluka, Jeffrey, ed. 2000. *Death Squad: The Anthropology of State Terror*. Philadelphia: University of Pennsylvania Press.

Smith, Jordan. 2004. "The Bakassi Boys Vigilantism, Violence, and Political Imagination in Nigeria." *Cultural Anthropology* 19 (3): 429–455.

Sorenson, John. 1991. *Imagining Ethiopia: Struggles for History and Identity in the Horn of Africa*. New Brunswick, NJ: Rutgers University Press.

Stambach, Amy. 2000. *Lessons from Mount Kilimanjaro: Schooling, Community, and Gender in East Africa*. New York: Routledge.

Svolik, Milan. 2012. *The Politics of Authoritarian Rule*. Cambridge: Cambridge University Press.

Taddia, Irma. 1994. "Ethiopian Source Material and Colonial Rule in the Nineteenth Century: The Letter to Menelik (1899) by Blatta Gabra Egzi'abher." *Journal of African History* 35 (3): 493–516.

Treiber, Magnus. 2009. "Trapped in Adolescence: The Postwar Urban Generation." In *Biopolitics, Militarism, and Development: Eritrea in the Twenty-First Century*, edited by David O'Kane and Tricia Redeker Hepner, 92–114. New York: Berghahn Books.

———. 2010. "The Choice between Clean and Dirty: Discourses of Aesthetics, Morality and Progress in Post-revolutionary Asmara, Eritrea." In *Urban Pollution: Cultural Meanings, Social Practices*, edited by Evaline Durr and Rivke Jaffe, 123–143. Oxford, UK: Berghahn Books.

Trevaskis, G.K.N. 1960. *Eritrea: A Colony in Transition: 1941–1952*. London: Oxford University Press.

Tronvoll, Kjetil. 1996. *Mai Weini: A Highland Village in Eritrea. A Study of the People, Their Livelihood and Land Tenure during Times of Turbulence*. Trenton, NJ: Red Sea Press.

———. 1998. "The Process of Nation-Building in Post-war Eritrea: Created from Below or Directed from Above?" *Journal of Modern African Studies* 36 (3): 461–482.

Tronvoll, Kjetil, and Daniel Mekonnen. 2014. *The African Garrison State: Human Rights and Political Development in Eritrea*. Oxford, UK: James Currey.

Trouillot, Michel-Rolph. 2001. "The Anthropology of the State in the Age of Globalization: Close Encounters of the Deceptive Kind." *Current Anthropology* 42 (1): 125–138.

Turner, Victor. 1969. *The Ritual Process: Structure and Anti-structure*. Chicago: Aldine.

UNHCR. 2000–2011. UNHCR Statistical Yearbooks. Available at www.unhcr.org/pages/4a02afce6.html. Accessed May 3, 2013.

———. 2014. Sharp Increase in Number of Eritrean Refugees and Asylum Seekers in Europe, Ethiopia and Sudan. Briefing Notes. November 14, 2014. Available at www.unhcr.org/5465fea1381.html.

———. 2015. 2015 UNHCR Subregional Operations Profile East and Horn of Africa. Country Pages: Eritrea. Available at www.unhcr.org/pages/49e4838e6.html.

UN News Centre. 2014. "Number of Eritrean Asylum-Seekers in Europe Soars from Past Year." UN News Center, November 14. Available at www.un.org/apps/news/story.asp?NewsID=49343#.VGouxFfF96Y.

U.S. Department of State, Bureau of Democracy, Human Rights, and Labor. 2011. "Country Reports on Human Rights Practices for 2011: Eritrea." Available at www.state.gov/documents/organization/186404.pdf. Accessed November 15, 2013.

———. 2012. "Country Reports on Human Rights Practices for 2012: Eritrea." Available at www.state.gov/j/drl/rls/hrrpt/humanrightsreport/index.htm?year=2012&dlid=204118. Accessed November 15, 2013.

Verdery, Katherine. 1996. *What Was Socialism and What Comes Next?* Princeton, NJ: University of Princeton Press.

Vincent, Leonard. 2014. "Eritrea: Conversation with the Resistance Movement inside Asmara." Horn Affairs, October 26. Available at http://hornaffairs.com/en/2014/10/26/eritrea-interview-resistance-activists.

Wacquant, Loïc. 2009. *Punishing the Poor: The Neoliberal Government of Social Insecurity.* Durham, NC: Duke University Press.

Weber, Eugen. 1976. *Peasants into Frenchmen: The Modernization of Rural France, 1870–1914.* Stanford, CA: Stanford University Press.

Wedeen, Lisa. 1999. *Ambiguities of Domination: Politics, Rhetoric, and Symbols in Contemporary Syria.* Chicago: University of Chicago Press.

———. 2008. *Peripheral Visions: Publics, Power, and Performance in Yemen.* Chicago: University of Chicago Press.

Weldehaimanot, Simon, and Emily Taylor. 2011. "Our Struggle and Its Goals: A Controversial Eritrean Manifesto." *Review of African Political Economy* 38 (130): 565–585.

Wilson, Amrit. 1991. *The Challenge Road: Women and the Eritrean Revolution.* Trenton, NJ: Red Sea Press.

Wilson, Fiona. 2001. "In the Name of the State? Schools and Teachers in an Andean Province." In *States of Imagination: Ethnographic Exploration of the Postcolonial State,* edited by T. B. Hansen and F. Stepputat, 313–344. Durham, NC: Duke University Press.

Woldemikael, Tekle. 1993. "The Cultural Construction of Eritrean Nationalist Movements." In *The Rising Tide of Cultural Pluralism: The Nation-State at Bay?* edited by Crawford Young, 179–199. Madison: University of Wisconsin Press.

———. 2009. "Pitfalls of Nationalism in Eritrea." In *Biopolitics, Militarism, and Development: Eritrea in the Twenty-First Century,* edited by David O'Kane and Tricia Redeker Hepner, 1–16. New York: Berghahn Books.

———. 2013. "Introduction: Postliberation Eritrea." *Africa Today* 60 (2): v–xix.

World Bank. 2003. *Eritrea Education Sector Improvement Project: Project Information Document.* Available at www.worldbank.org/infoshop. Accessed May 3, 2006.

Young, Crawford. 2007. "Nation, Ethnicity and Citizenship." In *Making Nations, Creating Strangers: States and Citizenship in Africa,* edited by Sarah Dorman, Daniel Hammett, and Paul Nugent, 241–264. Leiden, Netherlands: Brill.

Zigon, Jarrett. 2008. *Morality: Anthropological Perspectives.* New York: Berg.

Index

actors, middle, 16–17, 19–21, 202, 209; defined, 16; (limited) power of, 16, 19, 21, 32; teachers as, 16, 200, 205

actors, state, 4, 84, 111, 194, 202, 209, 212n8, 217n1; disillusioned, 17, 19; power or sovereignty of, 11, 17, 62–63, 172, 191, 198, 201; teachers as, 152, 157–158, 172, 174–175, 178, 181, 205, 212n9; violence or use of force by, 3, 11, 16, 19, 32, 87–88, 157–158, 183, 191, 202, 205, 212n6

Addis Ababa University, 106

Adi Abeto, 83–84, 87, 175

Afar, 28, 37, 161, 167–169, 179, 218n7

affect, 6, 12, 49, 60, 82, 124–125, 208. *See also* emotions

Africa, 9–11, 35; state formation in, 41–42

Agamben, Giorgio 19, 62, 84, 92, 156–157, 170, 178, 211n5, 217n1–218n3

Amharic, 26, 139

Anderson, Benedict, 10, 22, 212n11

anticolonialism, 35, 43, 45

Appadurai, Arjun, 10, 13, 200, 209, 211n1

Arabic, 44, 215n4

Arabs, 40, 43

arbitrariness, 64, 68; of detention, 7, 59, 65, 212n8; of punishments, 15, 62, 66–67, 71, 184; of round-ups, 65; of state, 156, 177, 184, 212n8; students' experience of, 156, 159, 172, 176–178

Aretxaga, Begoña, 3–4, 13, 59, 73–74, 86, 181, 212n7

Asmara, 14, 26–27, 48, 50, 137, 164, 194; as capital, 37, 48, 71; Department of General Education in, 26, 178; *gifa*, 57, 60, 77, 83, 175; Sema'atat Square in, 33; teachers in, 62, 71–72, 74, 80, 137–138; teacher training in, 89, 97; transfers to, 185, 193; University of Asmara, 56, 71–73, 83, 98, 100–101, 106

Assab: Assab Kebir, 163–164; Assab Seghir, 168; border war's impact on, 2, 27–28, 218n5; Campo Sudan, 163–164, 166, 196, 207; demographics of, 27–28; Eritrean, 29, 36; Ethiopia or Ethiopians and, 27–29, 166–167; evacuations of, 1–4, 71–72, 129, 195; fieldwork in, 18, 25–27, 137, 212n9; history of, 36; imagined geography of, 163–164; military camp in, 129, 133, 195; Ministry of Education in, 171; port in, 1–3, 28, 113, 164, 166; rumors in, 83; teachers or schools in, 18, 26–28, 72, 85, 128–129, 137, 149, 163–164, 167, 175, 195–196, 212n9, 217n9, 218nn5–6; transient population of, 18, 28–29

assessment, 115–116, 118
asylum, 196, 206–208, 214–215n9
attendance, 118, 135–136, 189, 216n7
authoritarianism, 1, 7, 9–10, 32, 147, 203–204, 212n7. *See also* states: authoritarian
Awate, 81, 208

Bakhtin, Mikhail, 142, 147
bare life, 92, 170, 204, 206, 217n1
beer, 2, 14–15, 48, 165
biopolitics, 31–32, 90, 112–121, 156, 197, 200; defined, 23
bodies: authoritarian regimes' power over, 12–14; civilian or citizen, 64–66, 68–69, 77, 88, 172; coerced, 60, 68–69; disciplined, 22, 61, 66, 113–114, 117, 162, 214n4; docile, 54; president's, 148; state or nation and, 16, 54, 62, 73, 76–77, 88, 123, 183; students', 114, 117, 123, 157–158, 162, 176, 178, 181, 183, 187, 190
books, 50, 97, 139, 141, 183. *See also* textbooks
borders, 8, 22, 35, 66, 156–157, 194, 198–199, 203
border war, 11, 30, 54–55, 84, 211n4; criticism of management of, 55; deaths in, 50, 208; end of, 6, 11, 50, 195, 200; impact on Assab, 2, 27–28, 218n5; military or national service and, 3, 6, 18, 65, 68, 85, 127, 200, 214n6; outbreak of, 2, 5, 27–28, 85; teachers in, 93
Bourdieu, Pierre, 162, 215n2
bright future, 20–21, 90–91, 93, 101, 105, 107–110, 124, 161
British Military Administration (BMA), 37–39, 43
brutality, 50, 55, 59, 84, 181, 186
bureaucrats, 15–17, 19, 92, 158, 191, 201

camp, 2, 9, 56, 169, 201–206, 209; Assab as, 129, 133; Eritrea as, 156–157, 197–199, 202–203
carcele, 57–59
carnivalesque, 142–143, 146–147, 153–154
children, 9, 105, 111, 115, 125–126, 132, 204; Afar, 28, 168; children *are* nation, 103–104, 124; corporal punishment of, 179–180, 182; disciplined, 149, 180; parents or adults and, 47, 110, 168–169, 171–173, 189–190; "running away," 47; sacrificed, 47, 49, 102; sorted, 169–173; Tigrinya, 167–168
Christians, 17, 28, 37–40
citizens: bodies of, 64–66, 68–69, 77, 88, 172, 183; coerced, punished, or imprisoned, 3–4, 11, 13, 24, 60, 69, 84–85, 88, 127, 203–206; conscripted, military, or militarized, 21–22, 31, 85, 88, 104, 107, 112, 125–126, 156; diasporic, 206–207, 209, 213n14; docile or compliant, 12, 77; educated, 8, 20–21, 31, 92–93, 104–105, 107, 112, 126, 152, 154, 157, 159, 190, 212n11; evading, emigrating, or resisting, 12–13, 66, 88, 125, 142, 206–207; everyday encounters by, 157, 191, 201; excluded, 42; force used against, 4, 8, 11, 13, 77, 86, 200, 217n1; good or ideal, 50, 90, 103–105, 142, 151–152, 206, 209; imagining state and/or nation, 3–4, 10, 14, 17, 54, 62, 174, 191, 206, 213n12; PFDJ view of, 8; producing, 125–127, 149, 152, 154, 157, 159, 190, 205; rights and/or duties of, 21, 62, 152, 156, 207; sacrificial, 50, 147, 207; service and, 53, 56, 68–69, 76, 85, 88, 127, 200; in strong or maddening state, 7, 59, 84
citizenship, 8, 16, 104, 143, 147, 149, 152, 205–207, 209
civil servants, 14–18, 69, 72, 77–80, 83, 91, 217–218n2; teachers vs., 18, 132; transfers of, 18, 53, 64, 69, 71
class, social, 16, 34, 36, 38–40, 43, 45
classrooms: cleaned, 135–136, 189; debates in, 142–147; (dis)orderly, 104, 136, 138–142, 144, 146–147, 153–154, 159–160, 167–168, 184; military training in, 96; nation and, 5, 20, 124; nonstudents in, 171; overcrowded, 90; repeaters in, 115–116; rituals in, 124, 135, 140; section 8D, 171, 175–177
clientilism, 10, 132
coercion: arbitrary, 15, 62, 66; authoritarian, 7, 11, 13–14, 204, 212n7; camps or encampment and, 198–199, 202–203, 209; cycles of, 13, 16, 77, 80, 82, 88, 124, 153–154, 200–202, 205; defined, 64; evasion of, 12–13, 63, 77, 79, 81, 86, 203; impact on nation-state making or imaginaries, 4–6, 11–14, 25, 30, 61, 70, 73, 175, 200, 203, 206, 211–212n6;

limits or inefficiency of, 13; and punishment, 15, 60, 62–63, 70–71, 80, 82, 85, 175; state effects of, 60–64, 66, 68–69, 77, 82, 184, 202; state or government, 4, 7, 11–12, 16, 18, 30–31, 53, 57, 59–60, 63–64, 70, 77, 81–88, 156, 175, 190, 200–201, 207, 211–212n6 (*see also* states: coercive); of subjects (*see* subjects: coerced or punished); and teachers, 19, 31, 127, 156–158, 178, 183, 191, 202
colleges, 94–95, 98
colonialism, 27, 35–38, 41–43, 45, 213n1
commandement, 77–78
communitas, 134, 138, 141, 152–153
conscription, 64, 195, 202, 214n6, 217n2; arbitrary, 67; for 18 months, 3; impotence and, 77, 88; limitless, 3, 6–7, 129; military, 67, 69, 71, 84, 127, 129, 175; for nation of soldiers, 6; National Service, 13, 18, 20, 22, 66–68, 70–72, 88, 200, 203, 214n6; people vulnerable to, 78, 214n2; schools as conduit for, 7, 152–153, 202; of teachers (*see under* teachers)
constitution, 11, 55–56, 150–151, 215n10
control: coercion and, 8, 12, 60, 82, 198; lack or loss of, 64–65, 69, 76, 78, 81–82, 92, 155, 186–187, 190, 202–203; military, 3, 6, 42, 214n4, 217–218n2; of population or citizens, 55–56, 60, 64–65, 68–69, 76, 79–80, 82, 87–88, 157, 218n3; retaking, 156, 170, 174, 188, 202; sorting as means of, 170; sovereign, 156–157; of space or territory, 157, 159–163, 198–199, 202; by state (actors), 3, 35, 38, 42, 55, 68–69, 76, 78, 82, 88, 157, 190, 193, 197–198, 218n3, 218n9; of symbols, 13; by or of teachers, 32, 76, 136–137, 140, 142, 147, 155–156, 159–163, 168–173, 179, 184, 186–190, 202, 216n7; Tigrinya words for, 160
corporal punishment: authority, sovereignty, or control and, 177, 179, 181–187, 190; avoided or limited, 168, 179–180; debates over, 178–179, 184–185; illegality of, 178, 185; in military, 71, 181, 201; of National Service trainees, 3, 70; pedagogical use of, 180–183; of students, 20, 159, 177–187, 190, 201; two notions of, 183; ubiquity in Eritrea, 178, 186
crackdowns: 1970s, 55; 2001, 11, 55–56, 59

curriculum, 108; civics, 48–49, 51, 102, 149–152; to create national subject, 21; new, 26, 31, 89–91, 94, 96, 100, 215n4, 216n5 (chap. 3); office of, 26; simplified, 99–100; Texas standards-based, 89, 96, 215n1

debates: about being national or Eritrean, 24, 31, 143, 148, 200; about *mengisti*, 15–16; political, 55, 146; student, 24, 31, 97, 141–149; teacher, 119, 158–159, 178, 184–186, 189, 191–192, 201
demobilization, 6, 18, 68, 128, 200
democracy, 168, 192, 213n2; authoritarianism vs., 203–204; classroom debates and, 142–144, 146–147; imprisoned or punished subjects and, 205–206; lack of, 55–56, 146–147, 151; skepticism about, 11, 150–151
Derg regime, 27–28, 49
desert, 3, 27, 56, 65, 71, 74, 167, 193
detention, 58–60, 68, 78–79, 176, 198–199, 201, 212n8
development: defense or military and, 6, 8, 22–23, 53, 56, 75, 111; education and national, 21–23, 91, 107, 112, 134; by EPLF/PFDJ, 23, 34, 43–44; National Service and, 6, 9, 53, 68, 103; self-sufficiency and, 5, 35, 56
developmentalism, 22–23, 35, 53, 91; defined, 22
development projects, 6, 23, 53, 68
diaspora, 25, 44, 55, 67, 148, 196, 206–209, 213n14, 215n10
dictatorships, 27, 58, 148, 199
discipline: biopolitics vs. 112–118, 120–121; bodily or physical, 3, 12, 22, 61, 66, 113–114, 117, 162, 214n4; civics and, 150–151; committee on, 184–185; encampment for, 156; EPLF, 35, 45, 55; flag ceremony and, 124; Foucault on, 12, 22, 66, 113–114, 214nn4–5; military, 53, 55, 66, 76, 86, 214nn4–5; National Service as, 53, 66, 75; in schools, 8, 20–21, 90, 104, 112–118, 120–121, 124–125, 153, 157–158, 161–164, 172–173, 180–181, 186–187, 190, 218n5; self-discipline, 161; spatial, 22, 66, 113–114, 163–164, 191; temporal, 22, 66, 113–114; Wedeen on, 212n7

disorder: anti-structure, 135; carnivalesque, 142, 146–147, 153; classroom or school, 20, 31, 104, 122–125, 134–149, 152–154, 158–160, 167–168, 184, 189–190, 218n5; coercion and, 12; Douglas on, 162–163; and flag ceremony, 122–124, 142; moral crisis of, 184, 202; nation or national and, 124–125, 142, 148–149, 152; teacher–student hierarchy and, 138, 142, 146
dissidence: in 2001, 11, 55–56, 59; in 2013, 56
docility, 12–13, 54, 61, 66, 77, 125, 214n6, 217n11
Douglas, Mary, 135, 162–163
duty, national, 6–8, 56, 77, 91, 149

education: access to, 28, 94–95, 99, 171; competition in, 94–95, 99–100, 106–108, 112–116, 171; goals, meaning, or value of, 26–27, 90, 92, 94, 105, 116, 138; government (dis)interest in, 7, 100–101; indigenous, 102; job-oriented, 94, 97; as liminal phase, 126; militarization and, 7, 16, 21–24, 31, 92–93, 100, 120, 124–126, 175, 212n10; military training and, 7, 20–22, 27, 31, 90–91, 93–98, 100, 107, 120–121, 138–139, 169; Ministry of Education (*see* Ministry of Education); moral, 20, 119, 181; nation and, 7, 16, 92, 100, 124, 149; National Service and, 27, 53, 69, 72–73, 90–91, 95, 98, 108–112, 120–121, 126, 139; PFDJ/EPLF role in, 23, 43–45, 100; political, 43–45, 53, 126; problems in, 115, 169; quality of, 20–21, 94, 107; rewards of, 105, 107–108, 112–113, 116, 131; in rural or remote areas, 11, 23, 147, 167; teleological orientation of, 21, 92
education reform: described, 7, 90–91, 93–94; government/state role in, 15, 100; paper vs. practice, 90, 96–100; for population not individual, 114; resistance to or criticism of, 24, 93, 107–108; "wastage" eliminated, 94, 98, 100, 107–108, 115
effervescence, 5, 7, 14, 24, 30, 35–36, 200, 211n3, 212n7
elections, 11, 56, 142, 146, 148, 150–151
elites: educated, 90–91, 100, 106, 112, 121; middle actors vs., 16; political, 38, 42, 55; teachers as, 17, 19

emergency, state of, 3, 63, 83–86, 211–212n6, 217n1
emotions, 219n10; authoritarian regimes and, 6; being Eritrean, 46–47; conflicting, 60, 82, 194; of independence or post-independence years, 5, 30, 47; for nation, 13, 55; transfers ascribed to, 72–73
English, 26; teachers of or classes in, 25, 97, 143, 146, 153, 215n4; textbooks on, 50; word "control" in, 160; word "soldier" in, 75–76
equality: of educated and uneducated, 23; ethnic, 11; gender, 11, 34, 44
Eritrea: as camp, 156–157, 197–199, 202–203; compared to other states, 9–11, 35, 41, 125, 132, 148, 203–206; demographics of, 37; Eritreans vs., 39; ethnic groups of, 9, 17, 22, 37, 43–44, 55; highlands of, 2, 17, 28, 37–40, 52, 128, 167, 218n6; history of, 36–39, 102; independence of, 5, 8, 10, 39; languages of, 26, 37, 44; leaving, 6–7, 26, 64–66, 68, 80–81, 194–197, 201, 206–208, 217n2; lowlands of, 2, 17, 37–40, 44, 52, 72; as maddening state, 12, 59–60, 83–86, 88, 159, 181, 211–212n6, 212n7; as prison, 6, 64, 66, 70, 197, 205; rural areas of, 11; scholars on, 5, 68, 213nn13–14; as "siege state," 84–85, 199, 211–212n6; strong or struggling, 7, 10
Eritrean Liberation Front (ELF), 35, 38–44
Eritrean Liberation Movement (ELM), 39
Eritrean-ness, 9, 42
Eritrean People's Liberation Front (EPLF), 33–46, 216n5 (chap. 4); dissent not tolerated by, 55; education or literacy emphasized by, 23, 43–44, 100; ELF vs., 40–43; name of, 5, 34, 44 (*see also* People's Front for Democracy and Justice [PFDJ]); nationalism of, 5, 10, 34–37, 40–46, 54; "Our Struggle and Its Goals," 42–43; quotidian strategies of, 51, 54; socialism or communism of, 45; state or nation building of, 36, 40, 44–45; textbooks and, 49–50
Eritreans: defining, 8, 24, 34, 42–43, 49, 51–52, 103; moral values of, 51, 91, 152, 162, 173–174; quotidian experiences of, 46, 50–51, 54
etatization, 69, 77, 214n7

Ethiopia, 47, 50, 55, 65, 68, 92, 164, 196; Assab and, 27–29, 166–167; border war with (*see* border war); colonial history of, 35–37; Eritrea ruled by, 36–40, 43, 45, 50–51, 59, 106; Eritrea's independence from, 5, 8, 28, 43; Soviet Union and, 28

Ethiopians, 37–40, 45–46, 49–51, 59, 169, 218n5; in Assab, 27–28, 167; Ethiopian soldiers, 47, 49

ethnicity, 3, 9, 11, 16–17, 21–22, 28–29, 36–38, 41–44, 55, 167, 199, 215n3

evacuations, 2–4, 26, 71–72, 129, 195

evasion, 76–82; of coercion, 12–13, 63, 77, 79, 81, 86, 203; culture or climate of, 31, 80, 125; cycle of coercion and, 13, 16, 30–31, 77, 80, 82, 88, 124, 153–154, 200–202, 205, 209; defined, 80; of military service, 217n2; of National Service (*see* National Service: evaded or delayed); resistance vs. 81–82; "sleep late" strategy of, 80, 82; solidarities around, 12, 80, 82, 86, 88; strategies of, 12, 80–82, 88; by teachers or in schools, 24, 80, 123–125, 158, 190

examinations, 112–118, 128, 215n1; as discipline, 114–115, 117–118; end-of-semester, 114; for entry into secondary school (national), 91, 95, 99, 112, 114, 134, 171–172; for entry into university (matriculation), 91, 95, 98, 112–114, 134; stringent selection, 114–117; students' or teachers' views of, 113–115

fighters (*tegadelti*), 24, 30, 43–48, 51–55, 83, 102, 148–149; all Eritreans as, 30, 47–48, 52–54, 124; educated people vs., 23, 25, 101, 126; ELF vs. EPLF organization of, 41, 44; joining, 46–48; punished, 75–76, 101; sandals of, 1, 33–34; *tegadelti*, 23–24, 33, 48, 53; *tegadelti* vs. *agelglot*, 76; women, 44

flag ceremony, 27, 52, 54, 104, 122–124, 142

Foucault, Michel, 12, 22–23, 61, 66, 113–114, 214nn4–5

freedom, 51, 82, 107, 126, 150, 196, 201; teachers', 67, 76

"Freedom Fridays," 81–82

G-13 or G-15, 55–56, 214n1

gender, 9, 11, 16–17, 21, 29, 34, 36, 44

gifa (round-ups), 11, 175, 193; affective response to, 82; arbitrary, 65, 78; coercive, 6, 60, 64–65; evading, 77–82, 153, 204; "last," 87–88; mass or widespread, 59–60, 64, 68, 78, 83, 86–88, 175; rumors about, 80, 86–88; state or government and, 15, 58–60, 84, 86, 191, 202; in 2002, 60, 64, 68, 78, 80, 86

government: biopolitics (*see* biopolitics); as coercive or punishing, 18, 60–64, 67–72, 76–77, 80–87, 127; control by, 68–69, 78–79, 81–82; defining Eritrean-ness, 49; dependence on, 132–133; diasporic citizens and, 206–207, 209, 213n14; and dissent or criticism, 55–56, 59, 125, 196, 207–208; force used by, 87; as inefficient or impotent, 79–80, 87, 203; (lack of) legitimacy of, 76, 203; *mengisti*, 6, 15–16; nation-building project of, 153, 203, 209; new, 42, 53; officials of, 56, 60, 65, 68, 92, 124, 195; policies or programs of, 6–7, 11, 15, 17, 20–24, 28, 52, 63, 85, 94, 98–101, 107–111, 115, 132, 167, 175, 196, 208, 216n5 (chap. 3); in pre-border-war era, 11, 52, 55, 214n6; protective, 87, 199, 211n6, 212–213n12, 214n6; quotidian strategies of, 51; rhetoric of, 51–53; surveillance by, 30; teachers and, 17–18, 75; uncertainty about, 15, 111; University of Asmara and, 98, 101; "writes in pencil," 62, 90

Great Britain, 37–38

"growing up,": authority and, 133–134; children or students, 31, 124–125, 137, 202; Eritreans, 125; as markers of being, 130–132; as a nation, 124, 134; National Service preventing, 125, 128, 131–133, 202; teachers, 31, 128–134, 137, 197, 202; "youth," 131–132

Gupta, Akhil, 19, 61, 211n1

habitus, 162, 215n2

Haile Selassie, Emperor, 38, 106

health, 11, 43, 118

Hepner, Tricia Redeker, 23–24, 41, 206–207, 211n3

Herzfeld, Michael, 19, 76, 211n1

hierarchies, 14, 45, 54, 216n5 (chap. 4); liminality and, 135, 153; school, 138, 140, 142, 146–147, 161, 164, 167, 169

higher education, 17, 22, 98, 105–107, 116, 201; government changes in, 90–91, 98; National Service and, 69, 73, 91, 95, 120; rewards of, 105; statistics on, 95
history, 26, 33, 36–38, 151, 216n5 (chap. 4); military history or history of The Struggle, 21–22, 43; as school subject, 50, 97, 102, 149, 215n4; teachers of, 151
holidays, 27, 47, 49–50, 54, 193
homework, 118, 178, 184–185
Hoyle, Peggy, 48, 52–53
humor, 12, 77, 82, 150. *See also* jokes; mockery
Humphrey, Caroline, 157
hyphen in nation-state, 4, 7, 10, 32, 200, 209

ID cards, 58, 79, 83, 85, 87, 175, 207, 219n11
identification effects, 61, 64, 66
ideology: dissemination of, 9, 44–46; national, 9, 14, 30, 35, 40–41, 45–46; of revolutionary movements, 54
imaginaries: coercive state, 5, 86, 211–212n6; conflicted or plural, 4–5, 14, 178, 188–190; impotent state, 189; national imaginaries or imaginaries of nation (*see* national imaginaries); punishing state, 60, 73, 87, 153; state, 10–11, 13–14, 16, 32, 60–63, 68, 73, 87–88, 158, 175, 178, 188–190, 201–202, 205, 212n6; teacher state, 190; violence's or coercion's impact on, 4, 6, 11, 32, 87–88
imagined communities, 3, 10. *See also* imaginaries; nation(s): imagined; states: imagined
impotence, 31, 63, 75, 80, 82, 124–125, 147, 152–153, 189–190, 197, 201–203, 209; cycle of, 13, 82, 88; Mbembe on, 12, 77–78; of state, 12–13, 17, 19, 88; of subjects, 12
imprisonment, 46, 49–50, 56–57, 65, 78, 195, 200, 202–203, 206–207, 209, 212n7, 215n10; in United States, 204–206. *See also* prison
independence: of Ethiopa from Italy, 36; euphoria of, 54, 211n3; of other African nations, 10, 35, 42, 106; war/The Struggle for, 5, 9, 22, 25, 27, 30, 33–34, 37–47, 51, 82, 200, 208

Independence Day, 50, 54
India, 61–62, 108, 174; teachers from, 212n9, 216n3
individuating effects, 61, 64, 69
intellectuals, 39, 55, 118
Internet technology (IT), 94, 97, 102
irony, 150–151
Isaias Afewerki, 5, 15, 40, 43, 55, 101, 103, 144–148, 153–154; everyman, 48, 148
Italians, 27, 36–37, 57
Italy, 36–37, 208

jail, 50, 57–59, 155, 177. *See also* imprisonment; prison
jokes, 77, 80, 82, 89–90, 124, 135, 142–143, 149, 152–153, 182
journalists, 11, 56, 59, 64
Junior Secondary School (Assab), 26, 155–156, 169, 171–172, 179, 190
junior secondary schools, 74, 95–96, 99, 151, 167, 171, 218n8

Kesete, Semere, 56, 71
Kibreab, Gaim, 102–103

Lampedusa, 207–208
law(s): corporal punishment, 178–179, 185–187; force of, 62, 156, 204, 217n1; rule of, 15, 62, 71, 201; service, 3, 6, 68; state of exception, 156–157, 159, 172, 177–178, 191, 217n1; "written in pencil," 90
legibility effects, 61
legitimacy: cannibalized or undermined, 12–13; of nation, 8, 12–13, 32, 42; of nationalism, 54; of officials or leaders, 32, 55, 147–148; of regimes, 13, 35, 54, 77, 211n4; of state, 8, 86, 88, 153, 218n9; of teachers or educational administrators, 101, 175
liminality: communitas or anti-structure and, 133–135, 138; defined, 126; limitless or permanent, 125–126, 133, 138, 152–153, 162, 195, 202, 216n2; of National Service, 125–129, 133, 152–153, 195, 202; of students, 118, 125–127, 153; of teachers, 17, 131, 133–134, 141; of "warm-up" time, 135–138
literacy, 23, 43, 100
loyalty, 8, 11, 13, 41–42, 53–55, 61, 66, 207

martyrs, 48–50, 208–209
Martyrs Day, 49–50
Massawa, 2, 28, 71–72
Mbembe, Achille, 12–13, 63, 77–78, 82, 147, 203, 211n5
McLaren, Peter, 134, 216n6
media, 46, 62, 67, 168
mengisti, 6, 15–16
Mengistu Haile Mariam, 27. *See also* Derg regime
middle actors. *See* actors, middle
militarism, 18, 22–23; defined, 212–213n12
militarization, 6, 66, 129, 197; defined, 213n12; education and, 7, 16, 21–24, 31, 92–93, 100, 120, 124–126, 175, 212n10; mass, 5, 8, 16, 18, 24, 29, 125, 199; nationalism and, 92; resistance to, 125; state effects of, 68
military, 42, 82; active-duty, 18, 29, 58, 71, 76; eligibility to serve in, 214n2, 219n11; future and, 21, 91, 93; history of, 21–22; identification, isolation, or totalization effects of, 66, 214n4; indefinite service in, 68–69, 109–110, 129; military camps, 156–157, 195, 198; military commanders or personnel, 16–17, 55–56, 58, 65, 76, 79, 86, 111, 158, 170, 191, 201, 213n12; military conscripts, 3, 6–7, 67–69, 71, 83, 85, 129, 202; military culture, ethos, or legacy, 53–54, 70–71, 199; military discipline or drills, 9, 66, 86, 111, 123–124, 214nn4–5; military experiences fused with everyday, 22; military punishment, 70–72, 111, 181, 201; nation and, 92, 112, 124, 126–127, 212n10; revolutionary, 54–55; round-ups by, 65, 79
military training: education and, 7, 20–22, 27, 31, 90–91, 93–98, 100, 107, 120–121, 138–139, 169; harshness of, 3–4, 6, 14, 67, 70–71, 109, 111, 181; "in Sawa," 67–68, 76; of teachers, 4, 6, 14, 70–72, 127–128, 133, 216n4 (chap. 4)
Ministry of Defense, 73
Ministry of Education, 7, 26, 133, 158, 174–175, 188–189; Assab boarding school, 29, 137; central office of, 73, 79; curriculum of, 49–51, 96, 149, 150; and implementation of policies, 115, 121; local or regional offices of, 74, 171–172; passing grade set by, 99, 120; policy documents of, 94–96, 115, 172; professional teachers hired by, 18; supervisors or officials in, 2, 15, 73–74, 79–80, 89, 102–103, 117, 149, 171–172, 189
Ministry of Information, 56, 215n10
Mitchell, Timothy, 61, 66, 214n5
mockery, 24, 31, 123–124, 142, 145–148, 152–153, 182, 202
morality: crisis or concerns of, 21, 31, 158, 167, 169, 172–173, 177–178, 184, 190, 201–202, 218n9; educated people and, 91, 104, 107, 121; fortitude and, 48, 50–51, 149; smoking and, 173–174; space indexes and, 159, 162–167; teachers and, 20, 24, 31–32, 103–104, 106–107, 119, 152, 157–159, 162–167, 169, 172–174, 177–178, 180–181, 186–187, 190–192, 201, 218n9; violence and, 19–20, 178, 180–181, 186–187, 191, 201, 205, 218n4
mourning, 27, 49–50, 197, 208
Muslim League, 38–39
Muslims, 17, 37–38, 52

nation(s): in Africa, 41–42, 213n2; attachment to or feelings about, 10, 21, 55, 61, 66, 124–125, 152; building (*see* nation-building project); cannibalized, 13, 200, 203, 209; defense of, 3, 6, 8, 13, 21, 23, 34, 49, 56, 63, 66, 68, 75, 84–86, 92, 100, 110, 199; defined, 10; development of, 22–23, 53, 75, 91, 106–107, 112, 134; duty to, 6–8, 56, 77, 91, 126, 149; embodied, 54, 123–124; future of, 90, 92–93, 101, 107, 109–110, 112, 124, 192; hyphen in nation-state, 4, 7, 10, 32, 200, 209; identification with, 64, 66; imagined, 3–4, 10, 32, 91–92, 206 (*see also* national imaginaries); leader as embodying, 148; militarized, 22; sacrifice for, 8, 13, 21, 36, 42, 46–53, 93, 104, 112, 121, 151, 200, 209; schools and, 30, 31, 149, 212n10; sovereign, 8, 157, 198; teachers or schools producing, 5, 16, 101, 103, 152, 197, 212n9; uncoupled from state, 4, 10–11, 24
national identity, 40–41, 43, 45, 149

national imaginaries, 3, 112, 124; coercion's impact on, 4, 6, 11; conflicting, 112; non-official or alternative, 10, 14, 32, 37; origin or production of, 4

nationalism, 123, 152; African, 10, 42, 213n2; alchemical, 193, 206–207, 209; American, 206; Anderson on, 22; generation of, 206; hollow, 13; militarized, 92; populist, 10, 30; revolutionary, 8, 35–36, 44, 54, 212n7; teachers, schools, or education and, 25, 29, 149, 205

nationalism, Eritrean, 14, 22, 24–25, 29, 46, 56, 143, 213n14 (introduction), 213n1 (chap. 1); China's impact on, 40; core elements of, 56, 142; "drama" of, 76; effervescent, 7, 211n3, 212n7; EPLF or ELF, 37, 40–42, 54; genesis or history of, 5, 30, 36–38, 213n1; questioning of, 147–148; quotidian, 34, 36, 46, 51–52, 54; revolutionary, 8, 30, 35–36, 40, 44, 212n7; versions of, 5–6, 10, 27, 32, 37–38, 42, 50, 101, 125, 148, 152–153, 200

National Service: in Assab, 129–130; developmentalism and, 23, 68; eligibility for or exemptions from, 62, 65, 79, 132; evaded or delayed, 79–81, 99, 170–171, 202, 207, 218n2; exit visas contingent on, 65, 217n2; goals of, 9, 22, 53, 102–103, 124; identification or individuating effects of, 66, 69; laws or policies about, 3, 6, 85, 95–96, 103, 218n2; as liminal phase, 126–128, 133, 152–153, 202; limitless or indefinite, 6, 18, 64–65, 68–69, 85, 101, 109, 120, 124, 127, 131–133, 138, 152–153, 202; militarism and, 23, 53, 66–67; nationalism and, 52–53; National Service conscripts, 13, 18, 20, 22, 66–68, 70–72, 88, 200, 203, 214n6; as punishment, 56, 71–72, 214n6; punishments during, 70–72; rigors or hardship of, 3, 53, 67–68, 126; spatialization effects of, 18, 66; start or early years of, 9, 11, 56, 110, 214n6; students and, 23, 31, 54, 90–91, 93, 95, 98–100, 108–112, 120–121, 124, 126, 138–139, 152, 171, 202, 216n4 (chap. 4); teachers and, 3, 18, 27, 31, 67, 70, 72–75, 93, 110, 127–129, 132–133, 137–139, 216n4 (chap. 4), 217n9; television coverage of, 9, 214n6; totalization effects of, 66; unpaid, 6, 74–75, 127, 132, 137

nation-building project, 8–11, 16, 19, 22, 25, 52, 74, 153; EPLF/PFDJ's, 34–36, 40, 43–45, 100, 200, 203

nation-state: African, 41–42; Eritrean, 32, 35–36, 213n14; European, 212n10; hyphen in, 4, 7, 10, 32, 200, 209; making of, 10, 14, 24–25, 35, 92; refugees and, 216n2; sovereignty of, 157, 198

nonstudents, 164, 168–171

normalization, 21, 59–60, 84, 113–114, 116, 123, 201

obedience, 12–13, 53, 77, 147, 158–159, 168, 183, 214n6, 217n11

O'Kane, David, 23, 211n4

opposition, 11, 39, 56, 81, 174, 206–209, 215n10

party: coercion or force used by, 8, 36; culture of, 48; defining Eritrean-ness, 8, 34, 41, 148, 200; developmentalism and, 33; egalitarianism and, 23; ideology of, 44, 51, 200; Isaias Afewerki as face of, 148; militarism or militarization and, 5, 22, 36, 124; nation-state or nationalism and, 5, 8–9, 25, 30, 34, 36, 45–46, 51, 54, 125, 151–153, 199–200, 213n1; opposition to or questioning of, 11, 55–56, 59, 148; PFDJ (*see* People's Front for Democracy and Justice [PFDJ]); scholarship on, 24, 46, 54; state, government, or *mengisti* and, 10–11, 15, 132, 200, 206; Unionist Party, 38

Passeron, Jean Claude, 162, 215n2

patrimonialism, 10

patriotism, 7, 9, 13, 42, 48–50, 67, 92, 110, 149, 151, 206

Peace Corps, 9, 25

peasants, 44–45

pedagogy, 90, 94, 96–97, 118, 179–184, 192, 212n9

People's Front for Democracy and Justice (PFDJ), 46, 51, 55, 199; and arrest of critics, 11, 55; delegitimized, 8, 11; developmentalism and, 22–23; education and, 7, 22–23, 100; egalitarianism and, 44, 216n5 (chap. 4); leaders of, 9, 11; "Open

Letter to Members of the People's Front for Democracy and Justice," 55; paranoia and, 11; quotidian strategies of, 34, 51; state or nation building of, 5, 7–10, 34–36, 42, 44, 46. *See also* party

police, 16, 18, 201, 204–205, 219n2; military, 79; in schools, 155–156, 158, 175–177; sovereignty of, 170, 191

policies, 62, 159–160; promotion, 7, 23, 34, 36, 42, 90–91, 94–96, 98–100, 107, 112–121, 130, 172, 215–216n4; reform, 90, 142, 169–170; state or government, 4, 6–7, 11, 15–17, 44–45, 63, 69, 109, 132, 196, 201, 208, 217n1

policies, educational, 7, 91–102, 171–172, 175, 215–216n4, 218n8; disorder and, 124–125; foreign donors and, 216n5 (chap. 3); implementation of, 26, 90–91, 95–96, 98–99, 113, 115, 119, 121, 124–125; military and, 20–21, 23–24, 91, 93, 95, 100, 107–109, 124, 126, 169, 175; rationale for, 93–94, 100, 102, 121; teachers and, 20, 24, 31, 74, 93, 96, 99–101, 107–109, 112–121, 158, 172, 196

ports, 1–3, 28, 113, 164, 166

power: authoritarian, 11–12; coercive, 12–13, 61; disciplinary or biopolitical, 13–14, 113–114, 124, 212n7; imaginary power of state, 87; impotent, 78, 147; inverted, 142, 146, 153; legitimacy and, 55, 78; of middle actors, 16, 19, 21, 32; of military or guards, 54, 159–160; of nation or power to nationalize, 4, 92; productive, 12; and spaces, 162, 201; of state (actors), 3, 15–17, 19, 24, 61, 63, 65, 69–70, 73–74, 84–85, 158, 177, 183, 205, 212n6; symbolic, 13–14, 212n7; of teachers, 17, 19, 32, 130, 140–141, 156, 175, 178, 183; technologies of, 174–175, 214n4

prejudices, 19, 157, 192, 201, 205

prison, 6, 49, 57, 64, 66, 70, 199, 205; state as, 6, 64–66, 70, 197–200, 202–203, 205

progress, 5, 35, 43, 92, 111, 118–119, 128, 158, 163, 199

promotion policies, 7, 23, 34, 36, 42, 90–91, 94–96, 98–100, 107, 112–121, 130, 172, 215–216n4

punishment: arbitrary, 15, 62, 66–67, 71, 184; collective, 71; corporal (*see* corporal punishment); discourses of, 62–63, 70–72, 86; encampment and, 199, 203; evading, 80–82, 88, 187, 204; by government or EPLF/PFDJ, 6, 15, 30, 55, 62, 64, 70, 85 (*see also* states: punishing); imaginaries and, 60–64, 73, 87–88, 111–112, 153, 175, 206; military, 70–72, 111, 181, 201; National Service (*see* National Service: as punishment; National Service: punishments during); Sawa as, 73, 108; seeming like, 70, 72; service as, 56, 71–72, 76; of students, 24, 114, 173–174, 177–178, 183–184, 190, 201, 203; subjects of (*see* subjects: coerced or punished); by supervisors, 70, 72–75; transfers and, 74–75, 185

quotidian, the, 8, 16, 34, 36, 46, 51–52, 54, 63

Red Sea: North, 71; South, 14–15, 18, 50, 74, 155, 167, 181

refugees, 208, 214–215n9, 216n2

religion, 3, 16–17, 21–22, 29, 34, 37–43, 105, 199

resistance: in Africa, 35, 42; evasion vs., 81–82; impotence and, 12, 77–78; little, 56; punishment for, 30; by students, by teachers, or in schools, 20, 24, 31, 124–125, 145, 153, 202

rights, 3, 21; civics curriculum on, 150, 152; denied or violated, 82, 156, 212n8; in state of exception, 62, 177, 217n1; students', 186, 192; teachers', 187

ritual(s): flag ceremony, 27, 52, 54, 104, 122–124, 142; life cycle or initiation, 27, 126, 133; liminal phase, 126, 133, 138 (*see also* liminality); macro- or micro-, 134, 138, 152, 216n6; national, 13, 46, 52, 123–126, 134, 213n12; National Service as, 124, 126; resisted or subverted, 12, 77, 124, 153; school or classroom, 27, 31, 123–125, 134–136, 138, 140, 149, 152–153, 216n1, 217n11

rule of law, 15, 62, 71, 201, 204

rumors, 2, 30, 70, 80, 83, 86–88, 111

sacrifice, 6, 21, 46–54, 207, 209; of children or students, 49, 104, 154; in civics curriculum, 48–49, 102, 149, 151; EPLF/PFDJ or state demand for, 5, 8, 34, 36, 42, 46, 49–51, 56, 62, 200; fleeing Eritrea as, 207, 209; forced, 13, 53, 56, 62; of future, 21, 104, 112; military sacrifice or sacrifice of soldiers, 21, 92, 101, 107, 112, 121; nationalized, 49–50; National Service as, 53, 153; patriotism and, 48–50; rhetoric of, 53; self-sufficiency and, 5, 34, 48; service and, 42, 54, 56, 62–63, 76, 121, 153–154; The Struggle, 5, 8, 34, 46–49, 53, 102; willing, 8, 34, 47–48, 51–52, 63, 75–76, 102–103, 149, 200. *See also* subjects: sacrificial
sandals, 1, 33–34, 51, 54
Sawa, 29, 72–73, 95, 117, 120–121, 134, 170, 176; media coverage of, 9, 67; new policy about, 90–91; "in Sawa," 67–68, 76; students or school in, 7, 24, 67, 90–91, 98–101, 107–112
Schmitt, Carl, 19, 92, 157, 217n1, 218n4
schools: American, 96, 134, 205, 215n1; built or opened, 22, 94, 100–101, 218n8; camps or sovereignty and, 157–158, 181, 184, 198, 201–202; coercion in, 88, 154; in developing world, 91; directors of, 2–3, 26, 75–76, 97, 117, 119–120, 134–136, 155–156, 159, 172, 180, 184–185, 187–189, 218n6; discipline or biopolitics in, 21–23, 104, 114, 124–125, 157, 218n5; disorder in or control of, 32, 109, 124–125, 134, 136–138, 140, 146, 152, 154–155, 158–161, 163, 170, 172, 174, 187–190, 202, 218n5; doing well in, 93, 104–105, 112–113; English-medium, 26; evasion or resistance in, 30–31, 99, 125, 153–154, 170–171, 175, 202; grades in, 94–95; imaginaries and, 4–5, 163; lack of resources in, 90, 97, 100; late start of, 134–138, 189, 202, 217n9; liminality or communitas in, 135–136, 141, 152–153; lockouts or walls and, 155–156, 159–163, 169–170, 172–173, 175–177, 190, 201–202; military, militarization, or Sawa and, 7, 21–22, 24, 67, 90, 94, 98, 124, 175, 202, 212n10; as (moral) spaces, 8, 20, 104, 155, 157–158, 160, 162, 165, 169, 172, 174, 181; National Service and, 23, 95, 111, 138, 152, 202, 217n9; nation or state and, 8, 22, 31, 93, 121, 123, 125, 149, 152–153, 191, 212n10; new subjects taught in, 97, 100; politics of, 25; problems in, 26, 74, 120, 218nn5–6; society and, 104, 215n2; sorting in, 114, 169–176, 178, 201; state institutions, 8, 14; statistics on, 95, 115; teleological orientation of, 21

science, 97, 149, 203
Scott, James, 81, 162, 191
secondary education, 28, 84, 94–96, 106, 112–113, 115, 117, 126; military training and, 20–21, 90–91
Senior Secondary School (Assab), 7, 25–26, 83, 97, 122–124, 134, 137, 151, 156, 161, 173, 190, 196; demographics of, 28
senior secondary schools, 7, 94–99, 112, 171, 215n4, 219n11
service: defined, 3; demanded, 62, 64, 68–69, 76, 88, 112; as duty, 6, 13; eligibility for, 79; evading, 78–80, 99, 170–171, 217n2; exit visa and, 65; indefinite or limitless, 6, 11, 68, 75, 131, 134; laws about, 3, 6; for nation or state, 42, 53, 213n12; as punishment, 6, 71–72, 76, 155; "in Sawa," 67; service projects, 19, 34, 53, 56, 69; sexual abuse of women in, 111; support for, 9, 56, 110, 214n6; unpaid, 6, 127–128
shida, 1, 33–34, 51, 54
shortages, 90, 137–139, 165, 188
slogans, 45, 50
smoking, 168, 173–174
soldiers: Adi Abeto incident, 83; Eritrean, 5–6, 28–29, 47, 76; Ethiopian, 47, 49; killed, sacrificed, or wounded, 65, 92, 212n11; occupation of Ministry of Information by, 56, 215n10; police and, 18; production of, 21, 31, 90, 100; protecting nation, 3, 92; punishment of, 72, 74–76, 101; round-ups by, 65, 80, 85; soldier subjects, 21–22, 31, 66, 68, 91–92, 107, 112, 121; student, 7, 16, 21, 31, 90, 93, 100, 108, 110, 112; as symbols (*see* symbols: fighters, martyrs, or soldiers as); teachers or educated people and, 16, 75–76, 101, 104, 133, 152; training of, 22, 214nn4–5 (*see also* military training); words for, 75–76. *See also* fighters; military

sovereignty: defined, 157; EPLF, 35–36; exception or devolution and, 19, 92, 156–157, 175, 178, 198, 201, 211n5, 217n1, 218nn3–4; sovereign nations, 8; sovereign soldiers or military, 92; sovereign state (actors), 4, 7–8, 10, 35, 172, 191, 198, 201–202, 218n3; sovereign teachers, 31, 157–159, 172–173, 175, 178, 181, 183–184, 186–187, 190–191; violence or force and, 178, 187, 211n5; waning, 198–199

spaces: carnival, 147; etatized, 69, 77; exception or encampment and, 156–157, 201, 209; imaginaries of, 10, 163; informal, 14; liminal, 118, 135, 152; morality of, 20, 159, 162–166, 190; national, 50, 61, 65–66, 142, 198, 209; political, 142, 156, 198; public, 77, 164, 166; school or classroom, 8, 20, 114, 116, 136, 143, 146–147, 157–158, 160–163, 165, 169, 172, 181, 184; sovereign, 158, 201–202; state effects and, 61, 65–66; time and, 10, 61, 66, 69, 77, 113–114; walled or controlled, 159, 161–163, 172, 190–191, 198, 202–203

spatialization effects, 61, 65–66

state actors. *See* actors, state

state effects, 60, 64, 66, 68, 77, 82, 183; coercive, 30, 61–63, 66, 69, 184, 202; theories about, 61

state of emergency, 3, 63, 83–86, 212n6, 217n1

state of exception, 19, 31, 62, 84–86, 156–159, 191, 204; in camps, 156–157, 201, 217n1; sovereign deciding on, 92, 157; teachers deciding on, 158, 172, 175, 177–178, 186, 190–192, 201

state(s): African, 35, 40–42, 132, 213n2; authoritarian, 4, 7, 11–14, 77, 79, 183, 191–192, 203–204, 212n7; benevolent or caring, 4, 10, 12, 19, 54, 59–60, 63, 77, 82, 84, 86–87, 112, 159, 181; cannibalizing nation, 12–13, 200, 209; coercive, 4–8, 11, 14–16, 59, 60–62, 68, 70, 82, 84, 86, 177, 183–184, 190, 193, 197, 200, 202; control by, 55, 87–88, 193; defined, 3–4, 10, 211n2; double body of, 73; EPLF/PFDJ, 44, 46; hyphen in nation-state, 4, 7, 10, 32, 200, 209; illegitimate or delegitimized, 12–13, 63, 78, 80, 175, 218n9; imagined, 3–6, 10–19, 24, 31, 54, 60–62, 73, 77, 86, 91, 158, 174–175, 178, 188, 191, 201, 203, 205, 212n8, 213n12, 214n3 (chap. 2); inept or impotent, 12–13, 17, 19, 80–81, 88, 125, 189, 191, 197, 201–203; maddening nature of, 3, 12, 57, 59–60, 63, 83–86, 88, 159, 181, 211–212n6, 212n7; nationalism and, 29–30, 34, 209; nation fused to, 4–5, 9–10, 42–43, 200, 211n4 (*see also* hyphen in nation-state); paternalistic, 59–60, 86–88, 92; as people not "things," 61, 214n3 (chap. 2); prison or carceral, 64, 70, 200, 204–206; protective, 2–3; punishing, 6, 8, 24, 30, 60, 62, 73, 76, 86–88, 111, 153, 175–176, 184, 190–191, 200, 204–205; ridiculed, 12–13, 77; scaling of, 61–63, 74; "seeing like" or "seen as," 162, 174–175, 189–191; siege, 84, 195, 199, 211–212n6; sovereign, 8, 35, 157, 201; state institutions, 8–9, 13–14, 34, 42, 46, 132, 154, 174, 175, 181, 188; The State vs., 15, 201; strong or weak, 7, 41–42, 87–88, 218n4; struggling, 7–8, 203; teacher or educational, 31–32, 158, 174–175, 190–192; technologies of, 113–114, 116, 118, 121, 174; use of force by, 3–4, 11–13, 61, 82, 84, 156, 158, 177, 191–192, 201; violent, 6, 14–16, 60, 85, 177, 181

statistics, 113, 118

Struggle, The, 22, 33, 46–48, 50–54, 56, 148, 150–154, 200, 207; definition or name of, 5, 7–8, 52; education and, 101–102; EPLF pamphlet on, 43; nationalism and, 24–25, 30, 37, 39–40, 42; National Service and, 34, 53, 66; start or origins of, 39, 43; values of, 34, 36, 101

students: 6th-grade, 151; 7th-grade, 149, 172, 184; 8th-grade, 95, 99, 170–172, 174–176, 188, 218n8; 9th-grade, 163; 10th-grade, 50, 143; 11th-grade, 7, 95, 98–99; 12th-grade, 7, 67, 90, 94–95, 98–100; acting like, 31, 115, 140, 163, 165, 169–170; at-risk, 117–118; coerced, 16, 64, 109, 202; controlled, 136, 155, 157, 159–161, 163, 166, 168, 170, 173, 186, 189, 216n7; disciplined, 104, 114, 117, 149, 157, 162–164, 218n5; disorderly, 122, 125, 130, 139–140, 142, 153, 158,

students *(continued)*
170, 175, 177, 187–188; failure of, 91, 95, 99, 112, 115–120, 172, 184, 215–216n4; future of, 31, 92–93, 100–101, 105, 108–109, 112, 114, 119; and "growing up," 31, 124–125, 137, 202; high school, 9, 53–54, 67, 91, 93, 105–106; ID cards for, 79, 175, 219n11; incomplete, 118–120; individual vs. all, 113–114; late or truant, 123, 136–137, 153, 155–156, 173, 177, 189–190; locked out, 155–156, 158, 169–170, 175–177, 190; monitored, 118–120, 136, 160, 163; moral or good, 162–166, 173–174, 178, 186, 190; nation or state and, 4–5, 16, 22, 102–104, 110, 123–124, 143, 147–152; older, 172–173, 175–176, 188; protests by, 55–56, 71, 98, 215n10; punished, 24, 176, 178, 186 *(see also* corporal punishment); repeaters, 99, 108, 115–116, 170–172; as soldiers in the making, 7, 16, 21, 31, 90, 93, 100, 108, 110, 112; sorted, 114, 169–176, 178, 201; spoiled, 166–169; statistics on, 28, 95, 115, 122; teachers and, 27, 31–32, 117–118, 133–134, 136, 138, 140–142, 153, 163–169, 177; university, 9, 53, 56, 69, 91, 95, 98, 100, 106, 108, 113–114, 127–129, 134, 216n4 (chap. 4); working, 128, 130, 168

subjects: bodies of, 12, 16, 183; coerced or punished, 3–4, 12, 61–63, 66–67, 81–82, 86–88, 181, 200, 203–206; educated national, 21, 24, 31, 91–93, 107, 123, 125, 154; loyal or docile, 8, 12, 54, 61, 66, 125 *(see also* docility); military or soldier, 21–22, 31, 66, 68, 91–92, 107, 112, 121; national, 13, 20–21, 34, 36, 42, 75, 91–93, 112, 121, 124–125, 149, 153; sacrificial, 24, 34, 49–50, 92, 147, 200, 207; state, 12, 16, 40, 61, 63–65, 77, 203, 214nn4–5; theories about, 22

suffering: military, 67, 92, 109, 133; opposition groups on, 206, 209; valorized and/or nationalized, 34, 46, 49–51

summer service *(ma'atot)*, 9, 22–23, 53–54, 69, 95–96

supervisors, 2, 70, 72–76, 78–80, 175

surveillance, 11, 30, 64, 114

symbolism, 29, 75–77, 92, 98, 106–107, 112, 148, 205, 207, 212–213n12; authoritarian regimes or coercion and, 12–14; EPLF use of, 45–46

symbols, 46, 54, 75–78, 98, 123, 209; camel as, 51–52; fighters, martyrs, or soldiers as, 50, 75–76, 92, 213n12; map as, 66; national, 42, 48, 50–52, 75; quotidian or everyday, 51; *shida* as, 33–34; teachers as, 19

teachers: authority of, 14, 23, 31, 133–134, 136, 138–142, 146, 153–154, 159, 167–169, 177; citizens made by, 103–104, 107, 157, 190, 205; civics teachers, 148–153; coerced or controlled, 127, 158, 161; coercive, 183, 202; conscription or military training of, 4, 6, 14–16, 18, 65, 71–72, 93, 127–128; junior secondary school, 26, 131, 155–156, 169, 171–172, 188; late arrival by, 20, 75, 80, 135, 137–138, 202, 217n9; lion-like, 185–187; as middle actors, 16, 200, 205; morality of, 20, 24, 103–104, 106, 119, 157–159, 162–167, 174, 177–178, 181, 190; National Service of, 3, 18, 27, 31, 67, 70, 72–75, 93, 110, 127–129, 132–133, 137–139, 216n4 (chap. 4), 217n9 *(see also* teachers: service teachers); nation-state or imaginaries and, 4–5, 16, 25, 32, 93, 101, 103; parents and, 32, 110–111, 130, 158–159, 174–175, 181, 189–190; playful, 141–142, 153; policies or curriculum and, 16, 20, 24, 31, 89–90, 93, 96, 100–101, 121; professional, 18, 73, 127–128, 133; punished, 70–72, 74–75, 178, 184–185, 205; punishment by *(see* corporal punishment; punishment: of students; students: punished); role of, 21, 99–100, 115, 119, 181, 212n9; Sawa, 24, 67, 72, 111; senior secondary school, 99, 106, 173; service teachers, 18, 73, 75, 91, 127–129, 131, 133, 139, 141, 143, 217n9; shortages of, 90, 97; sovereign, 31, 157–159, 172–173, 175, 178, 181, 183–184, 186–187, 190–191; as state (actors), 19, 31–32, 152, 158, 174–175, 177, 181, 183, 189–192, 201, 205; status of, 17–19, 110, 130–133; struggles of, 8; students

and, 27, 31–32, 117–118, 133–134, 136, 138, 140–142, 153, 163–169, 177; training, 18, 26, 89, 96–97, 100, 106, 118, 179, 185; transferred, 18, 28, 54, 72, 74–75, 185, 193
technologies: biopolitical or disciplinary, 115–119, 121; of categorization, 190; of power, 174–175, 214n4; of the state, 80, 84, 89–90, 113–114, 118, 121, 200, 202
tegadelti. *See* fighters
television, 9, 47–48, 50, 208, 215n10
tertiary education, 90–91, 94, 98, 100, 121
textbooks, 139, 149; unavailable, 96–97, 100, 152
Tigrinya (ethnic group), 17, 28, 37, 40, 167–168
Tigrinya (language), 26, 75–76, 160, 164
time, 66–67, 69, 77, 104, 113–114; etatization of, 69, 77, 214n7; in schools, 104, 109, 135–137, 155–156, 169; wartime, 84–86
torture, 50, 58, 65, 71, 196, 201, 207, 212n8
totalization effects, 61, 64, 66, 69, 133
Treiber, Magnus, 79, 164
truancy, 137, 153
Turkey, 125, 212n10
Turner, Victor, 126, 134–135, 138, 216n2

United Nations, 39, 195; High Commission on Refugees, 214–215n9
United States of America, 58, 168, 212n11; carceral state in, 204–206; schools or teachers in, 134, 196, 205, 215n1

universities, 106–107; Addis Ababa University, 106; University of Asmara, 56, 71–73, 83, 98, 100–101, 106

Verdery, Katherine, 69, 77, 214n7
vigilantes, 17, 188, 202, 211n5, 218n4, 218n9
violence: anticolonialism and, 35; benevolence or paternalism vs. 60, 87, 92, 159, 177, 181, 187; coercion and, 64, 88, 157, 178, 203, 205; culture of, 70–71; military, 14–15, 92, 202; morality and, 20; necessary, 84–85, 87–88; school, 8, 32, 154, 157–158, 177–178, 180; state (actors) and, 3–4, 6, 11, 14, 16, 19, 30, 32, 83, 85, 87–88, 92, 158, 181, 201, 211n5
virtue, 16–18, 21, 48, 90, 101, 113, 133, 146, 191
visas, 65, 193–194, 196, 201, 207

warrior ethos, 5
Warsai Yikaalo Development Campaign (WYDC), 6, 11, 68, 124, 127, 144
Warsai Yikaalo School, 98
Wedeen, Lisa, 10, 13–14, 148, 203, 211n5, 212n7, 214n8
Wi'a, 71–72, 74
Woldemikael, Tekle, 54
women, 34, 44–45, 53, 111, 174, 219n10

youth, 34, 44–45, 67, 69, 95, 103, 216n5 (chap. 4); category in Eritrea, 131–132

zombification, 12, 78

Jennifer Riggan is Associate Professor of International Studies in the Department of Historical and Political Studies at Arcadia University.